BL/
NEWSPAI
AMERICA'S WAR FOR
DEMOCRACY,
1914-1920

BLACK NEWSPAPERS AND AMERICA'S WAR FOR DEMOCRACY, 1914–1920

WILLIAM G. JORDAN

The University of North Carolina Press

Chapel Hill and London

© 2001
The University of North Carolina Press
All rights reserved
Manufactured in the United States of America
Set in New Baskerville and Block types
by Tseng Information Systems, Inc.
The paper in this book meets the guidelines for
permanence and durability of the Committee on Production Guidelines
for Book Longevity of the Council on Library Resources.

Publication of this work was aided by a generous grant from the
Z. Smith Reynolds Foundation.

Library of Congress Cataloging-in-Publication Data
Jordan, William G.
Black newspapers and America's war for democracy, 1914–1920 /
by William G. Jordan.
p.   cm.
Includes bibliographical references and index.
ISBN 0-8078-2622-7 (alk. paper) —
ISBN 0-8078-4936-7 (pbk. : alk. paper)
1. Afro-American press—History—20th century.   2. Afro-American
newspapers—History—20th century.   3. World War, 1914–1918—
Press coverage—United States.   I. Title.
PN4882.5 .J67   2001
071'.3'08996073—dc21   00-052778

05   04   03   02   01   5   4   3   2   1

FOR WENDY

CONTENTS

ILLUSTRATIONS

ACKNOWLEDGMENTS

Over the years during which this project took shape, I have relied on the help, encouragement, and guidance of many individuals. My graduate adviser, Harvard Sitkoff, read many drafts of the manuscript and offered incisive criticism and guidance. Others read all or part of the various drafts or supported me in other ways, from providing child care to helping me figure out my word-processing program. With apologies in advance for inadvertent omissions, I thank Marcia Carlisle, Charles Clark, Joyce Denning, Jeff Diefendorf, Les Fisher, Mike Foley, Raymond Gavins, Julie Graham, Bill Harris, Susan Herbst, Stacy Hogsett, Nancy Jerauld, Jennifer Jordan, Ryan Madden, Bob Mennel, Edith Murphy, Beth Nichols, David Richards, and Lucy Salyer.

Librarians, archivists, and others also helped me at numerous points along the way. They include Jane Boesch at the Phillips Exeter Academy Class of 1945 Library; librarians at the special collections departments at the W. E. B. Du Bois Library, University of Massachusetts, Amherst, and Mugar Library, Boston University; and librarians at the reference and interlibrary loan departments at the University of New Hampshire (UNH) Library. I also thank UNH History Department secretaries Jeanne Mitchell and Lee Szeliga and the Class of 1945 Library word-processing department. I received generous financial assistance from the UNH History Department, Graduate School, and Central Research Fund; the Colonial Dames of America; and the American Historical Association's Beveridge Grant. The PEA library provided office space (with air-conditioning) at a crucial moment in the life of this project.

Last but certainly not least, for her patience and support, I thank my wife, Wendy Aldrich Jordan.

BLACK NEWSPAPERS AND AMERICA'S WAR FOR DEMOCRACY, 1914-1920

America must be told. The time is at hand for the people—
all the people—to know the truth, and the whole truth, about
our condition and our aspirations and our demands. . . . AGAINST A
SOLIDLY UNITED, GENERAL, NATIONAL, UNCEASING CAMPAIGN
OF PUBLICITY IN ALL FIELDS AND DEPARTMENTS, PREJUDICE
AND ITS KINDRED IMPS WILL RUN LIKE A SCARED HOUND.
AMERICA MUST BE TOLD.

Nahum Daniel Brascher
"Getting America Told," *Chicago Defender,* June 7, 1919

INTRODUCTION
GETTING AMERICA TOLD

Yes, this man was fighting, fighting with words.
He was using words as a weapon, using them as
one would use a club. Could words be weapons?
Well, yes for here they were. Then, maybe, perhaps,
I could use them as a weapon?

RICHARD WRIGHT
Black Boy: A Record of Childhood and Youth

Richard Wright's epiphany, after reading H. L. Mencken's *Book of Prefaces* in 1927, started him on an illustrious career in which he used words to attack American racism in novels, short stories, and essays. One hundred years earlier, in 1827, two other black men embarked on a similar quest when they established the first African American newspaper, *Freedom's Journal*. John B. Russwurm and Samuel E. Cornish said they planned to defend free blacks by refuting "the calumnies of our enemies . . . by forceful arguments."[1] Since that time, African American writers, editors, and publishers have used black newspapers to defend black people and attack racism.

To them, the black press has been a "defender of the race," ever ready to counter attacks on African Americans in the mainstream "white" press, to make the case for black equality and civil rights, or to point out the injustices inherent in America's race relations. As the *Chicago Broad Ax* put it, black newspapers have served African Americans by "constantly struggling as best they can to fight their battles for them."[2] Even black readers have seen the black press in this light. A reader criticized the *California Eagle* at a public forum in Los Angeles in 1917 because that black weekly had failed to respond to a recent attack on African Americans in the *Los Angeles Record*, a local daily. "It was confidently expected that we should be on the job every minute and make this fight for the race," the *Eagle* noted. The *Eagle*'s editorial writer agreed that "with such copperhead sheets as the Record, we should ever be in a position to hurl these attacks back into their teeth."[3]

But the idea that the black press could fight for African Americans begs some fundamental questions. How and in what situations have

African Americans used words in their newspapers as weapons of defense or offense? And how effective have these weapons been? This book seeks to answer these questions in the context of World War I and at the same time to develop insights into the black response to that war and the turmoil that followed it.

In the years from the outbreak of war in Europe in 1914 to the height of the Red Scare in 1920, African Americans needed a great deal of defending. A majority could not vote and were relegated to segregated and inferior public accommodations, and dozens were lynched every year. When America went to war, black soldiers served in poorly trained, segregated units, usually labor battalions, and after the war, several black veterans died at the hands of lynching parties in the South. Meanwhile, the mainstream American media not only largely excluded black opinions but also reflected and reinforced widely held racist assumptions and stereotypes.[4] Faced with such dire circumstances, black journalists waged battle on behalf of "the race" by printing indictments of America's racial injustices, monitoring and criticizing the white media and the statements of white leaders, praising messages complimentary to blacks, and condemning racist utterances. Sometimes they reprinted and rebutted articles, addressing white authors as "you." Most important, they chose their words and shaped their arguments not simply with black readers in mind but to awaken the consciences of white readers as well.

Like black editors and readers, historians of the black press have seen it as an arena of conflict between black and white and have sought to evaluate the strategies employed in that conflict and to understand its impact on the larger struggle between the races. Beginning with I. Garland Penn in 1891, nearly all historians of the black press have recognized its role as the "champion" of an "oppressed people" or as a "fighting press." According to Frederick G. Detweiler, Gunnar Myrdal, Vishnu V. Oak, and others, black newspapers have demanded democracy, protested injustice, challenged white statements on race, presented positive images of black people, and sought to perfect American democracy. A recent study by Charles A. Simmons examines the responses of editors of four black newspapers to financial, physical, and political pressures from whites to modify their editorial policies. Simmons shows how black editors resisted or succumbed to these pressures but does not explore how the black press might have affected white Americans.[5]

The focus of most historical accounts turns quickly from the way black newspapers championed the cause of African American freedom to the role of the black press within the black community. Some examine the efforts of black newspapers to fight racism indirectly by creating solidarity within the black community, bolstering black self-esteem, promoting militant consciousness, or advocating protest.[6] Others see a more conservative role, suggesting that the press served as a "safety valve," relieving black anger and discontent rather than directing it against oppressive systems.[7] Myrdal defined the black press as an instrument of the "Negro upper classes" for spreading conservative values, establishing group control and identity, channeling black anger, and teaching readers how to think and feel. The black press, which Myrdal called "the greatest single power in the Negro race," taught American ideals to black readers while showing that white Americans rarely lived up to them. In this way, the press fostered discontent and militancy and encouraged blacks to demand full citizenship.[8]

Of primary interest to many historians of the black press has been the way black newspapers have acted as both a "mirror" of black life in America and an institution that "*defines the Negro group to the Negroes themselves.*"[9] Some of the most provocative work on African American newspapers has focused almost exclusively on this reflective quality. E. Franklin Frazier argued that the major function of the black press was to provide psychological compensation for the black bourgeoisie's inferiority complex by printing white praise of blacks and exaggerated accounts of black achievement.[10] Albert Lee Kreiling offered the more affirmative interpretation that black newspapers created mythical symbols for mostly urban blacks in a secularizing society. The strident protests against racial injustice were less important for the way they attacked racism than for the psychological and cultural service they performed for the blacks who wrote and read them, Kreiling argued. After all, northern black newspapers spent more time denouncing racial injustice in the distant South than in their own cities, where they could have had greater impact. The posture of outrage against southern lynchings, according to Kreiling, was part of a collective ritual that replaced traditional religious rituals, provided meaning and identity, and asserted the independence and manhood of the African Americans who participated. During World War I, the black press continued to perform such ritual functions for African Americans while also offering guidance on how to respond to the government's call to arms.[11]

Thus, to a large extent, the black press has occupied a "parallel public sphere," not fully part of the mainstream of public opinion and debate that links society and state but a separate arena where African Americans have worked out among themselves alternatives to the dominant culture's views of their identities and interests.[12] But no impermeable barrier separated black discourse from the rest of the public sphere. Although blacks had a diminished voice, their arguments frequently seeped into the main currents of public discussion. Black editors knew this to be true because of the letters white people wrote them, the attacks of white mobs on southern black newspapers in response to militant editorials, the patronage some black newspapers received from white-dominated political parties, and occasional critiques of black newspapers in white publications or by white politicians.[13] During and shortly after America's involvement in World War I, black editors knew white people were reading their newspapers even more closely because of comments on the black press issued by federal investigatory agencies, the U.S. Congress, southern officeholders, the state legislature of New York, and white individuals.

Although small in number compared to black readers, white readers influenced the character of the black press in important ways. Because black editors were more concerned with exercising as much power as possible than with simply expressing ideas or laying out a consistent ideology, they took care to frame their arguments in ways that would be convincing to white Americans—especially powerful ones.[14] Such efforts could succeed only in an environment in which power was not monopolized by central authorities through the use of physical force. Although the federal government did mobilize coercive forces against dissenting citizens during World War I, individuals had room to criticize the government—and even the war effort—within limits.[15] But even within those limits, black editors knew they did not speak in a vacuum in which they could define the terms of debate as they wished. Instead, they shrewdly borrowed terms and ideas from others involved in the current political discourse and bent them to serve their own ends. In an arena in which deviant political views were marginalized or ignored, they sought to present their ideas as akin to mainstream political views.[16] This strategy sometimes served their ends well. Some of the most widely used political phrases of the war years proved to be easily adaptable to the cause of racial justice.[17] Black editors could easily turn a war to "make the world safe for democracy" into a war to make the "south safe for the Negroes" or transform southern lynchings into "atrocities" akin to the enemy's misdeeds.[18] But some of the words black journalists used served the interests of the federal government better than the interests of African Americans. Phrases like "loyalty," "patriotism," and "100 percent Americanism" could be used to bolster black claims to citizenship. Yet the self-sacrificing loyalty demanded by the national government during the war suggested that blacks should not insist on racial justice as a condition of their participation in the country's defense. The use of such words created difficult dilemmas for black writers.

Although calculated efforts to adapt popular political dogma to serve black interests may have determined much of the content of black newspapers during the war, other factors also came into play. Most important, the threat of physical coercion by white individuals and institutions regulated the content of the black press, as it always had. During the nineteenth century, white mobs had attacked black editors from time to time in response to certain kinds of editorials. Such attacks served as warnings to all black journalists in the region. In the North, coercive pressures were not as naked or as common before World War I, but they nevertheless played a role in shaping the discourse of black newspapers there. White advertisers and political parties, for example, could withhold crucial funds. The advent of a world war dramatically increased the attention of white Americans to the black press. Southern leaders read black newspapers and tried to suppress them at the same time that the Espionage and Sedition Acts gave the federal government the power to monitor and intimidate black editors throughout the country. During those years of widespread prowar frenzy, it must have seemed possible that even in the North black newspapers might be the victims of vigilante violence if they opposed the war.[19]

Thus, during World War I, the black press served as a frontier between black and white in which the terms of racial coexistence were negotiated and renegotiated through written and verbal exchanges that were conditioned by the ever-present threat of force.[20] This thesis sheds light on African American militancy, the role of black newspapers in black protest and American life, and, most directly, the African American response to World War I.

Historians have been deeply divided over how to characterize the black response to this war. Some argue that militancy was negligible during World War I, that African Americans generally followed the advice of W. E. B. Du Bois in 1918 to "forget our special grievances and close our ranks"—supporting the war and soft-pedaling protest out of a combination of "deeply-felt patriotism," hope that the war would accelerate racial progress, and fear that failure to comply would lead to brutal persecution.[21] Other historians have been more inclined to emphasize the militancy of African Americans, whether in opposing the war or in using it as an excuse to intensify demands for racial equality.[22] Both sides have recognized the diversity of opinion among blacks, depicting one group as dominant and the other as the exception that proved the rule.[23] But it has been too easy to see the black reaction to the war as simply dividing along the lines of the old Booker T. Washington/W. E. B. Du Bois, accommodation/protest dichotomy, with Du Bois on the other side this time.[24] Such categories mask the profound ambivalence displayed by the black press as a whole, as well as individual writers, leaders, and newspapers, and they gloss over the indeterminacies characteristic of any text.

To arrive at a fuller understanding of black protest ideology, one must move beyond the overt meanings of the relevant texts and consider what their authors wanted to accomplish by writing them—how they hoped to affect their audiences, both black and white.[25] Black ambivalence toward the war was not simply a product of indecision or imprecise thinking. Rather it flowed from writers' efforts to use language to motivate powerful white readers to attempt to improve race relations in America. The success or failure of black thinkers must therefore be judged by the impact of their words rather than by the logical consistency of their arguments. The editorial policies of the black press during World War I must be evaluated as a response to a national emergency in which the threat of force was always present. By that measure, most of the black newspapers examined in this book must be viewed as having succeeded in bringing black concerns to the public attention while not inviting repressive measures against either the black press or African Americans as a group.

The chapters in this book have been arranged chronologically; since each chapter deals with a different theme, however, there is considerable overlap. Chapter 1 provides a history of the black press from its beginnings in 1827 to the early twentieth century, focusing on blacks' use of the press as a weapon and whites' counterattacks against it. It also introduces the publications used in this study.

Chapters 2 and 3 examine the strategies black newspapers used to promote black advancement in the context of World War I. Chapter 2 shows that shortly after the outbreak of war in August 1914, writers began to draw parallels between what was going on in Europe and the condition of blacks at home. They exposed the hypocrisy of American outrage at alleged atrocities in the war zones and indifference to the lynchings of blacks in the South. Chapter 3 reveals that after America's entry into a war that Woodrow Wilson said would make the world safe for democracy, black writers were able to draw even stronger parallels. Democracy would have to be assured at home before the United States could bring it to Europe. But in pointing out the inconsistencies between Americans' actions and Wilson's democratic ideals, black writers did not reject these ideals or refuse to participate in the war until democracy had been extended to all African Americans. To varying degrees, black newspapers supported U.S. participation in the war or at least advocated black cooperation in the war effort while prodding the government to live up to its own ideals.

Chapter 4 examines the response of white America, especially the federal government, to the black press's wartime strategies. Although white readers usually rejected black arguments for equality, their clear preference for censoring black newspapers generally went unrealized. In fact, by the summer of 1918, it seemed that black newspapers had struck an effective balance between making demands and pledging loyalty. Although the government had instituted some repressive measures and some publications had softened their demands for racial justice, high-level federal officials had begun to act on the "Bill of Particulars," a list of fourteen demands made by black editors. A few white southerners had begun to form antilynching organizations. Most important, President Wilson, who three years earlier had implicitly endorsed the racist film, *Birth of a Nation,* condemned lynching in a speech and praised the democratic spirit of the black press.

Finally, chapter 5 explores the relationships between black newspapers and white Americans in the year or so after the Armistice—a period when radical doctrines swept the land, race riots broke out in cities across the country, and government agencies clamped down on dissent. Black editorialists during this time tried to control the public image of what many were calling the "New Negro," a more assertive and angry African American, more proud and politicized than blacks had been before the war. As white Americans looked increasingly to the black press for a definition of the New Negro, the black press sought to send them a clear message: that African Americans were fully deserving of full citizenship rights, that they were prepared to stand up and fight for such rights, and that the act of doing so would purify American democracy.

This book is based on a close reading of six leading weekly black newspapers, including three from the North (the *Chicago Defender,* the

Cleveland Gazette, and the *New York Age),* two from the former Confederacy (the *Richmond Planet* and the *Savannah Tribune),* and one from a border state (the *Baltimore Afro-American).* It also relies on evidence from a less systematic sampling of other black newspapers: the *Appeal* of St. Paul and Chicago, the *Boston Guardian,* the *California Eagle,* the *Chicago Broad Ax,* the *Cleveland Advocate,* the *Indianapolis Freeman,* the *Norfolk Journal and Guide,* and the *Washington Bee.* Frequent reference has also been made to the monthly organ of the National Association for the Advancement of Colored People (NAACP), the *Crisis,* edited by W. E. B. Du Bois. Although in the strictest sense, the *Crisis* does not qualify as a black periodical because it was controlled by a predominantly white-run organization, no study of the black press during World War I can ignore this highly influential journal. Black newspapers commented on its content frequently, and the government and white Americans viewed it as a faithful representative of black opinion. Moreover, its black editor exercised a good deal of independence in determining the *Crisis's* content. The monthly *Messenger* and other radical publications that sprang into existence during the war — mostly in New York City — fall even further out of the scope of this study because they were not published throughout the entire period and were not typical of the black press. Still, reference to the *Messenger* is made in the later chapters because it loomed large in the government's view of the black press.

The periodicals examined in this book are intended to be a representative sampling of the black press, including not only newspapers from different geographic regions but also newspapers of different sorts. These journals range from the highly influential and well-circulated *Crisis* to the relatively obscure *California Eagle.* The *Baltimore Afro-American,* the *Chicago Defender,* and the *Norfolk Journal and Guide* would become national, mass circulation leaders of the industry between 1915 and 1925. The *New York Age,* one of the leading black weeklies of the time, would decline in influence after World War I. The *Cleveland Gazette* and the *Chicago Broad Ax* were typical of many nineteenth-century black newspapers in that they were run almost single-handedly by and reflected the outlook of their owner-proprietors, Harry C. Smith and Julius Taylor.

All but the monthly *Crisis* and *Messenger* were published weekly, and all but the *Crisis* were controlled exclusively by blacks. Few of the publications made much money; the majority operated on a shoestring. Only the *Defender* approached a regular circulation of 100,000 before 1920.[26]

8   INTRODUCTION

These publications make up a reasonably typical cross section of the black press during World War I, including some newspapers that would lead black journalism in the years that followed the war and others with deep roots in the nearly 100 years of the industry's history that preceded it.

CHAPTER 1
ABOLITIONISTS, ACCOMMODATIONISTS, AND THE NEW NEGRO, 1827–1914

The inauguration in 1913 of the first Democratic president in sixteen years marked a significant transfer of political influence among African Americans at the same time that it shifted power from one political party to another.[1] Booker T. Washington, who ran a well-known institute for black students in Tuskegee, Alabama, had served as the chief spokesman for African Americans to Republican presidents Theodore Roosevelt and William Howard Taft. Washington had been consulted on the appointments of blacks to federal office and had advised the presidents on race policy. He was known among blacks as the great accommodator for his philosophy that African Americans should accept their status as second-class citizens with few civil or political rights while seeking economic progress through self-help. He was also known as the Wizard of Tuskegee for the imposing political machine he had built with donations from white patrons, whom he approached with great deference and humility.

With Woodrow Wilson in the White House, however, the Wizard lost his exclusive access to the presidency, and a small group of maverick black leaders who had endorsed the Democrat in the general election now had the ear of the chief executive. The new group opposed the Tuskegee philosophy of accommodationism and refused to shrink from demanding all the rights they believed African Americans deserved. In November 1914, a delegation led by William Monroe Trotter, editor of the weekly *Boston Guardian* and organizer of the National Equal Rights League, met with Wilson in the Oval Office.

Alarmed by reports of racial segregation in the Post Office Department, the Treasury Department, and the Bureau of Printing and Engraving, Trotter had met with Wilson in 1913 and had been assured that his administration had no segregation policy and would investigate reports that black civil servants had been treated unfairly. Now Trotter was back a year later with further evidence of segregation and discrimination.

Trotter said he had come "to renew the protest" and to ask Wilson to abolish segregation in his administration. He pointed out that black voters had shown their disapproval of the policy by voting against Democratic candidates in the recent midterm elections. "Only two years ago you were heralded as perhaps the second Lincoln, and now the Afro-American leaders who supported you are hounded as false leaders and traitors to their race," he said. "Have you a 'new freedom' for white Americans and a new slavery for Afro-American fellow citizens?"

Affronted by such bold criticism, Wilson scolded Trotter. "I don't want politics brought into it at all," he said. "I am not seeking office." Trotter's talk of electoral support struck the president as "blackmail." Wilson lectured Trotter, defending the segregation of federal employees as a well-intentioned measure to prevent friction between white and black employees and as a way of preventing employees of both races from feeling "uncomfortable." Solving the race problem would take generations, the president concluded, and it would happen faster "if these questions aren't raised."

But Trotter persisted. Black employees had been "humiliated and indisposed" as a result of segregation, he said.

"If you think that you gentlemen, as an organization, and all other Negro citizens of the country, that you are being humiliated, you will believe it," Wilson sputtered.

Trotter pressed the point. The humiliation was not imagined, he insisted; segregation "creates in the minds of others [the impression] that there is something the matter with us—that we are not their equals, that we are not their brothers." He went on to contradict the president: "This segregation is not due to any friction between the races, but is due to race prejudice on the part of the official who puts it into operation."

When Trotter again raised the issue of Wilson's declining popularity among black voters, the president rebuked him sharply. "If this organization wishes to approach me again, it must choose another spokesman," he said. "Your tone, sir, offends me. . . . You are the only American citizen that has ever come into this office who has talked to me in a tone with a background of passion that was evident."

Wilson's rebuke left Trotter "thunderstruck," he said later.[2] He could only reply, "I am from a part of the people, Mr. President."

"You have spoiled the whole cause for which you came," the president said.

"Mr. President, I am sorry for that," Trotter apologized. Then, amazingly, he pressed his point further, making a statement that Wilson's stenographer missed about America professing to be Christian. Wilson again cut him off. "I expect those who profess to be Christians to come to me in a Christian spirit," he snapped.

Trotter began to backtrack, but just barely. "If my tone has seemed so contentious, why my tone has been misunderstood," he said. "I was simply trying to show how my people feel." He explained that his organization's support of the Democratic ticket in 1912 had led blacks to brand members as "traitors to our race."

Then, positioning himself as intermediary between the black population and Wilson, and perhaps seeking some reconciliation with the president, he said: "We have tried to get the colored people to reason in this matter. Their feeling is more [intense on this issue] than on others. Any portrayal, we found, led them to resent this thing. We would be false, Mr. President, false to ourselves and false to you, if we went out and led you to believe that we could convince the colored people that there was anything but degradation [in segregation]."

On his way out of the White House, an agitated Trotter told newspaper reporters about his encounter, calling the president's contention that segregation would prevent friction among employees "entirely disappointing." The incident made the front page of the *New York Times* and appeared in newspapers across the country. Although many commentators condemned Trotter's treatment of the president, progressive writers focused most of their criticism on Wilson's defense of segregation.[3]

The president himself admitted that Trotter had gotten the better of him. At the very least the editor had brought a concern of blacks into public awareness. At best he had won an important debate with the nation's most powerful leader and forced him to make a change in policy. "I was damn fool enough to lose my temper," Wilson confessed. "I raised that incident into an issue that will be hard to down." Wilson's secretary, Joseph Tumulty, while scolding Trotter for breaching White House etiquette by relating his conversation to reporters, had to admit that the editor's appeal had been "most eloquent."[4] Still, Wilson seemed reluctant to meet any demands made by Trotter, no matter how worthy. A few months after the encounter with Trotter, Wilson's secretary gave him a newspaper clipping featuring an account of Trotter's protest of the racist film, *Birth of a Nation*. Wilson agreed that

THE NEW NEGRO

he would issue a statement expressing his disapproval of the film if he "could do it without seeming to be trying to meet the agitation which . . . was stirred up by that unspeakable fellow."[5]

Trotter's encounter with the president illustrates the power of the black press and foreshadows its relationship with Wilson during the war. First, black editors like Trotter borrowed phrases—like "new freedom"—from influential whites and found ways to apply them to the cause of racial justice. Wilson never meant his "New Freedom" or his war to make the world safe for democracy to apply to African Americans, but Trotter and the black press forced him to confront the logic of those connections. Second, black journalists like Trotter, editor of a well-known newspaper and organizer of several race advocacy groups, frequently augmented their journalistic efforts through "back channels"—direct face-to-face appeals or behind-the-scenes organizing and lobbying.[6] Black journalists since the antebellum period had been participating in political activism on the state, local, and national levels. During World War I, three dozen black editors would meet with Wilson administration officials to hammer out an agreement on race policy during the war. Third, journalists often offered themselves to white America as arbitrators between African Americans and the white world—Trotter was "simply trying to show how my people feel"—and white leaders often accepted them in that role or even sought them out for it. During World War I, black editors warned the government about the growing militancy of the black population and suggested ways to diminish it. Finally, and perhaps most important, in spite of their relative powerlessness, black journalists sometimes got the better of white leaders as powerful and eloquent as Woodrow Wilson. Although Wilson controlled more resources of physical coercion than Trotter, in the public sphere they engaged each other on a more equal footing. In fact, Wilson did end up curbing segregation in federal offices, probably in response to Trotter's plea. Similarly, during the coming war, the Wilson administration could not simply dismiss published black demands no matter how persistently officials might criticize their tone.

Trotter's run-in with Wilson also seemed to signal a new era in black journalism and leadership. With Booker T. Washington's influence waning, more aggressively militant black journalists and leaders found their voices, arguing eloquently for racial justice. Washington had maintained harmonious relations with powerful whites, including Presidents Roosevelt and Taft, by speaking the contemporary language of economic progress while declining to publicly challenge the most distressing signs of racism. Trotter, by contrast, paid little attention to economic issues, refused to accommodate racism or sacrifice ideals for short-term political gain, and rarely spoke in muted tones.

When Washington died a year after Trotter's meeting with Wilson, leaders who combined some aspects of both approaches would fill the leadership vacuum. Editors like W. E. B. Du Bois of the *Crisis*, James Weldon Johnson of the *New York Age*, and Robert S. Abbott of the *Chicago Defender* emerged as the figures who would lead African Americans into the twentieth century. Like Trotter, they believed it was essential to demand black rights forthrightly, but sometimes they found it necessary to modulate the stridency of the tone with which they addressed white America. Yet they shared much in common with editors, publishers, and writers who had been producing black newspapers in America for nearly 100 years. These black journalists had been protesting and accommodating; lobbying politicians; making both bold and conciliatory statements; and quoting, lecturing, and winning and losing arguments with whites since the black press began. Many of the practices the black press would employ during World War I had been devised and utilized long before the war began.

THE ANTISLAVERY ROOTS OF THE BLACK PRESS

Du Bois, Abbott, Johnson, and Trotter each practiced journalism in a different way. Du Bois edited a monthly magazine bankrolled by a white-run organization. Abbott owned a financially successful black weekly and hired others to do most of the writing and editing. Johnson wrote editorials for a black-owned weekly. Trotter owned, published, edited, and wrote much of the content of a small weekly, barely making ends meet. But all of these men functioned within a tradition of black journalism that stretched back to 1827.[7]

In that year, on March 16, two free black men, John Russwurm, a Jamaican immigrant, and Reverend Samuel Cornish, began publishing *Freedom's Journal* in New York City. Excluded from the public sphere, the founders of the journal wanted to create a forum in which they could respond to attacks on free blacks by the proslavery editor of the *New York Enquirer*. Russwurm and Cornish defined their new venture as a "channel of communication between us and the public" and an instrument of "defense of five hundred thousand free people of colour."[8] Other antebellum black journalists established publications to respond to white newspapers. Martin R. Delany founded *The Mystery* in Pittsburgh in 1843 after local dailies refused to print blacks' letters.[9] When William A. Hodges attempted to rebut the *New York Sun*'s attacks on black voting rights in 1846, the daily newspaper charged him $15 to print an edited version of his letter. An editor explained to Hodges the place of blacks in the public sphere: "The *Sun* shines for all white men and not for colored men." If he wanted a public forum for his ideas, he would have to publish his own newspaper. A year later, Hodges established the *Ram's Horn*.[10] As their most renowned colleague, Frederick Douglass, put it, black publishers wanted to establish a mode of communicating not just among themselves but with white America for the purpose of "renovating the public mind, and building up a public sentiment, which should send slavery to the grave."[11]

Sending a message to white America was not black journalists' only motive for publishing during and after the antebellum period. They also hoped to unify and educate black Americans. The editors of *Freedom's Journal* said they wanted to link "together by one solid chain, the whole free [black] population, so as to make them think, and feel and act, as one solid body, devoted to education and improvements."[12] They advocated uplift of African Americans through moral and intellectual improvement and cooperative ventures. Russwurm took such nationalistic impulses to their logical extreme, calling for the colonization of all black Americans to Africa. Like most editors of black newspapers, however, Cornish saw African Americans as a permanent part of the United States and accordingly sought to communicate not only with other blacks but with white America as well.[13]

Black publishers, editors, and writers who sought to change white attitudes through their writing, however, faced formidable barriers. Most white Americans, both North and South, accepted the doctrine of white supremacy unthinkingly. The Victorian worldview, which began to take shape around the time of *Freedom's Journal*'s founding and lasted into the first years of the twentieth century, divided the world into dichotomous and hierarchical elements, splitting the human race into civilized and savage people, one clearly and unalterably superior to the other. White Americans thus denied African Americans, whom they categorized as savage, a common humanity with themselves. Even most northerners who favored emancipation of the slaves—including Abraham Lincoln—believed freed blacks had to go back to Africa because they could not live in harmony with civilized whites.[14]

African American journalists protested against overtly racist ideas, but they did not seek to renovate the public mind by attacking the basic assumptions of Victorianism, which would have been part of their own intellectual makeup. Instead, while agreeing that the world was made up of civilized and uncivilized people, they sought to categorize African Americans as civilized by publicizing the doings of respectable, middle-class blacks. They ignored the masses of lower-class blacks and defended the virtue and honor of black women. At the same time, black newspapers offered lessons to black readers in how to live up to middle-class values and thus demonstrate their civilized humanity. As one historian has concluded, antebellum black editors sought both to guide black behavior and to "mold white attitudes" by documenting "the abilities and successes of free blacks."[15] They did so, however, within the limits imposed by contemporary opinion.

Antebellum publishers in this sense set patterns for black newspapers that would persist into the twentieth century. They addressed both black and white audiences, and they oriented arguments for black rights within the framework of contemporary mainstream political and cultural beliefs, accommodating some and protesting others. Similarly, during World War I, black newspaper publishers would use their papers both to advise African Americans on how to respond to the war and to exhort white America to fulfill the war's idealistic purpose by granting civil rights to loyal black citizens. And again, they would do so within the limits imposed by the contemporary political climate.

ACCOMMODATORS AND AGITATORS

In spite of the continuity between antebellum and World War I newspapers, the intervening period brought important changes to the black press. Emancipation marked a watershed, bringing the end of the antislavery movement in the North and the legalization of black literacy in the South. Free blacks established their first newspaper, *L'Union*, in the former slave states in Union-occupied New Orleans on September 27, 1862, just five days after Lincoln announced the Emancipation Proclamation and three months before it took effect. Meanwhile, with slavery outlawed and abolitionism victorious, northern black journalists had to find a new raison d'être.[16]

In the southern states, the transformation was more immediate and dramatic: African Americans established their first newspapers in Virginia, North Carolina, Tennessee, and Alabama in 1865; Mississippi in 1867; Arkansas in 1869; and Florida in 1870.[17] In the North, the end of Reconstruction spurred a dramatic increase in black journalism. Between 1879 and 1895, African Americans outside of the South established numerous influential newspapers—many of which would have long and distinguished careers. These included the *California Eagle* (at first called the *Owl*) in 1879; the *Washington Bee* in 1882; the *Cleveland*

Gazette and the *New York Globe* (later renamed the *New York Freeman* and finally the *New York Age*) in 1883; the *Philadelphia Tribune* in 1884; the *Appeal* of St. Paul and Chicago in 1885; the *Indianapolis Freeman* in 1888; the *Baltimore Afro-American* in 1892; and the *Broad Ax* of Salt Lake City in 1895 (which moved to Chicago four years later).

After the end of Reconstruction, the black press declined in the South, losing both its economic viability and its political relevance, whereas the opposite occurred in the North. By 1910, although 89 percent of blacks lived in the South, only 63 percent of black newspapers were published there.[18] Yet some black newspapers did flourish and pursue political objectives in the South, whereas some northern newspapers refrained from militant protest. Each black newspaper in the country developed a balance between militancy and accommodation shaped by a combination of internal and external factors, including the personality and ideology of the publisher, the state of race relations in the local area, the relationship of the publisher to local political parties, recent events, and the requirements of a particular situation or moment. Still, after the withdrawal of federal troops from the former Confederacy, most black newspapers in the South became less political, less militant, and more interested in the social and economic advancement of individuals. Three factors contributed to this trend: the imposition of new legal restrictions, the ascendancy of the ideology of industrial capitalism, and the escalation of vigilante violence.

First, legal innovations across the South made black political activism increasingly futile. Most important, new constitutions in southern states effectively disfranchised the majority of black citizens through a system of poll taxes, literacy tests, and other barriers to voting. State laws also created a system of legal segregation of the races—in housing, public transportation, schooling, marriage, and even cemeteries —that paralleled and reinforced blacks' political exclusion. The national government sanctioned this disfranchisement and legal apartheid, and the Supreme Court handed down a series of favorable rulings culminating in *Plessy v. Ferguson* in 1896. Faced with the futility of political action, black leaders changed their focus.

A second factor that contributed to the decline of political activism from the black press in the South was the rise of the success ideology of American industrial capitalism, which elevated personal advancement over collective action. Most Americans viewed their country as a land of opportunity that rewarded virtue, hard work, and ability with success. Andrew Carnegie's "Gospel of Wealth," the lectures and writings of William Graham Sumner, and the novels of Horatio Alger all reinforced this belief. Led by Booker T. Washington, many blacks throughout the country came to see their salvation in hard work and economic pursuits rather than in collective protest for equal rights.[19]

Washington became influential in the South in the 1880s and 1890s. His 1895 address at the Atlanta Cotton States and International Exposition catapulted him into the national spotlight and made him the most visible black leader in the country. In that famous speech, Washington counseled survival through accommodation to rather than protest against the South's system of white supremacy. He advised blacks to stop protesting for equality and civil rights and to focus instead on self-improvement and uplift, especially in the economic realm. If blacks proved themselves economically useful, Washington naively reasoned, whites would welcome them as full citizens. Washington, whose rise to fame and power had been facilitated by white patrons, interpreted the Social Darwinist ideas of Carnegie, Sumner, and Alger for a black audience. His Alger-like autobiography, *Up from Slavery*, became a best-seller after the turn of the century.[20]

Embraced by African Americans across the country, the ideology of personal success had its greatest impact in the South, where the height of its popularity coincided with disfranchisement and gave editors something more hopeful to write about than politics. Southern papers increasingly focused on material success, often (but not always) to the exclusion of politics. Following Washington's lead, black newspapers encouraged political passivity to promote harmonious relations between the races, promising better business opportunities and greater prosperity for blacks. Accordingly, one southern newspaper pledged it would never print "anything that has a tendency to bring about unpleasant relations between the races."[21]

These ideas became so pervasive before the turn of the century that even a young W. E. B. Du Bois could agree with Washington that the degraded condition of blacks rather than race prejudice kept them down and that self-help, hard work, and upright behavior were the keys to advancement of the race rather than federal or even state legislation.[22] Matthew M. Lewey, editor of the *Florida Sentinel*, summed up the philosophy of black uplift even before Washington's Atlanta address. African Americans, he wrote, should "rely entirely upon ourselves in the development of manly character, aspire to excel in everything, work hard day and night, get money, educate our children, don't beg but depend upon our own brain and muscles."[23]

To the extent that the Tuskegee philosophy promoted individualism and self-reliance at the expense of collective consciousness and action, it helped to keep African Americans mired in a degraded status, and newspapers that espoused it served the interests of the white ruling class. Blacks, after all, had been oppressed as a group, and only group action could eliminate the barriers that prevented them from having a fair chance.

Yet the African American version of the success ideology contained a germ of collectivism, fostering a nascent black nationalism that held that individuals must help to elevate the race through service and charity to the black community.[24] Editorials in black newspapers encouraged readers to patronize black-owned businesses and to feel pride in the race. An African American should "love his race and do his part to advance its interests," the *Savannah Tribune* said.[25] Newspapers promoted love of race by running profiles of blacks who had become successful in business, politics, arts, and other endeavors; citing the contributions of blacks to American and world history; and reporting on the social and economic advancements of the race as a whole. *Nashville Globe* publisher Richard Boyd sold black dolls to teach "children how to look upon their people."[26] Despite these tendencies toward race pride and group action, the success ideology and disfranchisement combined with a powerful third factor, vigilante violence, to keep southern black newspapers quiescent.

Toward the end of the century, white mobs lynched scores of black citizens every year, and sometimes these mobs directed their ire against newspaper publishers. In 1887, publisher Jesse C. Duke of the Montgomery *Baptist Leader* had to flee Alabama with a mob at his heels after he wrote in response to the lynching of a black man for alleged rape of "the growing appreciation of the white Juliet for the colored Romeo."[27] R. C. O. Benjamin, editor of the *Birmingham Negro American* and a self-proclaimed "chronic disturber of the peace," was forced into exile that same year for defending Duke in print. In 1889, after Mansfield E. Bryant, "the most aggressive and fearless editor in the country," predicted in his *Selma Independent* the outbreak of a race war in which blacks would emerge victorious, he was arraigned on charges of making "incendiary utterances," narrowly escaped a lynching, and finally fled to Nashville.[28]

But Tennessee was no haven. In 1892, white Memphians drove Ida B. Wells out of the South after she wrote an unequivocal attack on lynching in her newspaper, the *Memphis Free Speech and Headlight*. White Memphis newspapers had already reprinted some of the *Free Speech's* more incendiary polemics, including Wells's 1891 call for violent retribution against lynchers. Angry white readers responded to the editorial by threatening the paper's publisher, who left Tennessee to escape a lynching, leaving the paper to Wells and J. L. Fleming. A year later, after the lynching of three successful black businessmen in the city, Wells advised her readers to leave Memphis (2,000 did) and to boycott streetcars. In addition, she began printing a series of forthright exposés challenging the most common justification for lynching—that it protected white women from rape. A few weeks later, after five black men had been lynched for allegedly raping white women, she wrote: "Nobody in this section believes the old threadbare lie that Negro men assault white women. If Southern men are not careful they will overreach themselves and a conclusion will be reached which will be very damaging to the moral reputation of their women." Fortuitously in Philadelphia at the time, Wells escaped harm when a mob organized by leading white citizens ransacked her office in response to the editorial. They were incited by the *Memphis Daily Commercial*, which reprinted Wells's editorial and commented: "The fact that a black scoundrel is allowed to live and utter such loathsome and repulsive calumnies is a volume of evidence as to the wonderful patience of Southern whites. . . . There are some things that the Southern white man will not tolerate, and the obscene intimations of the foregoing have brought the writer to the very outermost of public patience. We hope we have said enough." Wells's partner also escaped the city safely. Warned not to publish another issue, Wells abandoned her publication and lived the rest of her life in the North.[29]

A few years later, in 1898, another black editor had to flee for his life after writing an editorial on lynching. When Alex Manly of the *Wilmington Daily Record* of North Carolina wrote that many blacks had white fathers and dared to suggest that white women often accused their black lovers of rape as a way to save their reputations, white-owned newspapers reprinted the editorial. The *Raleigh News and Observer* distributed 300,000 copies as a leaflet. One white orator advocated " 'choking the Cape Fear River with the bodies of Negroes.' " In the end, a frenzied mob burned the *Daily Record*'s office, then rampaged through black neighborhoods, killing thirty African Americans and driving dozens more from the city.[30] As editors Duke, Benjamin, Bryant, Wells, Fleming, and Manly learned, southern whites were ready to use force to punish blacks for what they printed in their newspapers, a lesson not lost on the hundreds of black publishers doing business in the South.

Still, militant protest was never completely erased from the southern black press. Although discussion of topics like the rape myth had become more dangerous and protest was virtually eliminated in some areas—Mississippi, for example—militancy never vanished from southern black newspapers.[31] Alabama's *Birmingham Era* managed to survive, for example, even after defending Duke's remarks and printing examples of consensual liaisons between white women and black men. It even opposed a miscegenation bill under consideration by the state legislature.[32] The *Nashville Globe* disavowed social equality and embraced most of the Tuskegee program yet continued to advocate black participation in local politics.[33] Other southern newspapers like the *Dallas Express,* the *St. Louis Argus,* and the *Richmond Planet* maintained a militant posture. *Planet* editor John L. Mitchell Jr. continually "hammered away at the barbarity of southern [lynch] mobs without suffering reprisals from whites." He encouraged blacks to arm themselves in self-defense, criticized incompetent police and racist judges, and even warned of a bloody race war while avoiding discussion of the rape myth. After the turn of the century, however, even this gadfly "muted" his tone.[34] By 1900, even the most militant southern black newspapers had become more cautious as they declined financially.[35]

It is tempting to characterize the southern black press as accommodationist and its northern counterpart as militant, as some contemporaries did. New South prophet and *Atlanta Constitution* editor Henry Grady, for example, labeled a group of mostly northern black editors "Afro-American Agitators" because of their persistent and intense agitation for equal rights. Although Grady meant the label as a slur, the Agitators adopted it as a badge of honor.[36] The fact that most of these militants published in the North suggests that they faced fewer coercive pressures than southern editors. Indeed, two of the three major factors leading the southern press toward greater accommodation—disfranchisement and vigilante violence—were all but absent in the North.

Nevertheless, northern newspapers increasingly felt pressure to moderate their tone as well. Grady's interest in black publishing in the North reflected the growing concern of southern whites who realized that the ideas of militant Agitators in the northern states would filter south. Although southerners and industrial leaders with an interest in maintaining a docile black labor force in the South could not enact laws or form lynching parties to intimidate editors in northern cities, their influence and money, channeled through Booker T. Washington, were used to control the northern black press to a degree. Moreover, the success ideology so eagerly adopted by New South advocates exerted as much influence in the North as in the South. Thus, northern black newspapers, although generally more militant than their southern cousins, faced external pressures working against militancy.

The more successful Agitators included the editors of newspapers like the *New York Age*, the *Cleveland Gazette*, the *Indianapolis World*, the *Appeal* of St. Paul and Chicago, the *Chicago Broad Ax*, the *Washington Bee*, the *Chicago Conservator*, and even the southern *Richmond Planet*. These independent and outspoken advocates of civil rights boldly criticized racial inequities and railed against the precipitous decline in race relations—especially in the South. Most, like Calvin Chase of the *Washington Bee* and Harry C. Smith of the *Cleveland Gazette*, denounced Booker T. Washington. Julius Taylor of the *Chicago Broad Ax*, who sometimes praised Washington in the 1890s, attacked him bitterly after 1900 as a "moral pygmy" and the "Great Beggar of Tuskegee."[37]

Whereas Washington preached political passivity combined with unswerving loyalty to the Republican Party, Agitators advocated political activism and independence. Chase said blacks should split their votes between the Democratic and Republican Parties because the latter had "deserted, disowned, and frowned upon the colored people of the South in 1876."[38] Other publishers, including Taylor, Smith, and T. Thomas Fortune, publisher of the *New York Age* and the most prominent Agitator, only occasionally endorsed Democratic candidates, mostly remaining in the Republican camp.[39] Northern editors sometimes went beyond endorsing candidates and held office themselves. Smith, for example, served three terms in the Ohio state legislature. John Q. Adams kept the *Appeal* going with income from minor political appointments, and journeyman journalist Ralph Tyler split his time between journalism and political appointments.[40]

Some Agitators took their activism a step beyond the political realm, calling for armed self-defense and retaliatory violence.[41] Fortune advocated self-defense and endorsed retaliation after the Wilmington riot in 1898 and the Atlanta riot in 1906. "The trouble will go on in Atlanta," he told a white reporter, "until the Negro retaliates—until, driven to bay, the Negro slays his assailant."[42] In a letter to the *Brooklyn Eagle* in 1900, Fortune gave what his biographer, Emma Lou Thornbrough, called "his most effective defense of the use of retaliatory force": "The blackman's right of self-defense is identically the same as the white man's right of self-defense. . . . When the law does not protect me, as it does not in the South . . . what am I to do? Accept it all meekly, without protest or resentment? . . . Slaves do that sort of thing, and are worthy to be slaves, but free men, American freemen! Who expects them to do it?"[43]

THE NEW NEGRO

In contrast to Washington's acceptance of segregation and his belief in a temporary social separation of the races, most Agitators believed in assimilation, the unity of the human race, and even racial amalgamation. Agitators advocated racial designations that de-emphasized the distinctiveness of African Americans, and they opposed most separate black institutions, even when they would provide needed services. Smith, for example, campaigned against the creation of a separate hospital, a home for girls, and a YMCA for blacks in Cleveland.[44] He sought admission of blacks to existing mainstream institutions.

At the same time, most northern editors and publishers promoted the success ideology of Booker T. Washington. Like their southern counterparts, northern Agitators had faith in upward mobility and middle-class values. They supported industrial education as a promising path to black success and advocated land and business ownership as a means of black uplift.[45]

One of the most persistent advocates of the Tuskegee philosophy, George Knox, publisher of the *Indianapolis Freeman,* one of the top three black newspapers around the turn of the century, constantly preached the value of hard work, self-help, and uplift. Born into slavery, Knox made his fortune operating a chain of barber shops catering to affluent white customers, and like Washington, he used his own story to illustrate how an upright, moral, and productive life could overcome the limitations imposed by a racist society.[46] He also gained a reputation as an accommodationist because he believed most blacks should remain in the South; eschewed social equality; scolded blacks for vagrancy and lawlessness; and promoted black businesses and middle-class values of thrift, industry, and clean living. Unlike the Agitators, Knox expressed an often unfounded optimism, seeing "little reason to be dissatisfied with conditions in this country."[47]

Although Knox was not an Agitator, some of his views paralleled those of the Agitators: he espoused middle-class Victorian values, saw himself as more American than African, came to see a need for political independence from the Republican Party, and opposed bans on intermarriage. Both Knox and the Agitators supported vocational training while stressing the right of black students to pursue an academic education.[48] Unlike Washington, Knox openly participated in politics and even engaged in protest activities. He spoke out against lynching, for example, and after 1917 condemned the Ku Klux Klan and supported a federal antilynching bill.[49] Sometimes Knox seemed like a pure accommodationist, but at other times, he was as militant as anyone else.[50]

For their part, Agitators were not purely militant, and they seemed to grow less so as Booker T. Washington's power grew. Many northern Agitators, most notably Chase and Fortune, came to rely on the Wizard of Tuskegee for financial help, which compromised their editorial independence. Fortune never attacked Washington or the doctrine of accommodationism, which he argued was necessary in the South.[51] For a time, Fortune benefited from his alliance with Washington while maintaining a militant stance. But as he became more dependent on Washington for financial support, his editorials grew less biting. Washington secretly became one of the chief stockholders of the *New York Age*. In 1907, after suffering a mental breakdown, Fortune sold his share of the paper to Fred Moore, whom Washington also covertly subsidized.[52]

Chase, an outspoken critic of Washington beginning in 1895, accepted $100 to write a series of pro-Washington editorials in 1906 and continued to back him until 1915.[53] The *Washington Colored American*, the *Boston Colored Citizen*, the *Colored American Magazine*, and *Alexander's Magazine* also received "sustained cash contributions" from Tuskegee, while Knox's *Indianapolis Freeman* received an occasional loan. Washington also distributed Republican Party patronage to the black press, exerted significant control over two black press associations, and placed his own advertisements in black journals. He sometimes paid editors to publish press releases and editorials in their newspapers. Washington never exerted complete control over the black press, but he used his considerable financial clout to influence the editorial direction of many newspapers in the North.[54]

Thus, as the black press—North and South—entered the twentieth century, the balance between protest and accommodation was decidedly tipped toward the latter, in part because of the publishers' own conservative values and in part because of coercion from outside. Still, the basic mission of the black press remained intact. Black newspapers North and South continued to alert black readers to the need for action and forced at least a few white Americans to face the issue of race and confront the gap between American ideals and the practices of lynching, segregation, and disfranchisement.[55]

When Ida B. Wells began writing for the *New York Age* in the 1890s, she believed she had the "opportunity to tell the world for the first time the true story of Negro lynchings."[56] Most white Americans probably did not listen—but some did. Just as mobs responded to southern black newspaper editorials with violence, white Americans sometimes felt compelled to reply to northern black journalists like Fortune who were out of the reach of southern vigilantes. During Fortune's most productive years as an Agitator, the 1880s and 1890s, northern and southern white Americans responded to him. When Fortune called on blacks to arm themselves or retaliate with force, when he defended interracial marriage or called for the formation of the Afro-American League, white newspapers from the *Macon Telegraph* to the *New York Times* either praised him as a statesman or condemned him as "a very foolish Negro."[57]

At a time when African Americans were largely invisible to whites—hidden, as W. E. B. Du Bois put it, behind a "vast veil"—this small opening of dialogue may have been one of the few channels of discourse between the races.[58] Although most whites ignored the black press, not all did. And to the extent that black journalists forced white people to pay attention, they succeeded in poking holes in the veil, making themselves visible, and forcing whites to reconsider their assumptions about African Americans and race.

TOWARD A NEW NEGRO PRESS

At the turn of the century, black journalists were vacillating between protest and accommodation, pushed and pulled by their own uncertainty about the best path for the progress of the race, by external coercive pressures, and by the nature of their dialogue with white America. Yet in the years between the turn of the century and the start of World War I, the tide began to turn away from the accommodationism of Booker T. Washington and toward more militant protest against the status quo, especially in the North. William Monroe Trotter had delivered a one-two punch against Washington by establishing his outspoken anti-Tuskegee newspaper, the *Boston Guardian,* in 1901 and then attacking Washington at a highly publicized event in 1903. These and a series of other events and milestones within and outside of the black press pointed toward the emergence by 1919 of what historians have labeled the "New Negro."

Other black editors had been critical of Washington, but Trotter attacked him with a ferocity that no others dared. The bitter, personal, and unrelenting nature of Trotter's attack set the *Guardian* apart and paved the way for a vigorous protest movement centered in the North. A graduate of Harvard College, Trotter had been raised by his father, James, a prosperous federal officeholder who acquired a home in an affluent white Boston neighborhood and demanded that his son stand up to the boys he lived among and fight them if necessary. Absorbing the lesson well, Monroe grew up fully convinced that blacks deserved an equal place with whites in American society and ready to fight for it. After graduating magna cum laude from Harvard in 1895, he tried a succession of jobs while at the same time becoming increasingly involved in black protest activities. Finally, in 1901, Trotter embarked on his life's work as publisher of the *Guardian*.[59] In his paper, Trotter pulled no punches, referring to Washington as the "Benedict Arnold of the Negro race."[60] Although many other black editors combined journalism with direct political involvement, Trotter took protest further than most.

In 1903, Trotter's campaign against Washington gained the attention of blacks and whites after his orchestration of the "Boston riot." At a meeting of the National Negro Business League in Boston, Trotter and some associates disrupted the speeches of T. Thomas Fortune and Booker T. Washington by throwing red pepper onto the platform and shouting damning questions (unanswerable accusations, really) at the speakers. The police carted the culprits away, and Washington's supporters insisted on pressing charges. Trotter eventually spent thirty days in jail for his role in the incident. Reported in newspapers across the country, the riot made most whites aware for the first time of African American opposition to the Tuskegee program. As Trotter biographer Stephen R. Fox writes: "Few white men at this time agreed with the radicals' case, but at least they knew of its existence after the riot."[61] Most white philanthropist allies of Washington were appalled at the riot, yet it helped to open their eyes to the need for a civil rights advocacy organization that would be free of Washington's domination.[62]

Within the black community, the Boston riot's most immediate consequence was to move W. E. B. Du Bois, a former Harvard classmate of Trotter's and the leading black intellectual of his generation, toward an alliance with the "radicals" who opposed Washington. Du Bois soon afterward helped establish the militant Niagara Movement, a group of mostly northern black men united in opposition to Tuskegeean accommodation and in outspoken advocacy of civil rights. Beginning in 1905, the Niagara Movement distributed pamphlets, lobbied against segregation and discrimination, and published a short-lived journal, the *Moon*. The organization itself did not last long—becoming a victim of internal squabbling among Trotter, Du Bois, and others—but the organizational momentum of the Niagara Movement contributed to the establishment of two groups with similar goals: the NAACP, an interracial organization, and Trotter's all-black National Independent

W. E. B. Du Bois (*seated*) and William Monroe Trotter (*far right*), probably at the Niagara Movement meeting in Harpers Ferry, West Virginia, 1906. F. H. M. Murray (*far left*) and L. M. Hershaw (*center*) are also pictured. Courtesy Special Collections and Archives, W. E. B. Du Bois Library, University of Massachusetts, Amherst.

Political League, later renamed the National Equal Rights League (NERL).[63]

Trotter, unwilling to work under whites because he believed they would force him to compromise and temporize, maintained only loose ties with the NAACP after its founding and focused most of his efforts on the NERL. Trotter's influence may have reached an apex with his 1914 meeting with Wilson in the White House. Still, African Americans did not fully embrace the *Guardian* editor's uncompromising posture. His newspaper's circulation remained small, and he did not seem a fitting intermediary between black and white Americans. Even *Cleveland Gazette* editor and Agitator Harry Smith, one of the most persistent critics of accommodation, wrote that Trotter's brash conduct in the Oval Office may have hurt his cause.[64]

Still, when Washington died a year later, in November 1915, it seemed likely that the leadership of black America would fall to more aggressive individuals like Trotter. Indeed, by the time of Washington's death, African Americans (and perhaps even Washington himself) seemed to have arrived at a consensus that blacks must protest more actively for civil and political rights. Washington's twenty-year reign paralleled a steady erosion of black rights—civil and economic. Rather than winning goodwill, accommodationism seemed to have emboldened southern whites to further oppress African Americans. If Trotter could not assume the leadership role, certainly others like him would step forward. The so-called New Negro that took shape during World War I, however, was no Trotter. Although the assertive New Negroes of the 1920s appeared on the surface to be the intellectual descendants of radicals like Trotter, a closer look shows they actually combined something of Trotter and something of Tuskegee. New Negroes insisted on political involvement but shared Washington's faith in economics. They displayed Trotter's fondness for militant rhetoric but did not oppose pragmatic compromise. They believed simultaneously in equality and self-help, full citizenship and black nationalism. And as August Meier has pointed out, most of the northern intellectuals who eventually joined the NAACP had supported Washington earlier and continued to be influenced by his ideas.[65]

The NAACP and Du Bois seemed to be the most obvious candidates to take over Washington's mantle of leadership of black America in 1915. The protest organization had the financial backing of white philanthropists and was rapidly gaining black support across the country. During the war, membership rose dramatically. Du Bois inaugurated the organization's well-written and influential organ, the *Crisis*, in 1910. Unlike Trotter, however, Du Bois took a more moderate position as editor of the *Crisis*, and he was never completely independent. Du Bois edited and ran the monthly *Crisis* on a day-to-day basis, but the all-white NAACP executive board maintained oversight powers and gave Du Bois feedback through frequent criticism of his editorials and suggestions for changes.

The most interference came from Oswald Garrison Villard, a chairman of the NAACP's executive board in the organization's early years, whom Du Bois accused of acting out of unconscious racial prejudice.[66] But even NAACP executive board members Mary White Ovington and Joel E. Spingarn, allies in whom Du Bois saw "no shadow" of racial prejudice, disagreed pointedly with him over his tone.[67] Both Ovington and Spingarn—like Villard—sought to increase the executive board's control over the *Crisis*.[68] They also used friendly persuasion to influence Du Bois's writing. In one instance, Spingarn informed his "friend" that the NAACP board had come to see the *Crisis* editor as a spoiled child who refused to "play the game" and subordinate his own will for the good of the group. "Many" now believed Du Bois should be "eliminated" from the organization, he said. Spingarn hoped Du Bois would stay, but he suggested the editor become more agreeable.[69] Ovington advised Du Bois to stop offending whites in his editorials and reminded him that his job depended on pleasing white readers.[70]

The organization's white leaders, who wanted to have at least one visible black founder, chose Du Bois because of his brilliance as a scholar and his eloquence as a writer and perhaps also because he seemed more willing to placate whites than other militant journalists like Trotter and Ida B. Wells, both of whom were kept at arm's length. Villard had observed that in contrast to the behavior of other black activists, whose contentiousness he found distasteful, Du Bois's "attitude and bearing" at the 1909 founding conference were "faultless."[71] Significantly, some of the most important black leaders of this period, including Washington, Trotter, and Marcus Garvey, criticized white domination of the NAACP and Du Bois.[72]

In spite of white interference, Du Bois spoke out for black equality and against racism in a clear and militant voice. He frequently outmaneuvered NAACP board members to get his way and wrote about taboo subjects like social equality and armed black self-defense.[73] Yet his proximity to white people altered the dynamic of his effort. The Crisis was certainly more measured than the Guardian. In accepting the editorship, Du Bois, for example, had agreed not to use the journal to attack Washington and to "avoid personal rancor of all sorts."[74] Du Bois was surrounded closely by the white audience he hoped to reach, a reality of which his colleagues often reminded him. White individuals, therefore, had a more direct impact on Du Bois than they had on other black editors. At the same time, the NAACP proved to be an important conduit for the black press to reach white America. Du Bois frequently repeated or summarized editorials from the black press in the Crisis, which gained more notice than most black weeklies. In addition, black viewpoints sometimes passed into the mainstream press through Villard, publisher of a major New York daily, the Evening Post, and the influential Nation magazine.

Another journalist who seemed poised to assume an important leadership role in the post-Washington era, James Weldon Johnson, also developed ties to the NAACP. A southerner and an early and enthusiastic supporter of Washington, Johnson began writing editorials in the New York Age in September 1914, became field secretary in 1916 and secretary in 1920 of the NAACP, and was one of the most visible literary figures of the Harlem Renaissance during the 1920s. New York

James Weldon Johnson, ca. 1920. Johnson began writing editorials for the *New York Age* in 1914. Courtesy Special Collections and Archives, W. E. B. Du Bois Library, University of Massachusetts, Amherst.

Age publisher Fred Moore, a real estate investor with close ties to the Tuskegee machine and little experience in newspapers, was fortunate in his choice of Johnson, who would write the majority of *Age* editorials during the war.[75] At the age of forty-three, Johnson had already run his own short-lived daily newspaper in Jacksonville, Florida, and

THE NEW NEGRO

worked as a teacher, school principal, lawyer, member of a popular Broadway songwriting team, and U.S. consul to Venezuela and Nicaragua (patronage jobs secured by Washington). Johnson left the consular service in 1913, foreseeing limited opportunities for blacks under the new Wilson administration.

When Johnson sought employment at the *Age*, Moore explained that he wanted the paper to have a "conservative and constructive" editorial policy, and after Johnson accepted the position, Moore told Washington the new editor was "a good friend of ours." Nonetheless, Johnson's editorials, which unlike others in the black press appeared under a byline, never shied away from condemning racial injustice in all its forms and taking on southern racists, like Georgia Populist Tom Watson, and the South in general. He advocated protest, although not the use of physical force; called for group pride and solidarity; endorsed self-help; and espoused mainstream economic and political doctrines. Johnson clearly believed that one of the main objectives of an editorial writer should be to reach white as well as black readers. As the young editor of the *Jacksonville Daily American*, Johnson had done "his best, in his reasonable arguments, to direct the opinion of both races," according to biographer Eugene Levy. In one of his first editorials for the *Age*, he said black newspapers should be considered "organs of propaganda."[76] Indeed, Johnson's considerable talents as a polemicist and a diplomat made him well suited to represent black concerns to white America. Unlike most black editors other than Du Bois, he sometimes published articles in mainstream journals. The NAACP often chose him to represent the organization before important white officials, including the president of the United States.

His visit to the Oval Office in February 1918 illustrates his talents but also shows how his approach differed from Trotter's. Johnson led a delegation to the White House to plead for clemency for court-martialed black soldiers and ask Wilson to speak out against lynching. After Johnson made his measured appeal, the president sat back in his chair in a relaxed posture and engaged Johnson and the other delegates in a "sociable manner," reminiscing about his youth in the South and discussing the issue of the soldiers and the problem of lynching. Johnson, although a severe critic of the president, left the half-hour meeting with his "hostility toward Mr. Wilson greatly shaken." Like Trotter, Johnson received no firm assurances, but just as the administration had reversed some of its segregation policies after the Trotter meeting, Wilson commuted the death sentences of ten condemned soldiers after his encounter with Johnson. Unlike Trotter, Johnson had followed the proper etiquette of White House visits and managed to leave on good terms with the chief executive after voicing his demands.[77]

In spite of Johnson's important leadership role, the *Age*'s most vital years had passed and a group of mostly new newspapers would lead the black press into a new era of journalism, beginning in the war years. During the 1920s and 1930s, four journals, the *Chicago Defender*, the *Baltimore Afro-American*, the *Pittsburgh Courier*, and the *Norfolk Journal and Guide*, sold dramatically more newspapers than the *New York Age* or any other newspaper had before 1915, when no black newspaper could accurately claim a circulation of more than 20,000.[78] By 1920, the *Chicago Defender* was selling 230,000 copies each week.[79] These newspapers increased readership by adopting a bolder, more sensational style with a readable format that appealed to marginally literate, lower-class readers who had ignored the sedate black newspapers of earlier days.

The *Defender* blazed the trail and set the tone for the new mass circulation black press. Starting with no capital in 1905, publisher Robert Abbott made his newspaper the first highly profitable black publication with a regular circulation in excess of 100,000.[80] Perhaps the most important step in the *Defender*'s rise came in 1910 when an employee, J. Hockley Smiley, instituted the changes that would give the *Defender* its appeal. Copying Chicago's daily newspapers, especially William Randolph Hearst's *Herald Examiner* and *Evening American*, Smiley began using large headlines and bold illustrations along with sensational copy. Eye-catching headlines—some of which had no obvious connection to the text—spread across the entire front page. A sampling of front-page headlines during 1915 gives a sense of the flavor of the paper, as well as the topics covered:

Race Not Dismayed by Vicious Acts of Congress
Howard P. Drew, Champion Sprinter, Wins Five Races in One Day
Amanda Smith, Race Martyr, Sleeps Near Her Monument
Abolish Segregation in the City Fire Department
Rev. E. J. Fisher Noted Divine Passes Away
President of Haiti Assassinated
Eighth Regiment off for Annual Encampment
Brothers Lynched for Loving Race Woman
Royal Life Insurance Co. Banquets 1st Race Superintendent
Johnson-Jeffries Fight—Pictures May Be Shown in Chicago
World Weeps for Washington

The *Defender* even borrowed a masthead design from Hearst, which triggered a lawsuit in 1918. Like Johnson at the *Age*, Smiley made the paper an "organ of racial propaganda," as some of the headlines suggest.[81]

Yet at the same time that his paper protested racial injustice with a fury that rivaled Trotter's *Guardian*, Abbott admired Washington and endorsed the philosophy of self-help and individual uplift, and he took conservative stands on issues unrelated to race. The *Defender* opposed female suffrage in the early 1910s, supported Washington's National Negro Business League, provided moral advice to black readers, and expressed deep faith in the ideology of personal success.[82] At the same time, however, Abbott's editorials supported the NAACP and used strong language to protest racial inequality and oppression in the South.

The most important difference between the *Defender* and Washington was the paper's willingness to criticize southern whites and advocate black migration out of the region. Through an ingenious scheme of distributing the *Defender* via black railroad porters, the newspaper became known to hundreds of thousands of southern blacks and helped to guide the migration of perhaps as many as 1 million blacks out of the South during World War I. The paper lured migrants by sensationalizing and often exaggerating southern lynchings, continually highlighting other examples of racial oppression in the South, and portraying Chicago and the North as a land of racial justice and boundless economic opportunity.[83]

Although this message was designed primarily for blacks, the *Defender* often addressed white America as well. And as the *Defender* and other black newspapers gained more circulation and had a greater impact on black readers, influential white leaders became increasingly interested in them. During the war in particular, the federal government, southerners who thought the paper was stirring up trouble, and a variety of others felt compelled to respond.

Like Johnson and Du Bois, Abbott called on blacks to cooperate with the war effort, but unlike Du Bois and perhaps even more adamantly than Johnson, he continued to demand racial justice in return. The *Defender* reached more southern blacks than any other black publication during the war and thereby raised the ire of southern whites, who branded Abbott's condemnation of southern lynching disloyal to the nation's war effort. More than any other black newspaper, the *Defender* engaged in dialogue with white America over the meaning and purpose of the country's involvement in World War I.

Besides Trotter, Du Bois, Johnson, and Abbott, other black individuals, organizations, and journalists sought to step into the vacuum left by Washington and influence the direction of race relations in America during the war. Washington's successor at Tuskegee, Robert R. Moton, cooperated with the federal government by encouraging black participation in the war effort. Emmett Scott, Washington's personal secretary, became special assistant on race relations to the secretary of war. The editors of the *Pittsburgh Courier* and the *Norfolk Journal and Guide*, which, like the *Chicago Defender* and the *Baltimore Afro-American*, would become major publications with mass national circulations in the 1920s, also sought to assume leadership positions in their communities. *Pittsburgh Courier* publisher Robert L. Vann, who was also a lawyer, would eventually win an appointment to President Franklin Roosevelt's Justice Department. He supported the American entry into World War I and organized widespread black support of the Liberty Loan and Red Cross drives. The *Norfolk Journal and Guide*, founded in 1910, remained a small newspaper during World War I. Not until World War II, when the First Lady and White House staffers were said to read it, would the paper reach the peak of its influence. Publisher P. B. Young, however, fashioned a leadership role even in the early years, primarily in his own community, where he founded a branch of the NAACP. Like Trotter and Johnson, he would also meet with a president in the White House—Calvin Coolidge, in 1925. Despite Young's participation in the NAACP, his biographer considers him an adherent of Washingtonian accommodationism. Young opposed black migration out of the South and soft-pedaled black grievances during the war while enthusiastically backing the war effort.

As the *Journal and Guide* was getting its start, a number of other vigorous black publications arose that sought to provide leadership and represent black demands—some locally and some nationally. The *Amsterdam News*, established in New York in 1909, and the *Black Dispatch*, first published in Oklahoma City in 1915, for example, both advocated racial justice on a local level, whereas a group of more radical national publications, including the socialist monthly *Messenger*, established in 1917, and Marcus Garvey's *Negro World*, inaugurated in 1919, came later.

Two older newspapers shifted their focus during the decade. Charlotta Spears (later Spears-Bass) became the only female owner of a black newspaper when, in May 1912, she purchased the *California Eagle* of Los Angeles with $50 of borrowed money. From the start, she put the paper on a course of "social and political activism," fighting for equal employment of blacks in government jobs and campaigning against *Birth of a Nation* and discrimination in housing.[84] The *Baltimore Afro-American Ledger*, a minor paper with roots in the nineteenth century, underwent a series of changes in personnel, name ("Ledger" was dropped), and style during the 1910s. After 1917, the paper began emulating the *Chicago Defender*'s sensationalist reporting, and its circulation increased dramatically—to 19,200 by 1919.[85] These newspapers represent only a small portion of the black press.

As World War I started in Europe in 1914, hundreds of African American newspapers and magazines in cities from coast to coast rolled off the presses every week. Just as America stood on the verge of a transformative event, the black press was about to enter a new era. In the coming months, as Washington passed from the scene and the country edged ever closer to war, each black journalist struggled to devise a response to the national emergency that combined the accommodationist impulses of Washington and the militant style of Trotter. Meanwhile, new distribution methods, black migration from the South, and sensational journalism expanded readership dramatically, making some key black newspapers more financially viable and giving them more credibility among white readers as the voice of "the Negro," thus making them more powerful. Under these circumstances, whites, especially government officials, paid greater attention to the black press—perhaps more attention than they had ever paid before. Black editors used this new power to press their demands for democratic reform.

CHAPTER 2

PREPARING AMERICA FOR WAR, 1914–1917

When the European nations plunged into war in the summer of 1914, it was not apparent that these distant events would have a significant impact on African Americans. Yet black editors and activists across the country immediately began to sort out the implications of the war. Racial hatred had caused it, they argued; the participation of men of darker races in the fighting would demonstrate their bravery and loyalty; Japan's involvement spelled the end of the unchallenged white dominance of the world.[1]

In September 1914, in the second month of the war, the *Richmond Planet* printed on its front page an appeal to President Wilson and "the 80,000,000 white citizens of the Republic" from William Monroe Trotter's National Equal Rights League. The document, published more than a month before Trotter's contentious meeting with Wilson, claimed the war was bringing advancements for women, the Irish, Poles, Jews, and Finns in Europe whereas African Americans suffered "more cruel, more insulting proscriptions and persecutions" than the members of these groups. The appeal urged Wilson "to free his Colored fellow citizens, millions that they are, from the repression, lynching, disfranchisement, Jim-crowism and segregation, even segregation under the federal government itself, not wait—till the exigencies of some awful war make the relief an act of expediency, rather than of justice."[2] In an editorial entitled "The Opportunity of the Dark Races," the *Planet* highlighted the successes of black troops fighting under the French army and predicted that participation in the war on both sides would win "the dark races" the "rights and privileges to which they are entitled."[3]

From the very beginning of the war, African American editors like Trotter and John Mitchell, the editor of the *Planet,* used their newspapers to promote the notion that an expansion of black rights should accompany the war and to highlight the loyalty of blacks. These two impulses—democratic advocacy and nationalistic loyalty—sometimes came into conflict with each other. Indeed, the former resembled a strategy of protest, whereas the latter smacked of accommodation. On the one hand, black journalists persistently pointed out the flaws in American democracy. On the other hand, they portrayed blacks as unconditionally loyal to a flawed nation.

Black journalists were not alone in struggling to reconcile these two contradictory motives during World War I. Nationalism was a driving force behind the conflagration that engulfed Europe from 1914 to 1918. Contests among nations for colonial possessions and national power contributed to tensions among the nations of Europe, and Balkan nationalism generated the sparks that started the war. Love of country inspired millions of men to offer their lives in battle and civilians to support their nation's efforts through war work and the purchase of war bonds. Meanwhile, at a time when many Western countries were moving toward greater democracy, England and its allies —as well as political elites in the United States—came to see the war as a fight to assure the triumph of democracy over authoritarian political systems.

Often, these two impulses clashed. In the nations purporting to fight for democracy, propaganda encouraged intolerant and sometimes hysterical militaristic nationalism, and opponents of the war lost the freedom to voice their opinions. Yet for the most part, supporters of the war acknowledged no contradictions between the two impulses, demanding blind patriotism and promoting democracy with equal vigor. No one embodied these competing influences better than the American president, who defined his nation's war as one to make the world safe for democracy while defining loyalty narrowly, encouraging cultural conformity, approving legislation to limit free speech, and sponsoring a propaganda effort that stimulated hysterical nationalism and intolerance of dissent.

African Americans found themselves caught between nationalism and democracy in even more complicated ways than those confronting Wilson and other white Americans. As members of a group that sometimes claimed a nationalist identity separate from that of other Americans, how would they respond to demands for loyalty and sacrifice to a nation that denied them basic rights? Indeed, many African Americans ridiculed the notion that the war was about promoting democracy, resisted participation in the war, and refused to be swept

RULER---PROTEM

"Ruler—Protem." "We should be thankful we are not subjects of Europe,"
the caption below this cartoon reads. "We are not at war in this country; let
us hope that we never shall be—barring the eternal war of injustice,
prejudice and unfair political and industrial disqualification." From the start
of the war in Europe, black newspapers began to compare it to the
circumstances of blacks at home. From *Chicago Defender,* August 15, 1914.

up in the wave of nationalistic passion that came over many of their fellow citizens before, during, and after the brief period of American belligerency. As many as 50 percent of African Americans opposed the war on some level, according to one historian.[4] But blacks had always responded to the nation's calls to arms. Whatever the feelings of the black population, however, the African American press's response cannot be seen as a reflection of them. Black editors were not the "voice of the Negro" in the sense of representing the general consensus of black opinion. They were less interested in articulating even their own ideas than in becoming involved in the national discussion about the war in such a way as to promote policy decisions or attitude changes that would benefit African Americans. Like Wilson, they never resolved the contradictions in their position because tangible results were more important than the consistency of their ideas.

Thus, black journalists began trying to influence the discourse about the world war from the summer of 1914 to the spring of 1917, well before America's entry, and they did so not by challenging fundamental popular assumptions about democracy, the war, or nationalism but by putting their own spin on those ideas.

ATROCITIES ABROAD AND AT HOME

As the war in Europe quickly settled into a bloody stalemate in the late summer and early fall of 1914, most Americans decided the best course was to remain neutral, as President Wilson put it, "in thought as well as in action." That was no easy task, given that a majority of Americans had European roots on one side of the fighting or the other. Events in Europe, too, made impartiality difficult. Germany's invasion of neutral Belgium at the outset of the war and reports of atrocities against civilians there poisoned many Americans against the Central Powers and inclined public opinion toward the Allies, whose propaganda machinery in America effectively exaggerated and accentuated German offenses, including the German chancellor's impolitic description of an 1839 treaty between Germany and Belgium as a mere "scrap of paper." Shortly after the invasion, German troops burned a library in Louvain containing 650 medieval manuscripts and, in 1916, forced Belgian laborers to work in German factories. In February 1915, the Kaiser proclaimed that neutral ships on their way to England would be torpedoed without warning, provoking a formal protest from President Wilson, and in May, a German zeppelin dropped bombs on London. Constant German bombardment reduced to rubble the French gothic cathedral of Reims, one of the architectural treasures of

Europe, and rumors proliferated about German atrocities in Belgium and at the front. Meanwhile, Germany's ally, Turkey, began a forced resettlement of Armenians in April 1915, which resulted in an estimated 600,000 deaths (Allied propaganda put the number at 1 million). Allied outrages, including Russia's mistreatment of Jews and Britain's brutal suppression of the Irish independence movement and blockade of neutral trade with Germany, never made as big an impact on public opinion in the United States in part because the German propagandists did not have easy access to the U.S. media. The British, in fact, cut the transatlantic cable between Germany and the United States in August 1914.

Allied propaganda converged with German actions, turning U.S. opinion irrevocably against the Central Powers in May 1915 when, shortly after a German U-boat sank the British liner *Lusitania* with 128 Americans onboard, the Bryce Committee reported the "deliberate and systematically organized massacres of the civil population" of Belgium and the looting, house burning, and "wanton destruction of property . . . ordered and countenanced by officers of the German Army."[5] Although the British report contained many distortions and fabrications, most Americans accepted it as truth because of the solid reputation of its author, former British ambassador to the United States, Viscount James Bryce, and because the 300-page report seemed to have been thoroughly documented, with 1,200 depositions from Belgian refugees and 37 captured diaries of German officers. The *New York Times* said the "shocking" report made "further dispute [of atrocity stories] impossible." The *Nation* argued that Germany was now morally isolated from the rest of the world, "branded with a mark of infamy such as in our time has not been stamped upon the face of any people."[6]

Like most Americans, black editorialists generally seemed to have accepted the stories of German atrocities as true, although James Weldon Johnson accurately predicted in his *New York Age* column that stories of atrocities in Europe would eventually prove to be "exaggerated tales."[7] Moreover, black writers had little sympathy for the Belgian victims of German atrocities. The *Norfolk Journal and Guide* suggested the Belgians deserved what they got from the Germans as punishment for their own atrocities in their African colonies.[8] Johnson argued that "nothing she [Germany] did in Belgium can surpass what the Belgians themselves did in the Congo."[9] In spite of his consistent support for the Allies, W. E. B. Du Bois agreed in November 1914 in the *Crisis* that Belgium had a dismal record in the Congo.[10] "Those colored men whose hands were cut off in the Congo by the Belgians would be of some service to them today as the Crisis so beautifully puts it this week," wrote Calvin Chase in the *Washington Bee,* endorsing another article by Du Bois printed shortly before the United States entered the war. "The Belgians are reaping what they have sowed."[11]

Most black editorialists did not conclude, based on the Bryce report or the *Lusitania* sinking, that the Central Powers were any worse than the Allies or that Germany had morally isolated itself from the world.[12] Instead, the black press saw similarities between Germany and some Allied nations. The *Chicago Defender* and the *Savannah Tribune* noted that the British committed worse violations of American neutrality than the Germans. Americans did nothing about the British blockade of all trade with Germany, the *Tribune* noted, while "the least action of Germany is vehemently protested against."[13] The *Washington Bee* saw no friend of the black man in the Allies. "England, Russia, and Japan would put the colored man in servitude," Chase pointed out. "England has her black soldiers digging trenches."[14]

Some writers also minimized Germany's villainy. The Allies could not "state in definite terms" what they were fighting for, and Germany's foibles were overrated, Johnson added. Indeed, what happened in Belgium was a natural consequence of a military invasion.[15] Although most Americans were outraged at Germany's sinking of the *Lusitania* on May 7, even branding it an atrocity, the *New York Age* shrugged and agreed with the Germans who said that new weapons like the U-boat required new rules of international warfare.[16] The *Richmond Planet* pointed out that the ship had been " 'loaded down to the gunwale' with ammunition and supplies for the allies" at the time of the attack.[17]

But if black writers saw a few parallels between the Central Powers' alleged atrocities and the actions of the Allies, they saw a clearer correlation between such atrocities and American deeds. Black editorials frequently contrasted stories of atrocities in Europe with accounts of lynchings of African Americans in the American South. "As ghastly as are the horrors of the European war, man's inhumanity to man is not confined to our brethren across the sea," the *Chicago Defender* editorialized in February 1916 after the annual statistics on lynching revealed a particularly bloody year in the South.[18] In the three years before America entered the war, 1914, 1915, and 1916, vigilantes had lynched 126 African Americans in ten southern states. The *Baltimore Afro-American* noted that a black American would be hard-pressed to distinguish between German "ruthlessness on the high seas" and "ruthlessness in my home town." At least the Germans killed their enemies for good reason: they were engaged in a battle for national survival. "Why are Negroes killed in the South?—for stealing a pig, for swearing in public, or wanting to vote."[19] Lynching, Johnson argued in the *New York Age*, made "the Turkish treatment of Armenians look like deeds of mercy."[20]

Lynching, which had originated in the American Revolution when patriot Charles Lynch organized a vigilante association to rid his Virginia county of Tories, resembled European misdeeds in that it violated the rule of law, according to black editors. In the early nineteenth century, lynchings took place mostly on the frontier, where practitioners hoped to deter crime in areas of dispersed population and weak law enforcement. Lynchers targeted mostly whites until the Civil War, when Confederates lynched some slaves to prevent rebellion. During Reconstruction, lynchers attacked both black and white Republicans as a means of political intimidation. Even later, in the first four years of record keeping, 1882–85, white victims outnumbered blacks 401 to 227, but from 1886 onward, the number of white victims declined steadily, totaling no more than eight in one year after 1915.[21] Contemporary apologists claimed that lynching of blacks was necessary to deter black criminals and especially rapists who, they alleged, preyed on white women in sparsely populated areas. Social scientists have tied lynching to economic stress or class conflict, southern cultural ideals, and the drive to control blacks.[22]

As black editors read their own headlines about southern mobs seizing African Americans who had been accused of some trivial breach of southern racial etiquette from poorly guarded jail cells and carrying them off to be hanged or shot or burned to death, they wondered how Americans could so passionately condemn Germany's breaking of treaties with neutral countries or its breach of international laws of naval engagement while tolerating these increasingly bold and gruesome punishments of individuals denied fair trials here at home. "Is the constitution of the United States also a 'scrape [*sic*] of paper?,'" the *Baltimore Afro-American* asked, echoing the German chancellor's pronouncement on the treaty with Belgium.[23] Editors frequently compared Germany's sinking of neutral vessels carrying civilians with the lynching of innocents in the South. Johnson wrote:

It does seem like hollow hypocrisy that this nation is . . . ready to raise armies and navies to uphold the principle of international law which guarantees protection to non-combatants aboard merchant vessels; even when those vessels belong to belligerents; and yet, the fact that within its own boarders one of its own citizens is taken from the custody of the lawfully constituted courts and burned at the stake by a mob will not call for the raising even of a sheriff's posse.[24]

Both Germany *and* the South would eventually have to answer for these transgressions of written laws, the *Norfolk Journal and Guide* predicted.[25]

Long before the outbreak of war in Europe, writers in the black press frequently related lynching to foreign policy by arguing that it hurt the nation's international reputation. Lynching belied America's "boast of leading the world in the great march of nations," the *Pittsburgh Courier* wrote in 1912.[26] Even before the turn of the century, Ida B. Wells had used the black press and an international speaking platform to condemn lynching as a blot on the national character that belied its claim to civilization.[27] Now, at the same time that war was raging in Europe, lynching in America seemed to be getting worse. Although the number of individuals lynched each year declined after reaching a peak in 1892, the incidents became more spectacularly brutal after the turn of the century. Instead of simply hanging or shooting their victims, mobs of white men, women, and children might gather for the burning of a live victim, hack off body parts for souvenirs, tie the victim to a car and drag it through the streets, and then pose blithely for photographs with the charred and mutilated corpse. In a widely reported Waco, Texas, lynching in May 1916, Jesse Washington, a seventeen-year-old boy, had just been convicted of raping and killing a white woman when a mob seized him from the court in broad daylight, dragged him into the public square, burned him alive, and dismembered his corpse. The lynching attracted national attention and energized the NAACP's nascent campaign against lynching. The organization distributed a lengthy exposé entitled "The Waco Horror" to 700 newspapers, including 50 black papers.[28] But Waco was not an isolated event. Lynchers killed fifty blacks in ten southern states in 1915 and thirty-nine in 1916.[29]

In addition to drawing parallels between lynching and European atrocities from 1914 to 1917, editorialists used lynching as a reason to question the federal government's ability to act justly anywhere in the world, including Latin America, where President Wilson intervened in the affairs of three nations during these years. He sent the marines to restore order after civil wars in Haiti and the Dominican Republic and dispatched the army to Mexico, first in 1914 to protect American citizens in the country as various forces contended for control in the wake of the 1911 Mexican Revolution and again in 1916 in retaliation for rebel Pancho Villa's raid of an American town just over the border in New Mexico.

Even black editors who did not oppose American intervention in all three cases expressed doubts about America's ability to act in the interests of black inhabitants, especially of Haiti. "They have shown in their segregation policies in this country that the love of a black man is far from their thoughts," the *Chicago Defender* argued.[30] The *Baltimore Afro-American* criticized the intervention bitterly, casting America in the role of the Kaiser discarding Haiti's rights like a "scrap of paper."[31] The *Washington Bee* urged Wilson to "let Haiti be free."[32]

Some writers argued that America had no business sending troops to right wrongs in Latin America when southern blacks were receiving no federal protection from lynching. "Why Mexico, Mr. President?," a *Chicago Defender* correspondent asked after the Waco lynching; "we need the Army in Texas."[33] The same event led Johnson to reflect: "We talk about helping Haiti and Santo Domingo and Mexico to rise to a higher level of civilization and development; it is enough to make the devil gasp in astonishment, seeing that we have in our own country such a community as Waco, Texas."[34]

Intervention seemed misplaced in Europe, too, given the pressing need to address lynching at home. After the outbreak of war in Europe, black editorialists made three convincing arguments about the connection between lynching in America and events in Europe that used the mainstream discourse about the war to shed light on the situation of blacks in the South. These arguments were not meant primarily to inspire black readers to action but rather to make it impossible for white Americans who believed in the humanitarian ideals underlying their critique of European atrocities to continue to ignore the lynchings of blacks in America.

First, editors wondered why Americans were so much more concerned about atrocities far away than they were about lynchings right at home. The *Richmond Planet* pointed out that the brutal lynching of six black Georgians in January 1916 "awakened no answering cry of horror from those who have been solicitous about the atrocities of the Germans and the Turks in Europe."[35] In 1915, Johnson called America "a nation of hypocrites" for complaining about the destruction of "old churches in Europe"—a reference to the German bombardment of Reims—while ignoring lynching in the South.[36] After the State Department inquired about the situation of Jews in war-torn Poland in May 1915, the *Chicago Defender* printed a sarcastic editorial, "Distance Lends Enchantment," that predicted: "Our government will do all in its power to relieve them. We are not speaking from experience."[37]

Second, editorialists argued that a nation unable to prevent lynching within its borders could not stop atrocities thousands of miles away. Americans, a *Defender* headline proclaimed, should put "our own house in order" before condemning European atrocities.[38] Such appeals were usually presented as general advice to the nation. Occasionally, black newspapers addressed white Americans more directly. The *Savannah Tribune*, for example, reprinted an editorial from the *Atlanta Journal* criticizing white ruffians in Forsyth County, Georgia, for throwing stones at tourists who used black chauffeurs. "Georgia is a state founded upon law and humanity, not a place for Turkish deviltry and persecution," the *Journal* opined, referring to the Armenian massacre. But the *Tribune* pointed out that the *Journal* had ignored a much more serious crime against blacks right in Atlanta. A mob had invaded black homes located near a white neighborhood and forced their owners to move out. The Atlanta case was far worse because it punished individuals for thrift and industry. "Let this section stop blaming Germans for their alleged ill treatment of the Belgians, the Turks of the Armenians, and have a house cleaning first," the *Tribune* scolded.[39]

A third message about the link between lynching and the war in Europe held that lynching would hurt America's credibility among the nations of the world and its ability to act on behalf of humanitarian motives. The *Chicago Defender* suggested as early as August 1915 that the United States' "apparent helplessness . . . to keep the law and order within its borders" disqualified it from intervening in Europe.[40] Johnson had made this point in his editorial "Concerns Not Even the Sheriff," also in August 1915, and in June of the following year, he argued that William Jennings Bryan's call for America to "lift Europe out of the bloody night of war" by spreading Christian ideals was unrealistic because "there are still parts of the United States in which this dominion is not yet firmly established."[41]

Lynching made it clear to inhabitants of other nations that the country was morally incapable of acting as the "seat of the world's conscience." Americans should try to "see ourselves as others see us," the *Richmond Planet* said.[42] Lynching was a "disgrace to American civilization" that "disfigured American history," according to the *Baltimore Afro-American*.[43] The Turkish ambassador to the United States, A. Rustem Bey, had been recalled in 1914 after Wilson objected to his statement in the press that Americans had no right to criticize Turks for the Armenian persecution when Americans lynched blacks "daily." The *Afro-American* agreed, adding that Wilson "could never recall the damage done by the truth that was uttered."[44] The *Chicago Defender* claimed that the rest of the world laughed off America's protests against the Turkish treatment of Armenians because of America's treatment of blacks.[45] A *Defender* cartoonist suggested that lynching would make "foreign powers" point at the American republic "with scorn . . . as a barbarous nation."[46]

Some white writers also equated lynching with atrocities in Europe and worried about the impact on America's credibility in international relations. Editorials in such mainstream periodicals as the *Independent*, the *Chicago Tribune*, and the *New York World* acknowledged this, and black newspapers often commented on or reprinted them. A *Chicago Tribune* editorial called the July 31, 1915, burning of Will Stanley in Temple, Texas, an atrocity. "Texas is disgraced by it, and the south and the United States. All America suffers from it, as any one knows who has read or heard the frequent reference to the offense in the foreign press, in books, in the mouths of men and women famous and obscure."[47] The liberal *Independent* described alleged atrocities by German soldiers as "trifling indiscretions" compared with lynching and warned that Uncle Sam "cannot preach morality and civilization for others and himself remain uncivilized, unless he wishes to appear in the eyes of the world as the most consummate hypocrite in all history."[48]

Black editors reprinted these and similar editorials as hopeful signs of growing white sentiment against lynching, sometimes apparently monitoring opinion in the mainstream public sphere. Johnson thought a *New York Sun* editorial comparing the plight of African Americans to foreign affairs had been inspired by his own piece on a similar theme. He went so far as to print the two articles side by side. Wilson, the *Sun* argued, could serve humanity by doing something about the plight of African Americans rather than looking abroad. "Their lot is at least as interesting as that of the Filipinos." The *New York Age* editorial, written on the occasion of the Waco lynching, was different in tone and content. Yet Johnson thought the two pieces expressed "exactly the same sentiment. The fact that this sentiment expressed in the Age is revoiced in a paper like the Sun—a great paper, but markedly lacking in friendly feeling for the Negro—is doubly gratifying," he concluded. Whether or not the *Sun* had been influenced by the *Age*, this exchange reveals clearly Johnson's aim of influenc-

TO THE PRESIDENTIAL NOMINEE—

"No Citizen, Whatever Race, Color or Creed Is Safe Where Justice Sleeps and Anarchy Reigns and Where the Law Is Openly Defied."

"To the Presidential Nominee." "Shall the American Republic be pointed at with scorn by the foreign powers as a barbarous nation?," the *Chicago Defender* asked below this cartoon. "WE DEMAND PROTECTION from these murderers, even if the ENTIRE SOUTH MUST BE PLACED UNDER MARTIAL LAW. Why Mexico? Why bother about Germany or Japan? No civilized nation has disgraced itself with the above scenes in the past fifty years." From *Chicago Defender,* June 10, 1916.

ing not only African American readers but the mainstream press as well.[49] Most black papers engaged in this practice of writing editorials aimed at influencing white opinion and monitoring and critiquing the white press. The *Savannah Tribune*, for example, frequently reprinted editorials from white newspapers condemning lynching, such as the piece from the *Atlanta Journal* and an editorial from the *Worth County Local* that criticized a Georgia sheriff for handing over a prisoner to a lynch mob. "It is refreshing to note that more and more the newspapers of the state are becoming outspoken against lawlessness," the *Tribune* concluded.[50]

LYNCHING, BLACK LOYALTY, AND *BIRTH OF A NATION*

In spite of the optimism of Johnson and the *Savannah Tribune* concerning efforts to promote antilynching sentiment, the black press could not yet hope to counter the vast cultural machinery engaged in cultivating racist feeling and even justifying the practice of lynching. Since before the turn of the century, southern apologists for lynching had been churning out tracts with titles like *The Negro a Beast* or *The Negro: A Menace to American Civilization* that portrayed African Americans as inferior, criminal people who had to be kept in line with an occasional lynching. No one did more to popularize a rationale for lynching than Thomas Dixon, whose trilogy of best-selling novels— *The Leopard's Spots* (1902), *The Clansman* (1905), and *The Traitor* (1907) —depicted black men as depraved beasts. Dixon said he intended *The Clansman*, which became a popular play in 1905, to "teach the North . . . what it has never known—the awful suffering of the white man during the dreadful Reconstruction period . . . to demonstrate to the world that the white man must and shall be supreme."[51] Black journalists' hopes to counter such ideas and portray lynching as un-American seemed lost when, in 1915, the pioneering filmmaker, D. W. Griffith, released a film based on *The Clansman*. Although somewhat tamer than the novel, *Birth of a Nation* conveyed the same message and promised to reach a far wider audience. It depicted Reconstruction as a disaster imposed by vengeful and misguided radicals in Congress who hoped to overturn the social order by forcing on whites a ruling class of blacks who became "drunk with wine and power," corrupted the government, refused to work, and, worst of all, pursued white women.[52] In a climactic scene, a young white heroine jumps to her death to escape Gus, a white actor in blackface, who has proposed "marriage"—a code in the movie for rape. The Ku Klux Klan later lynches Gus, providing a fitting punishment. In the end, the South is redeemed by the rise of the Klan, which rescues not only the white population but also "good" blacks who are content to remain in their places as loyal and powerless servants. As Du Bois put it, the film portrayed the African American as either "an ignorant fool, a vicious rapist, a venal or unscrupulous politician or a faithful but doddering idiot."[53] Dixon said he hoped the film would "create a feeling of abhorrence in white people, especially white women, against colored men."[54]

The filmmakers' central aim was embodied in two plot twists. In one, the former Confederate protagonists, the Camerons, are arrested for membership in the Klan but manage to escape (with the help of their faithful former slaves) and flee to an old cabin in the woods. Inside, they discover two Union Army veterans. Instead of driving the Confederates away, the Union veterans welcome them. An intertitle proclaims that "the former enemies of North and South are united again in common defense of their Aryan birthright," and they all prepare to fight to the death against the Reconstruction government's approaching black militia. Meanwhile, Austin Stoneman, a Radical Republican who has been preaching racial equality, changes his mind when the malevolent mulatto lieutenant governor, Silas Lynch, tries to "marry" Stoneman's young daughter. Thus North and South are reunited in their determination to protect white women, keep African Americans in their place, and assure the continuation of white supremacy in America.[55] To a great extent, the film's vision of northern and southern whites allied to keep blacks subordinated did reflect the reality of the post-Reconstruction period, in which the U.S. Supreme Court ratified legal proscription of blacks in the South and the Congress and president did nothing to stop it. Dixon and Griffith wanted to solidify the alliance and push blacks even farther down.

Few white Americans found anything objectionable in the film. The *Chicago Tribune* said it was "in all essential episodes grounded on historical fact, representing the struggles of that terrible time in the south. . . . It presents what the south says and the north of our day, at least, is inclined to believe to be truth."[56] Woodrow Wilson, his daughters, and the cabinet screened it in the White House just ten days after its February release in Los Angeles. Although Wilson probably did not say, as historians have often reported, that "it is like writing history with lightning, and my only regret is that it is all so terribly true," the filmmakers used Wilson's White House screening as a way to lend legitimacy to their production.[57] For the same reason, they arranged another showing for Supreme Court Chief Justice Edward White, other justices, senators, and congressmen.[58] One might expect southerners like White and Wilson to agree with Griffith's slanted view of history. White allegedly confided to Dixon that he had ridden with the Klan in his youth. And Wilson, who believed black Reconstruction policies had led to the "veritable overthrow of civilization in the South," had written some of the historical accounts Griffith used in his research for the movie. The film intertitles even quoted Wilson.[59]

More surprising was the acceptance of the film by many liberal whites, some with a history of sympathy for blacks. George Foster Peabody, a pacifist and generous supporter of black education; California's reformist governor Hiram Johnson; critic Burns Mantle; foreign correspondent and novelist Richard Harding Davis; Pulitzer Prize–winning novelist Booth Tarkington; and S. S. Frissell, a supporter of the NAACP, all accepted the film as accurate. Watching the film, medical reformer Dorothea Dix advised, would "make a better American of you." Some reformers thought its historical theme was a vast improvement over the sexual and slapstick titillation of most other films of the day.[60] Reviewers praised the film, and enthusiastic moviegoers flocked to see it in theaters.[61]

Dixon's hope that the film would *"revolutionize northern sentiments"* against blacks seems to have been largely realized.[62] Mary White Ovington reported that as she left a New York showing she heard a man exclaim: "I would like to kill every nigger. I would like to sweep every nigger off the earth." A white Indiana viewer shot and killed a black teenager after viewing the film. Houston audiences shouted "lynch him!" during the scene in which Gus chases the young woman over the cliff. The number of lynchings nationwide grew significantly in 1915, and a revived Ku Klux Klan emerged.[63] The makers of the film seemed to be succeeding at unifying white northerners and southerners against blacks and spreading, in the words of Michael Rogin, "the screen memory, in both meanings of that term, through which Americans were to understand their collective past and enact their future."[64] African Americans hoped to promote a different view of the past and vision for the future, but their small newspapers seemed like no match for this new medium.

Undaunted, African Americans waged a major campaign to ban the film from theaters or, failing that, to discredit it with the public. Although the NAACP undertook much of the direct action, black journals undergirded the campaign from the beginning. Before the film's February 8 premiere at Clunes Auditorium in Los Angeles, the *California Eagle* warned that black voters would not support any official who opposed banning the film. Significantly, the paper objected to this

THE LAST CAT

"The Last Cat." A thrown shoe and a gun labeled "public sentiment" knock antiblack southern politicians Cole Blease, James K. Vardaman, and Benjamin Tillman Jr. in the form of stray cats from the fence, while only *Birth of a Nation* remains. Blease had been defeated in his bid for the U.S. Senate in 1914, but Tillman and Vardaman were serving terms when this cartoon appeared. From *Chicago Defender,* October 23, 1915.

"prejudice-making play" not only for the way it portrayed blacks but also for its depiction of white people. The film opened, but only after a judge ordered that a few scenes be cut.[65]

The film's widespread popularity in the next several months seemed to confirm the editors' worst fears and the filmmakers' fondest hopes that *Birth of a Nation* would spread southern sentiment on race and justify lynching in white northerners' minds. "Clunes' Auditorium is thronged each day with all sorts of cultured people applauding the glorification of mob-murder!," William Easton wrote in the *Eagle*. "Mr. Griffith and Thomas Dixon are conducting a day and evening school to teach all who will pay the price, how easy it is to 'lynch,' how gracefully it can be done, and what wonderful maneuvering it admits of." Moviegoers at one showing broke into "tumultuous applause, a sort of hilarious happiness," upon the entrance of the Klan, he reported.[66]

The NAACP's campaign against the film began in late winter as organizers braced for the March 3 premiere in New York City. Protesters demanded first that certain scenes, then whole sections, of the film be removed; called for a preview by black leaders; filed suit to prevent the film's opening; flooded the mayor's office; and mobilized widespread opposition to the film among blacks and liberal whites. Whites who lined up with the NAACP included not only its former chairman, Oswald Garrison Villard, publisher of the *New York Post* and the *Nation* magazine, but also muckraker Ray Stannard Baker, settlement house organizer Jane Addams, movie producer Lewis Selznick, Rabbi Stephen A. Wise, and movie reviewer Francis Hackett, who wrote a negative appraisal of the film in the *New Republic*.[67] The film opened, but the opposition again won a few cuts.

Protest culminated in Boston, where William Monroe Trotter used the leverage of black votes to pressure Mayor James Michael Curley to consider a ban. Curley ordered the filmmakers to cut five of the most objectionable scenes before allowing it to open in a downtown theater on April 10. Trotter, still unsatisfied, led a group of protesters to the lobby of the theater; after club-wielding police arrested ten protesters, including Trotter, a few others managed to get in and throw a rotten egg at the screen during the climactic rape scene. In the following days, Trotter led a protest gathering at Faneuil Hall and a march on the State House. The 2,000 angry blacks protesting on the State House steps won a promise from Governor David Ignatius Walsh that he would draft a new censorship law, all to no avail. The censorship board created by the new law ruled on June 2 that the film could run, and it played to large audiences until mid-October, thanks in part to the publicity generated by Trotter's campaign. Still, the episode may have had some ancillary benefits, as Curley later sought to reach out to black voters by appointing some African Americans to public office and promoting a federal antilynching bill.[68]

Meanwhile, protests continued elsewhere around the country, and some local officials did ban the film, at least temporarily: in Chicago and later throughout Illinois; Pasadena, California; Wilmington, Delaware; St. Louis; Massachusetts outside of Boston; Norwalk, Connecticut; West Virginia; and Ohio.[69] Black journalists, through their newspapers and organizations, clearly did wield some power, however little compared to the makers of the film. A closer look at one relatively successful local campaign spearheaded by *Cleveland Gazette* publisher Harry C. Smith offers a case study in how a black newspaper could affect important white leaders and provides further insight into how the black press worked to shape the public meaning of national wars, lynching, and patriotism just prior to the American entry into World War I. Smith addressed black readers about the film but constructed his arguments to convince influential northern whites. He coordinated his published statements with communications through back channels to important state officials. Finally, he seems to have succeeded in winning significant opposition to the film among high government officials.

In many ways, Smith's attack on the film mirrored the strategy of Griffith and Dixon. Whereas the filmmakers sought to unify North and South against black Americans, Smith sought to unify northerners and blacks against the South. The filmmakers portrayed blacks and Smith portrayed southern whites as uncivilized brutes. The filmmakers depicted southern whites and Smith depicted blacks as respectable, law-abiding victims. Both highlighted the support of their positions by figures of authority and utilized back channels to contact those figures to bolster their positions. Both sought to make their positions on the film resonate with contemporary politics and culture.

A charter member of T. Thomas Fortune's "Afro-American Agitators," Smith was an uncompromising integrationist; an opponent of all separate black institutions, even those created by blacks for their own benefit; an early and consistent critic of Booker T. Washington and the South; a charter member of the NAACP, as well as a wary observer and frequent opponent; and one of Trotter's most reliable allies. Smith began publishing his weekly *Gazette* in 1883, and when he died in 1941, it died with him, ending one of the most extraordinary careers in black journalism. In a sense, Smith set the standard for the independent black editor-publisher-proprietor, a standard no one else ever quite met. Piecing together his newspaper week after week with little help, Smith advocated bedrock principles that remained consistent over the years, struggled constantly to stay afloat financially, and engaged energetically in politics. In addition to using his paper to promote political views and candidates, Smith himself dived into the arena, winning three terms in the state legislature in the 1890s, where he promoted a number of civil rights bills, including a pioneering antilynching bill. After the turn of the century, Smith became disenchanted with the Republican Party and advocated the political independence of blacks, forming the Interstate League of Independent Colored Voters in 1902. Nonetheless, he received 60,000 votes in the Republican primary for Ohio secretary of state in 1920, sought the Republican nomination for governor repeatedly during the 1920s, and endorsed and worked for Republican candidates for local, state, and national offices. Smith maintained his political contacts and used his paper to try to manipulate important state officeholders, as his campaign against *Birth of a Nation* illustrates.[70]

During 1915, he gave more space to his campaign against the film than he gave to any other political topic, and he continued to lobby against it over the next two years.[71] Most of his coverage revolved around efforts to persuade state and city officials—especially Governor Frank Willis—to censor the film. He printed letters to and from Willis and other officials, editorials, petitions, news accounts, official pronouncements, and pieces from other papers relating to the film and his campaign to ban it. Smith portrayed the white governor as aligned with blacks against the outrageous film even before Willis had taken a decisive stand. He praised Willis so extensively for supporting censorship that editor Calvin Chase of the *Washington Bee* called Smith Ohio's Sancho Panza, referring to Don Quixote's squire.[72]

Smith saw Willis as an important authority whose opposition to the film gave greater credence to Smith's own criticisms. Further, the governor's stand with blacks against the white South discredited *Birth of a Nation*'s assertion of a unity of whites against blacks. Smith also printed articles written by white authors who affirmed the humanity of African Americans and attacked Griffith's film. One of these happened to be the state attorney general, E. C. Turner, who oversaw the censorship board.

When Turner upheld the board's decision to ban *Birth of a Nation*, Smith reprinted his statement in full. Turner focused more on the film's slander of the North than on its slander of blacks. He criticized the historical absurdity of portraying northern leaders consorting with black mistresses when white slave owners had caused most race mixing; the inclusion of scenes unflattering to Union generals William Tecumseh Sherman and Ulysses Grant and Union soldiers; the portrayal of the South as superior to the North; the representation of black soldiers as rapists; and the depiction of the outlaw Ku Klux Klan as heroic. "This picture is neither of a moral, educational, amusing nor harmless character," Turner concluded.[73] The statement gave the lie to Dixon's notion of a unity of whites against blacks.

In his own criticisms of the film, Smith, like Turner, did not dwell on the way the film injured African Americans. " 'The Birth of a Nation' is not only vile in parts but positively a dangerous film because it ridicules and reviles sacred historical figures (soldiers and statesmen) of this country, attacks loyalty, praises rebels and their organizations like the infamous Ku Klux Klan, and promotes the mob spirit wherever it is exhibited," he stated.[74] Just as other editorialists had pointed out the ways lynching damaged the nation's reputation, Smith framed the film as an attack on the North and on America's best ideals rather than on blacks. This was a conscious strategy to influence northern white opinion. Advising local black activists in 1917 how to most effectively attack the film, he explained that instead of stressing blacks' gripes, they should focus on how the film "ridicules the loyal Federal soldier of the war of the rebellion, insults the North and does far worse in the case of such abolitionists as Lovejoy. . . . Make it clear that somebody else's 'ox is gored' besides ours."[75]

In this case and others, when Smith addressed blacks concerning the film, he usually offered suggestions on how best to turn whites against it. In addition to showing how the film offended whites, he advised, black opponents should exhibit greater unity in their protests and, most important, behave respectably during demonstrations.[76] When an Ohio court ruled in early 1917 that the film must be shown in Cleveland, Smith blamed the decision on a last-minute protest by a "mob" made up of the "lowest Negroes," some recruited from saloons. Not only did the protesters make a "weak demonstration," but on their way home, they vandalized a streetcar and some shop windows. "The decent respectable, law-abiding Afro-Americans of this city repudiate them," he declared, calling for the "arrest and punishment" of the mob members. According to Smith, the judge who heard the case on Monday afternoon handed down his decision against censorship on Tuesday morning in part because of the actions of the unruly black protesters the night before.[77] The protesters, it seems, had reinforced the filmmakers' claim that blacks were lawless and uncivilized, qualities that Smith and the rest of the black press consistently attributed to white southerners.

Like editors of black periodicals all the way back to *Freedom's Journal*, Smith promoted respectable behavior among blacks as a way of earning citizenship rights at the same time that he publicized any evidence of such behavior as proof to whites that blacks already deserved those rights. Smith turned against Willis early in 1916 because he appointed as oil inspector a black saloon owner—someone Smith thought would not be a "satisfactory representative" of the race.[78] In the context of lynching and the *Birth of a Nation* controversy, proper black behavior became even more important. After all, Smith was arguing that African Americans were not prone to uncivilized violence, so lynching was not needed to keep them in order. Such efforts to emphasize black accomplishments and respectability should not be explained away merely as a reflection of the class bias of bourgeois editors or a desire to allay feelings of inferiority among middle-class blacks, as E. Franklin Frazier has argued.[79] Rather, they were part of a campaign to mold and "shape public opinion about ourselves," as James Weldon Johnson put it.[80]

Smith hoped to counter Griffith's attempt to portray a unity of interest of northern and southern whites against blacks. Instead of depicting the South as the victim of the North in the Civil War and Reconstruction, Griffith had portrayed the entire nation as the victim of blacks and Radical Republicans, who formed an evil alliance and seized power after the assassination of Lincoln.[81] In contrast, Smith portrayed the film, white supremacists, and the South as the enemies of loyal Union soldiers, fundamental American ideals, and true Americans—black and white. Smith and Griffith were engaged in a struggle over the meaning of key events in American history with direct bearing on the character and meaning of America in the present. Whereas the filmmakers set up a polarity in American life between civilized whites and uncivilized blacks, Smith sought to establish a polarity between the true and the false America. On one side—humanistic, democratic, and civilized—stood the North, the (loyal) Union, the Constitution, the Declaration of Independence, and abolitionism; on the other—inhuman, undemocratic, and violent—stood the South, the (disloyal) Confederacy, racism, disfranchisement, and Jim Crow.[82] At least in the context of the state of Ohio, Smith's vision seems to have won out.

Nationally, however, the censorship campaign against *Birth of a Nation* failed to achieve its major objective.[83] Historian Thomas Cripps sees the campaign, at least in its later phases, as misguided because it put blacks in the dubious position of opposing free speech and because their protests actually boosted the popularity of the film.[84] In Oakland, promoters allegedly paid a group of blacks to boycott the

PREPARING AMERICA FOR WAR

A SNAKE IN THE GRASS

What the North Thinks of Rev. (?) Thomas Dixon. Every Now and Then He Slips Back Unannounced with His Dastardly Work.

"A Snake in the Grass." A farmer in the background labeled "Uncle Sam" is walking alongside a fence called the "Mason Dixon Line" saying, "Them durn reptiles get thru this old fence right along." Thomas Dixon, author of the book that inspired *Birth of a Nation,* is the snake scaring the "Northern Public." From *Chicago Defender,* February 19, 1916.

film to generate publicity. Griffith predicted that the "silly legal opposition . . . will make me a millionaire if they keep it up."[85] Some black newspapers, including the *Washington Bee* and the *Chicago Defender,* opposed continued protest for this very reason—although not before condemning the film and refuting its argument. Booker T. Washington and his followers adopted this stance early on, and his personal secretary, Emmett J. Scott, put his energies behind the production of *Birth of a Race,* a film that would present the opposing view. Underlying these different tactics, however, lay a basic similarity—a belief in the absolute necessity of answering Griffith. Black journalists could not sit idly by and allow such a distorted statement on race relations to go unanswered, so they sought to respond, even if only, as the *Washington Bee* proposed, by letting "our conduct be of such a nature that [it] will put a quietus on the indictment."[86]

Birth of a Nation may have had a devastating impact on race relations, but the campaign against it did have a mitigating effect. Important liberals like George Foster Peabody reversed their early endorsement of the film, Hollywood producers in the future shied away from negative black roles, and southerners like Justice White and some of his congressional friends came to be embarrassed by their initial sanctioning of the film.[87] Even President Wilson felt it necessary to leak to the press the news that he disapproved of the "unfortunate production."[88] Such recriminations may have become necessary because the protests had changed the climate and made it unrespectable—or at least politically inexpedient—to support the racist film. Black opposition may have prevented *Birth of a Nation* from fully nationalizing southern race sentiment. At the very least, African Americans had their say, and Griffith's racist justification of lynching did not go unanswered.

AFFIRMING BLACK LOYALTY

The discourse about European atrocities and the battle over *Birth of a Nation* in the black press—two parts of a crusade to mold public opinion about the meaning and significance of lynching during the years immediately preceding America's entry into World War I—had direct relevance to the coming struggle. One related lynching to the war America was about to enter, and the other sought to establish the meaning of the last war and the significance of African Americans' participation in it before the nation embarked on another one.

As Smith and other black editors demonstrated that African Americans had helped to preserve and perfect the Union during the last war, they also sought to show that African Americans would loyally support the government in the coming war—in spite of their intense skepticism about America's fitness to fight a war for democratic principles in Europe or anywhere else. Therefore, despite his outspoken criticism of President Wilson and the war, Smith, like most of the black press, declined to resist America's slow but inexorable slide toward war from 1914 to 1917. From the start of the war in Europe, leaders began preparing the nation for participation by calling for a military buildup and promoting a definition of loyalty that urged individuals to place national duty ahead of personal or group interests. Black editors' support for these preparations ranged from mild to enthusiastic — but few, if any, opposed them outright.

Shortly after the war started in Europe, leaders like Woodrow Wilson and Theodore Roosevelt began preaching self-sacrifice and undivided loyalty and railing against selfishness and self-indulgence. African Americans might have rejected the notion that they had a duty to a nation in which they were granted second-class citizenship and often lacked the protection of the law. Indeed, that response would have been in keeping with their criticisms of foreign policy during this same period. But such a strategy would have gone against the tradition of African American participation in U.S. wars and might have led to even greater oppression of blacks during this war. Black participation in the American Revolution had led the northern states to abolish slavery, and black soldiers fighting for the Union Army had helped to justify the Emancipation Proclamation. Again in World War I, African Americans would contribute admirably to the war effort. It was not clear, however, what reward, if any, they would receive in exchange. At a time when *Birth of a Nation* was suggesting otherwise, the black press hoped to show that African Americans conformed to a demanding standard of loyalty that subordinated all other interests to national duty. And yet, at the same time, they would demand something in return.

Black newspapers sought to use notions from the mainstream political discourse about patriotism, loyalty, unity, and, in particular, Americanism and preparedness to advance the cause of racial justice. In a sense, though, these notions would use them. After all, the white leaders who coined the phrases that would lead America into war never meant for them to advance the interests of weak minority groups — quite the opposite. They hoped that members of such groups would abandon their particular interests and channel all of their energies into winning the war.

After the outbreak of war in Europe in August 1914, some influential individuals and organizations began to worry about the loyalty of the nation's so-called hyphenated Americans, the approximately 30 million first- and second-generation European immigrants, especially the 8 million German Americans who might refuse to fight a war against their former homeland.[89] Such worries added fuel to a campaign that had been under way since the 1890s to "Americanize" new immigrants.[90] Institutions as diverse as the Daughters of the American Revolution and Hull House had guided the Americanization campaign for a variety of motives, from eradicating radicalism among the new population to helping immigrants adjust to their new home. Until the start of the European war, the efforts of Americanization advocates like Frances Kellor were focused mainly on offering night classes in English to new immigrants and lacked broad popular support.

By the summer of 1915, however, the divided loyalties of hyphenated Americans had become a major concern, and Kellor headed a new organization, the National Americanization Committee, supported by businessmen and political leaders and dedicated to "stimulating naturalization, breaking the immigrant's ties with the Old World, and teaching him an American culture."[91] Since the mid-1890s, Theodore Roosevelt had been railing against members of groups who acted politically as an ethnic bloc. Roosevelt and other nativist American reformers stepped up their attacks on hyphenism after ethnic groups began to form political organizations to fight various reform movements they believed to be opposed to their own interests—such as immigration restriction, prohibition, and woman suffrage. Opposition to ethnic political blocs grew after 1900 as the movement to restrict immigration gathered steam and German and Irish Americans and other ethnic groups formed national organizations to oppose it. The onset of the war brought these tensions to a head.[92]

"There is no such thing as a hyphenated American who is a good American," Roosevelt told the Knights of Columbus at a speech at Carnegie Hall in October 1915. "The only man who is a good American is the man who is an American and nothing else."[93] Although somewhat less zealous, Wilson, too, sounded the alarm about hyphenates. In his annual message to Congress in December 1915, he warned that foreign-born citizens "have poured the poison of disloyalty into the very arteries of our national life. . . . Such creatures of passion, disloyalty, and anarchy must be crushed out."[94] Congress applauded these remarks enthusiastically.[95]

The issues of loyalty and Americanism became major themes of the presidential election of 1916. First as a candidate himself and then on the stump for Republican nominee Charles Evans Hughes, Roosevelt advocated a military buildup, American entry into the war, and an extreme brand of nationalist conformity. Roosevelt saw something "sinister" in identification with any nationality other than an American one and argued that "hyphenated Americans," along with pacifists, war profiteers, and those who advocated peace at any price, came "perilously near being treasonable to this country." He declared: "I do not believe in hyphenated Americans. . . . We have a right to ask all of these immigrants and the sons of these immigrants that they become Americans and nothing else."[96]

Wilson also called for national unity. Just before the Democratic convention in July, he outlined his definition of loyal citizenship in a speech entitled "The American Spirit" presented to the Citizenship Convention, a meeting organized by the Bureau of Naturalization in Washington. Although Wilson was referring primarily to German Americans when he criticized "certain men" who "draw apart in spirit and in organization from the rest of us to accomplish some special object of their own," his message could be applied to any ethnic minority with its own exclusive organizations and political aims. He asserted that forming ethnic organizations

> is absolutely incompatible with the fundamental idea of loyalty, and that loyalty is not a self-pleasing virtue. I am not bound to be loyal to the United States to please myself. I am bound to be loyal to the United States because I live under its laws and am its citizen, and, whether it hurts me or whether it benefits me, I am obliged to be loyal. Loyalty means nothing unless it has at its heart the absolute principle of self-sacrifice. Loyalty means that you ought to be ready to sacrifice every interest that you have, and your life itself, if your country calls upon you to do so. And that is the sort of loyalty which ought to be inculcated into these newcomers—that they are not to be loyal only so long as they are pleased, but that, having once entered into this sacred relationship, they are bound to be loyal whether they are pleased or not; and that loyalty which is merely self-pleasing is only self-indulgence and selfishness.[97]

In a speech delivered a few days later at the Washington Monument, Wilson added that such "disloyalty . . . must be absolutely crushed." At the same time, the Democratic National Convention adopted a platform plank, drafted by Wilson and conceived as the centerpiece of the campaign, that promoted Americanism and denounced hyphenism.[98]

On some level, Wilson and Roosevelt's formulation of national loyalty as incompatible with ethnic identity and superior to every other interest was antithetical to the interests of African Americans—if not downright impossible to implement. Oppressed as a group, they needed to agitate for redress as a group. Set apart because of their racial identity by whites, they could not renounce their blackness because whites would not ignore it. Still, black newspapers strove to adopt the language of Americanism and loyalty so pervasive in America during the years before and during World War I. African Americans, they argued, had no divided loyalties, no homeland other than the United States to whom they owed allegiance, and no reason to be disloyal. Journalist Ralph Tyler, writing in the *Appeal*, a black weekly in St. Paul, told blacks to use the term "colored American" rather than "Negro" or "Afro-American" as a way of de-emphasizing difference. "We are not Africans because we are native born and native sired Americans." The editor of the newspaper, John Quincy Adams, called on all ethnic groups to "wipe out forevermore the hyphen in American citizenship."[99] The *Baltimore Afro-American* speculated that, "in view of the bad odor attached to hyphens," it might soon have to rename the paper "simply THE AMERICAN."[100]

In general, however, the black press saw the hyphen issue not as one requiring a change in black identity but as one that highlighted the difference between recent European immigrants, with foreign languages and customs and attachments to European states, and African Americans, who were "American[s] first, last and always."[101] The *Norfolk Journal and Guide* printed at the top of page 1 the governor of Virginia's statement that "in your race there is no such thing as a hyphenated American."[102] The *New York Age* came out in favor of forcing immigrants to learn English.[103] European immigrants, the *Chicago Defender* argued, had "sworn allegiance [to America] as a matter of form and . . . would on the slightest provocation aid their fatherland against their adopted home."[104] African Americans, others argued, were farther removed from Old World culture and politics and would thus give their undivided loyalty to America. "Its language is our only tongue, and no hyphen bridges or qualifies our loyalty," one editorialist wrote.[105] Wilson probably felt safer with black soldiers guarding the White House after his declaration of war in 1917, the *Richmond Planet* commented, than he would have felt with "white ones, who are made up of so many nationalities."[106] Also, unlike recent immigrants, African Americans had proven their loyalty by participating in all of the nation's past wars, creating what the *California Eagle* referred to as "the splendid illustrious record of the 'black Phalanx' from Crispus Attucks and Bunker Hill to Carrizal."[107]

Most black papers also supported the campaign for a military buildup in preparation for American participation in the European war. Although the campaign was led by the politically conservative National Security League, which sought "to militarize American society" by strengthening the army and navy and instituting universal military training, some progressives, led by Roosevelt, also clamored for preparedness.[108] Roosevelt noted that abolitionists who had been peace advocates had come to support the Civil War, and he compared opponents of preparedness to Tories in the Revolution, Copperheads in the Civil War, and even John Wilkes Booth, Lincoln's assassin. Patriotism required preparedness. "We must prepare ourselves against disaster by facing the fact that we are nearly impotent in military matters," he warned.[109]

Initially opposed to an increase in military spending, Wilson adopted in the summer of 1915 a policy of "reasonable preparedness" that called for a $500 million shipbuilding program, a small expansion of the regular army, and the creation of a new reserve army—distinct from the National Guard—of 400,000. His preparedness address of November 4, 1915, met with opposition from some leading progressives and a group of about fifty congressmen, most of them former Populists from the South and the West.[110] In spite of their skepticism about America's moral fitness for fighting a war for democratic principles in Europe, most editorialists in the black press supported preparedness in one form or another, illustrating that the record of black loyalty to the nation in time of war would continue.

Shortly after the president submitted his proposal to Congress, the Western Negro Press Association issued a resolution "unqualifiedly" endorsing "reasonable preparedness." The association also called for the training of black officers and soldiers and promised that blacks "can be trusted to come to the Nation's defense at any time."[111] The *Savannah Tribune* criticized whites in Savannah for organizing a preparedness parade in June 1916 that excluded blacks. The organizers had forgotten the "important part" blacks had played in all past wars and "must play" in any future war, the editor said. "The Negro believes in preparedness but not in any preparedness scheme which does not take him into account."[112] The *New York Age*, the *Cleveland Gazette*, and the *Chicago Defender* all endorsed preparedness and accused some of those who opposed it of un-American sentiments. Pro-preparedness essays appearing in these newspapers focused their criticism on the southern Democrats in Congress who threatened to block Wilson's plan. The *Defender* lumped the "non-American 'solid South'" together with "hyphenated Americans," whose opposition to preparedness was making the nation a coward in the eyes of the rest of the world.[113] Similarly, the *Cleveland Gazette* claimed that the main opponents to preparedness were southern Democrats and that only the "patriotic action of the republicans in congress" would provide for the nation's defense. Editor Smith, who favored preparedness, argued that Wilson himself lacked the patriotic fervor to challenge Congress and push through the preparedness bill.[114] Nonetheless, Congress passed Wilson's preparedness legislation nearly intact the following summer.[115]

By standing on the side of military preparedness, these editorialists situated themselves in a position of loyalty to the country while placing their mostly southern enemies on the side of disloyalty, with "hyphenated Americans." At the same time, they ignored the fact than some of their strongest northern allies, pacifists such as NAACP cofounder Mary White Ovington, opposed preparedness. These black writers were trying to bend to their own purpose words that were intended to crush dissent, bolster national unity, militarize the nation, and facilitate the process of making war. They showed that blacks were more American than most citizens, would fight and die to defend their country, and had an unblemished record of loyalty that they intended to maintain in the coming war. Yet although these words proved to be of use to blacks in their fight for equal rights, they also retained some of the intent of the white leaders who first spoke them by placing blacks who "revoiced" them (to quote James Weldon Johnson) squarely behind a war they might legitimately have opposed and by inspiring some black writers to put winning the war ahead of black freedom and civil rights.

Some editorial writers admitted that they felt compelled to support the war completely even though they opposed America's involvement in it. Just before the declaration of war in 1917, for example, the *Appeal* expressed hope that America had the "wisdom" to stay out of the "horrible, inhuman, unnecessary war." But if it did not, the editorial continued, blacks would participate, "as they have never been disloyal to their native land."[116] Similarly, the *California Eagle* opposed the war but promised that blacks would nevertheless be loyal. Even before Wilson's declaration of war, the *Eagle,* which would later condemn Du Bois's editorial calling on blacks to postpone protest during the war, warned that "this is not the time for adverse expressions of non-patriotic sentiments."[117] After Wilson's declaration of war, Reverend William A. Byrd, a frequent contributor, wrote in the *Cleveland Gazette* that the war was being fought "not for national honor but for gain and sordid greediness" and that "the right or wrong of the matter has never entered the consideration." Yet, Byrd continued, African Americans "are going to take our part in this damnable war . . . to keep this country in safety from the foe without."[118] The *Chicago Broad Ax* denounced the war as economically motivated but, echoing Wilson's "American Spirit" address, endorsed a call for blacks "in this hour of peril" to "forget—all thoughts of self or race."[119]

This call was in keeping with Wilson's claim that a citizen had to subordinate "every interest that you have" to national loyalty. But most African American writers could not do that. A month after urging blacks to forget all thoughts of race, the *Broad Ax* said that if blacks were to fight in Europe, "we must be given some assurances of better treatment at home."[120] This dilemma dogged black writers throughout the war. How could they live up to Wilson's demanding standard of loyalty while continuing to work for the advancement of black human rights?

The editors of some journals, including the *New York Age,* the *Crisis,* and the *Chicago Defender,* who questioned America's ability to fight for democratic principles in Europe given the country's dismal record with blacks at home nevertheless supported the war from the beginning and advocated unqualified black participation.[121] Still, even these publications could not "forget—all thoughts of self or race" (although the *Crisis* advised doing so in the summer of 1918). They struggled to distinguish their group's advocacy of democratic reform from the interests of disloyal hyphenates and unreconstructed southerners and to justify their aims as compatible with the war aims and beneficial to the nation. In fact, however, the two causes sometimes came into conflict, and the intimation that African Americans would not support the war if their demands were not met was never far from the surface of their editorial pages. Editorialists went to great pains to frame their demands for democracy in a way that made them seem in harmony with the interests of the nation.

Just before the election of 1916, for example, the *New York Age* seemed to violate Wilson's principle of national unity and Roosevelt's dictum that to vote in an ethnic bloc was "to be a traitor to American institutions" when Johnson advised blacks to cast their votes solely on the basis of racial interests. "Nevertheless," Johnson explained, "in taking up this issue, we are not guilty of hyphenism. We are not seeking the advantage of any outside power at the expense of the United States. We are simply seeking, as Americans of undivided loyalty, to maintain our status and rights as citizens. If we do not succeed in doing that, all other issues will be of no importance to us."[122] Here, Johnson used clever reasoning to show that black group interests did not contradict the prevailing definition of loyalty.

Elsewhere, he and other editors emphasized loyalty rather than protest or democracy. When school officials in Des Moines, Iowa, sent Hubert Eaves, a black eleven-year-old boy, to juvenile court for protesting racial injustice by refusing to salute the flag, black editors who

"Loyalty." Although the *Richmond Planet* pledged to support the war effort in spite of lynching, in doing so this cartoonist drew a striking parallel between a black soldier's loyalty and southern states' lynching record in 1916.
From *Richmond Planet*, June 16, 1917.

thought it "risky" to display such disloyalty declined to defend him.[123] The *Appeal* and the *Chicago Broad Ax* scolded the boy's parents for "teaching treason."[124] Johnson congratulated the judge for ordering Eaves to go back to school and salute the flag.[125] These editors disagreed with the boy's reasoning that because the law offered him no protection, he essentially had no country. Eaves should distinguish between racists who failed to enforce the laws and the laws themselves. "Our laws are for the most part all right. It is the enforcement of them that we find all wrong," the *Richmond Planet* argued. "So long as we are American citizens, it would be well for us to salute the flag."[126]

Throughout the nineteen-month period of America's participation in the war, situations arose that highlighted the conflict between blacks' accommodationist pledge of national loyalty and their militant demands for democratic reform and showed how black journalists could both use and be used by mainstream political discourse. Like Johnson's explanation of his voting strategy, the black press tried again and again to reconcile the two impulses, sometimes achieving impressive results but never fully eliminating the contradictions.

CHAPTER 3
DAMNABLE DILEMMAS, 1917–1918

As Congress debated whether to issue a declaration of war against Germany during the first week of April 1917, federal agents claimed to have uncovered a network of German spies working in conjunction with "professional" African American revolutionaries and Mexican and Japanese agents to "set the country ablaze with a negro insurrection" in order to divert U.S. armed forces from the war in Europe. According to the *New York Tribune*, which broke the story on April 4, German spies had met with blacks in Greensboro, North Carolina, and New York City to discuss the "Plan of San Diego," a plot devised two years earlier in the California city by German spies, unnamed African American leaders, and Mexicans to seize Texas and hand it over to blacks. According to other published reports, federal officers in Alabama had already arrested white and black German agents posing as Bible salesmen to entice blacks in six southern states to flee to Mexico on a special train scheduled to depart on April 15.[1]

Hollis Frissell, the white president of a black institute in Virginia and a self-appointed spokesman for African Americans, and some white publications like the *Outlook*, the *Macon Telegraph*, and the *Montgomery Advertiser* dismissed the story and voiced "unhesitating confidence in the loyalty of the Negro" while recalling the loyalty of slaves to the South during the Civil War.[2] When the *New York Tribune* asked a black newspaper editor to comment on the alleged conspiracy, however, he did not simply dismiss it. Instead, George W. Harris, editor of the *New York News*, affirmed the basic truth of the story and added new information he had obtained "through subterranean channels." Agents paid by the German government, he said, had been "stirring up the Negroes against white people" in the South "for some time," nearly causing "serious trouble" in Georgia and the Carolinas and increasing the general discontent in Oklahoma and Texas.[3]

Harris by no means condoned the actions of the black "malcontents and agitators" who had joined the plot, but he understood why southern blacks might be receptive to such a plan. They had been robbed of the vote and treated poorly by the Wilson administration, and they expected to be "sacrificed at every turn" in the coming war. "The colored people generally do not believe they have been treated fairly since the Wilson administration has been in the saddle," Harris continued. "No one would be more loyal than the Negroes if they were treated fairly. Their disloyalty, if there is any, is not to the country or to the flag, but to the Wilson administration." Harris thus used the story about black disloyalty to direct white Americans' attention to the legitimate grievances of African Americans while at the same time affirming their fundamental loyalty and patriotism. He walked a fine line at a dangerous time. Days earlier, during his war message to Congress, President Wilson had said Germany had "filled our unsuspecting communities . . . with spies," and immediately after the speech, Attorney General Thomas Gregory began rounding up suspects.[4] Harris and other black editors who commented on this story hoped to reassure federal officials that African Americans were loyal and should not be prosecuted while simultaneously highlighting the need for government redress of black grievances.

Black newspapers affirmed black loyalty in the face of the German plot in a number of ways. They reported on mass meetings in which African Americans pledged support of the war and quoted black leaders—including W. E. B. Du Bois and William Monroe Trotter—who had endorsed the war effort. The *Baltimore Afro-American* even quoted a southern black attorney who repeated the dubious claim that blacks had proven their loyal nature by refusing to rebel against the Confederacy during the Civil War. Other evidence that proved the loyalty of blacks included the recent selection of a black regiment to guard the nation's capital, statements by whites expressing confidence in black loyalty, and black soldiers' service in the recent conflict with Mexico. The *Boston Guardian* said blacks would never fall for such a "far-fetched" plot. The *Cleveland Gazette* predicted that German agents working among blacks in the South would "have found, and quickly too, that 'Negroes' have too much pride in the flag, for which they have given their life's blood, to give such traitorous action any serious consideration." Blacks supported the war "because we stand for the flag and our nation and because here is our home."[5]

Some black newspapers, including the *Norfolk Journal and Guide* and the *Richmond Planet,* did not go beyond promising that blacks would remain loyal and would never engage in "treasonable conduct."[6] The *Crisis* focused on affirming black loyalty in the face of the reports, while also casting stones at the South. The whole story, Du Bois claimed, was a plot by the "Bourbon South" to stop black migration to the North. An estimated 700,000 to 1 million African Americans migrated from the South to northern cities during the late 1910s. Fearful of losing its cheap labor supply, Du Bois argued, "the slave-thinking South" hoped to persuade the nation that blacks were a menace and that martial law must be declared to keep them in their place. Du Bois then deflected the accusation of disloyalty back onto the white South, saying blacks had been far more loyal to the national government than white southerners. The African American "never has been a disloyal rebel. He never fought for slavery in a land of Liberty. He never nullified the basic principles of democracy," Du Bois wrote. Blacks would remain loyal despite being "enslaved, raped and despised."[7]

The *Baltimore Afro-American* and the *Cleveland Gazette* took their responses to the reports of black disloyalty further than other newspapers. Following Harris's lead, they did not completely dismiss the reports that some blacks had joined a rebellion in the South. Instead, they argued that simmering resentments among blacks there made the German plot plausible, even understandable. "Underlying" the Germans' plan "to stir up Southern 'Negroes' against the government," Harry Smith wrote in his *Gazette,* "is the fact that they have not been accorded near all to which they are entitled as American citizens." If blacks were the most loyal ethnic group in America, the *Baltimore Afro-American* agreed, they were "also the most proscribed against" and had more reason than any other group to rebel. The *Afro-American* listed many potential causes of black disloyalty and even concluded that "some few colored men in Georgia and Alabama have grown sick and tired of repression, and accepted the offer of the German agents to stir up a rebellion in the Southern States with the hope of winning complete franchise, freedom and political and social equality." But the author quickly added that most African Americans remained loyal and rejected the enticement "as far as can be ascertained."[8]

But blacks remained loyal not just out of love of country. Rather, they recognized "the folly of a rebellion that is not sure of success" at a time when evidence of disloyalty could be grounds for arrest. "Now is the time to continue our insistence upon right, and now is the time to demand guarantees before going to war willingly," the *Afro-American* editorial continued, "BUT NOW IS NOT THE TIME FOR REBELLION." Echoing the *Afro-American* and contradicting his own claim that blacks would support the war out of "pride in the flag," Smith agreed that African American loyalty grew out of the desire for self-preservation and group advancement. African Americans, he said, would not be "so unwise as to allow discretion to be cast to the winds and seek an unpropitious moment to show resentment." Smith concluded that "every Afro-American" viewed the war as an opportunity for "bettering our position" by showing "the metal of which we are made" and thus shaping public "sentiment." The *Baltimore Afro-American* and the *Cleveland Gazette* argued that blacks supported the war out of both national loyalty and group interest while at the same time implying that they might not support it at all if their grievances were not redressed.[9]

The responses of George Harris, the *Baltimore Afro-American,* and the *Cleveland Gazette* to the reports of black cooperation with German agents reflected an ongoing tension in the black press during World War I between conditional and unconditional loyalty, between pledges of national service and demands for redress of grievances. On the one hand, reports of rebellion among blacks in the South threatened the image of loyalty that the black press had always cultivated. On the other hand, the story highlighted justifiable discontent among African Americans and accented the need for the federal government to do something to assure their full and enthusiastic cooperation with the war effort. Indeed, these and other reports of black "unrest" would finally lead the government to begin to redress some racial injustices as a way of furthering the war effort. In the meantime, dilemmas similar to the one posed by the story of the German plot would confront African Americans repeatedly during the course of the war, and the black press would continue to devise responses aimed at shaping the nation's war policy in ways that advanced black interests. The black press would affirm black loyalty, especially in the face of evidence to the contrary; argue that the government must redress some key grievances to assure full black cooperation; turn accusations of disloyalty against its own enemies—usually white southerners; show that participation in the war would lead to advancement for African Americans; and, in spite of continuing criticism of governmental policies, declare support for the underlying principles of America and the idealistic justification for the country's entry into the war. As a whole, these responses cannot be classified as either accommodation or protest, serving the interests of the state or of blacks entirely. Black editors blended accommodation with protest and in so doing advanced the interests of both a modern industrialized state at war and a minority group living within that state. The black press served as a link between the two, providing a channel through which African Americans could make their demands known and through which the state could reach and propagandize African Americans. In the process, the black press also prodded America to live up to its highest ideals.

EMBRACING A WAR FOR DEMOCRACY

The country had been inching toward war since 1914, but Germany's resumption of unrestricted submarine warfare in 1916 made belligerency inevitable, and in January 1917, Woodrow Wilson appeared before the Senate to outline his vision of what would become his stated war aim: "Peace without victory." Speaking "on behalf of humanity" and a nation that had been established to "show mankind the way to liberty," he plotted a path to a just and lasting peace, a peace between equals, not one imposed by victors on the vanquished. Underlying Wilson's vision of a new world order was the principle that "governments derive all their just powers from the consent of the governed." Wilson saw in these "American principles" "no breach in either our traditions or our policy as a nation, but a fulfillment, rather, of all that we have professed or striven for." Three months later, on April 2, he appeared before Congress again, this time with a declaration of war "for the ultimate peace of the world and for the liberation of its peoples." It was in this speech that Wilson coined the phrase that would come to sum up the best hopes for the war and become a measure of it failings. "The world," he said, "must be made safe for democracy."[10] Between the great hopes of April 1917 and the bitter failures of the postwar world, the black press would adopt these words of Wilson's and do its best to put them to work.

Despite serious Republican opposition to the notion of "peace without victory" and Wilson's plans to establish a League of Nations, most Americans reacted favorably to both speeches. "Never before, it seemed, had a single speech evoked such overwhelming and almost unanimous praise in the United States," Wilson's biographer, Arthur S. Link, wrote of the first speech. "Never before, it seemed, had a single speaker succeeded so well in enunciating the political ideals and principles by which the American people in their better moments had tried to live."[11] Wilson had summed up, refined, and given eloquent expression to the idealistic impulses that had been gathering momentum since the outbreak of war in August 1914 but had lacked focus and clarity.

Although all black newspapers did not join in the "unanimous praise" of Wilson's vision, his war speeches helped them refine their arguments and better articulate a vision of how the war would help their own cause. Wilson's speeches clarified the principles behind America's participation in the war and unified the nation, to a large degree, behind these principles, which were compatible with their own drive for racial justice. After initially expressing skepticism, many black writers came to believe that Wilson's humanistic idealism, whether or not it was heartfelt, would lead to a readjustment of the racial circumstances in America. The act of fighting a war for democracy might in fact force America to see the contrast between its ideals and its practices and lead to the establishment of true democracy here. Like other groups, including progressives, conservative organizations, and "special interest groups of all kinds," in David M. Kennedy's phrase, black journalists "sought to invest America's role in the war with their preferred meaning, and to turn the crisis to their particular advantage," and Wilson had given them a powerful weapon for doing so.[12] They were able to highlight the gap between Wilson's wartime ideals and the treatment of African Americans; draw parallels between the war against autocracy in Europe and their war against racial oppression at home; paint the oppressors of blacks—especially white southerners—as enemies of America no less than Germany and the Central Powers; lay claim to being part of the America that upheld true democratic principles and was the source of Wilson's war aims; and, most important, make a convincing case that the government should take action to address the concerns of blacks—for example, by legislating against lynching—as a war measure. As the federal government assumed more and more power over more and more areas of life during the war, it became increasingly plausible that it might do something about race relations. Even many white Americans—some in the South—began to accept that notion. Although some government officials would brand the black press as disloyal for pressing demands during the war—for essentially arguing that blacks needed an incentive to be loyal—the Wilson administration would finally have to conclude that the black press was loyal and its demands were legitimate.

In their responses to Wilson's speeches, few white commentators would make the same connection between democracy in Europe and justice for blacks in America. Theodore Roosevelt, who had thought a peace without victory would "set back the march of civilization," called the war declaration "unanswerable" and on a par "with the great state papers of Washington and Lincoln."[13] Conservative senator

Speak Out, Mr. President!

"Speak Out, Mr. President!" President Wilson holds a note in his hand
addressed to Bishop Alexander Walters that reads: "Count upon me for
absolute fair dealing; for everything by which I can assist in advancing the
interest of the Negro in the U.S." The wording of the note is virtually the
same as the wording of a note Wilson wrote Walters during the 1912
presidential campaign that helped him win the support of Walters, William
Monroe Trotter, and other black leaders. From *New York Age*, July 19, 1917.

Henry Cabot Lodge, also an opponent, in January, of both peace without victory and the League of Nations, now thought Wilson had "expressed in the loftiest manner possible the sentiments of the American
people." Only six senators and fifty representatives voted against the
declaration of war, despite opposition among the general population
that Link described as "deep and wide."[14]

White editorialists ignored or glossed over the contradictions—so obvious to black writers—between America's war aims and its treatment of African Americans. The *New Republic*, in proclaiming in the wake of Wilson's war address that "the cause of the Allies is now unmistakably the cause of liberalism," conceded that the Allied nations "have much to do before their own houses are put in order, and democracy is by no means secure among those who proclaim it." But the editorial did not dwell on or specify the Allies' faults—much less America's. Instead, it predicted that the entry of the United States and the participation of a Russia now rid of its autocratic czar would "be a stimulus to democrats everywhere." Wilson, the progressive magazine gushed, had become the world's "most liberal statesman in high office" —notwithstanding his regressive race policies.[15] The liberal *Nation* agreed that the president was qualified to make the world "a fit place for civilized man to live in."[16] The *New York Tribune*, usually a critic of Wilson, praised the declaration of war lavishly as approaching "the ideal of the American people, the ideal of a President who should lead."[17] The *World's Work* compared the world war to the American Civil War, describing both as struggles for human freedom.[18]

African Americans, however, saw irony in the prospect of the United States fighting a war for democracy. Disfranchisement, lynching, and Jim Crow, along with Wilson's own dismal record on race, made the administration's war aims dubious, if not laughable. Black newspapers' editorials exposed the irony of Wilson's messages by pointing out the hypocrisy of exporting to Europe democratic freedoms that Wilson himself had a hand in denying to African Americans at home. After Wilson's January "peace without victory" speech, some black newspapers noted the discrepancy between Wilson's pledge to bring government by consent of the governed to Europe and the disfranchisement of blacks in the American South. " 'Physician heal thyself,' " the *Baltimore Afro-American* prescribed. Wilson himself held office, the editorial noted, "because in more than a dozen states colored men [who could be expected to vote Republican] were prevented from casting their ballots."[19] The *Chicago Defender* scolded Wilson for pledging democracy to peoples in foreign lands instead of applying it "locally," where he actually had the power to enforce it. "Somehow it doesn't seem quite consistent to wash someone else's clothes and leave your own soiled."[20]

Southern lynchings continued to hamper America's ability to fight for justice and democracy abroad, writers warned. Wilson's claim to speak for "humanity" rang hollow in light of his failure to "utter one word against this outraging of humanity within the territory over which he presides," the *New York Age* said. Wilson and other Americans deserved censure for their "smug hypocrisy" in expressing "horror at German 'atrocities' " or the Turks' "treatment of the Armenians" while they ignored the lynchings of blacks in the South.[21]

After the president's April 2 war message, some black papers continued to express skepticism about Wilson's humanitarianism and even to oppose the war. "When President Wilson uses fine words about going to war for the protection of humanity abroad, thinking Americans recall the humanity at home that craves protection," the *Baltimore Afro-American* said immediately after the declaration of war.[22] The *Richmond Planet,* like the *Cleveland Gazette,* usually functioning as a partisan Republican newspaper, criticized every move Wilson made toward war. Just days after Wilson's message, *Richmond Planet* editor John Mitchell pointed out that the president "was elected on the assumption that he kept us out of war." Mitchell said little about Wilson's ideals one way or the other, however.[23] The gruesome fatal burning of Ell Persons in Memphis in May spurred an investigation by James Weldon Johnson on behalf of the NAACP and led some black editors to wonder about America's commitment to Wilson's ideals. "This nation cannot escape bearing the brunt of the shame of such a disregard of law and the rights of humanity while it is 'fighting for humanity,' " William Byrd wrote in the *Gazette.*[24]

Yet black writers also began to embrace the Wilsonian idea of a war for democracy. Three weeks after its initial critical response to the war message, the *Baltimore Afro-American* called Wilson's promise to fight a war to establish democracy in Europe "a beautiful theory." "It is well that [at] the close of the nineteenth and the beginning of the twentieth century such noble words should be uttered, and that the fetters of those people who have been bound hand and foot for centuries should be stricken off and that the reign of freedom should begin; that every man should have the chance to be an[d] to do and to assist in the government under which he lives; that all men should have the 'inalienable right to life, liberty and the pursuit of happiness.' " Still, from all appearances, Wilson did not believe this theory should be applied here at home. He would need to recognize that to credibly carry this fight to Europe, America itself must practice "real democracy." For those unsure of the meaning of democracy, the *Afro-American* printed a lengthy dictionary definition. A week later, the paper predicted that the act of fighting a war to make the Central Powers democratic might force America to confront its own demons at home.[25] The black press's response to the American war effort, then, was characterized by a critical optimism.

Some black newspapers began to include a picture of the American flag on their editorial pages each week. In the *New York Age,* Johnson called Wilson's war message a "convincing" and "inspiring" document, one that if followed up with action could heal racial and ethnic divisions. "We, as a race, might take the President up on some of the references to 'humanity,' and point out their inconsistencies, as we so well know them; but, for the present, we pass that over." Wilson's message struck "a responsive chord in the great American public," Johnson argued, and the war would provide a "great trial" to determine if the nation could live up to its democratic ideals.[26] The *Chicago Defender* seemed won over by Wilson's rhetoric. Roscoe Conkling Simmons—columnist, orator, and newspaper promoter—wrote in November that "the white man can't break his own chains without loosening mine."[27] The *Cleveland Gazette,* more reluctant to praise Wilson on any account, argued that of all the Allied nations, "America must be the leader in real democracy." But to accomplish that, the *Gazette* and other black newspapers argued, the South would have to be made democratic.[28]

Despite voicing some reservations, then, black editorialists advised African Americans to support the war for a range of reasons, from patriotic loyalty to sympathy with Wilson's war aims and a belief that support would advance group interests. Mitchell advocated supporting the war to advance black interests, placing little faith in Wilson's ideals. He predicted that by heeding the motto "our country, right or wrong," blacks would turn "antipathy to the Negro" into "plaudits."[29] The conservative *Norfolk Journal and Guide* opposed U.S. entry into the war and complimented Wilson for keeping the nation out as long as he did. Once war was declared, the paper advocated total support for the war effort without commenting on the merits of Wilson's ideals.[30]

Others seemed to focus more on ideals than on practical considerations. The *Crisis* demonized Germany, embraced the war effort enthusiastically, and urged blacks to "join heartily in this fight for eventual world liberty." An editorial drafted by an NAACP conference of May 17–19, 1917, claimed that "permanent peace" depended on the "extension of the principle of government by the consent of the governed, not simply among the smaller nations of Europe but among the natives of Asia and Africa, the Western Indies and the Negroes of the United States." The editorial acknowledged that blacks, of course, had a right to resent their treatment in America and to feel ambivalent about participating in the war but that they should "never forget that this country belongs to us even more than to those who lynch, disfranchise, and segregate."[31] The *Chicago Defender* agreed that German autocracy was "the greatest enemy civilization has known" and had to be stopped. Simmons accepted Wilson's view that the war was a "world battle for liberty," in which black Americans should take part.[32]

More frequently, editors offered a number of different reasons for their support, including group interests and endorsement of Wilson's ideals. The *Savannah Tribune,* for example, asserted that all African Americans would back the war out of patriotism and a belief in the cause. "We entertain no thought save the supremacy of our nation's loftiest traditions and ideals—to these we subordinate all else, everything." Yet the *Tribune* also offered self-interest as a reason for supporting the war. By fighting side by side with white Americans, the *Tribune* predicted in another editorial, blacks would build "ineffaceable ties of blood-bought liberty."[33] At the *New York Age*, Johnson said blacks should fight to defeat the Germans' idea that force could triumph over right, but at the same time, he noted that doing so would strengthen their claim to full citizenship rights.[34]

INDECISION OVER THE OFFICER-TRAINING CAMP

The determination of most African American newspaper editors to fully support the war created an uncomfortable dilemma even before the declaration of war over whether to support the formation of a segregated officer-training camp. Early in 1917, white NAACP chairman Joel Spingarn, who had become a major in the army intelligence service, persuaded the military brass to establish a camp to train African Americans as army officers. Promoting the camp in letters to black newspapers, Spingarn reasoned that the army was not likely to integrate the officer corps in time for the war, so blacks had to choose between segregated training of black officers or no training at all. As a leader of America's most influential black civil rights organization, Spingarn opposed segregation, but he believed the advantages of the camp outweighed the evils of establishing one more separate institution. Blacks could not afford to miss out on the opportunities for advancement that came with military service, he argued. He reassured militant integrationists like Harry Smith that "common sense and patriotism need not be inconsistent with the most radical conception of the rights of every group of American citizens."[35] Editors who criticized the camp denounced it as a separate institution, but they were even more incensed that it had been proposed by blacks themselves and their representatives.

Like Spingarn, Du Bois and others—including three southern black editors—defended the camp as an imperfect means to a worthwhile end and advised blacks to sign up. African Americans regularly made such bargains, Du Bois and the *Norfolk Journal and Guide* argued, by participating in "Jim Crow" institutions when they were banned from white ones. "We continually submit to segregated schools, 'Jim Crow' cars, and isolation because it would be suicide to go uneducated, stay at home, and live in the 'tenderloin,'" Du Bois wrote. In this case, the choice was between the "insult of a separate camp and the irreparable injury" of having no black officers. Another reason for accepting the camp was to bolster claims of black loyalty by countering rumors that African Americans were plotting with German spies. Opposition to the camp would "add treason and rebellion to the other grounds on which the South urges discrimination against" blacks.[36]

Yet Du Bois and other black supporters of the camp, including the *Norfolk Journal and Guide,* the *Richmond Planet,* and the *Savannah Tribune,* accepted it only reluctantly, acknowledging the "discrimination which this proposed training camp implies."[37] The camp presented a "damnable dilemma," as Du Bois put it, which characterized nearly every attempt by African Americans to participate in the American war effort. Whether they tried to join the army as soldiers or officers, serve in the Red Cross as nurses or doctors, or take part in the Liberty Loan program, blacks faced segregation and discrimination. On the one hand, why should they subject themselves to such humiliations to support a war against a distant enemy? On the other hand, how could they lay claim to self-sacrificing loyalty if they did not participate in the war fully? And as Du Bois pointed out, the rumors of rebellion made it even more important to affirm such loyalty.[38]

But the camp controversy involved more than the principle of when and how to accept segregated institutions. Individuals who generally agreed in their opposition to segregation disagreed over the issue of how to respond to the camp proposal. Most of the mainstream race advocates (including most black editors) were integrationists who nonetheless supported some separate black institutions. All could agree, for example, that public transportation and government offices should be integrated. But no one denounced the black press or black colleges as Jim Crow institutions. Other institutions caused greater contention, however. Both Smith and Trotter denounced the establishment of black YMCAs and hospitals in northern cities.[39] Most other integrationists, including Robert Abbott of the *Chicago Defender,* James Weldon Johnson of the *New York Age,* and even Agitator Calvin Chase of the *Washington Bee*, like Du Bois, usually supported the formation of such institutions as necessary evils that would contribute to the quality of black life as long as African Americans were excluded from white institutions.[40]

But some of the black newspapers that usually tolerated separate black institutions demurred in this case. The *Chicago Defender* responded to Spingarn's proposal with an editorial entitled "'Jim-Crow' Training Camps—No!" But the emphatic "No!" masked a keen ambiguity. Less than a year earlier, the paper had supported the "lesser evil" of training black officers for black troops, and throughout 1917, it called on blacks to volunteer for military service in the segregated army. The newspaper even chastised blacks for not showing more enthusiasm. Yet in April 1917, the *Defender* not only rejected Spingarn's "Jim Crow" camp but also condemned separate black regiments led by white officers. Since the paper did not urge blacks to oppose the war or refuse to participate, it is unclear what the editorial intended black men to do.[41] In fact, the *Defender*'s position was more strategic than heartfelt. It let white America know that African Americans opposed this kind of segregation.

The *Chicago Defender* and the *Cleveland Gazette* both suggested that if blacks declined to enroll in the officer-training camp, the government might end segregation in the armed forces once casualties began to mount and black help became more crucial.[42] Smith also argued that instead of training new recruits, the army should promote black career soldiers to the ranks of officers.[43] But Smith opposed the camp mainly because he did not want blacks to be perceived as endorsing segregation. It was "bad enough to have segregated . . . military training camps FORCED on us by the government, but infinitely worse to ASK for them," he reasoned.[44] Like the *Defender*'s opposition to the camp, Smith's was inconsistent with his often strong support for the war. He backed preparedness fully, cheered Ohio's army recruitment campaign, and publicized evidence of black loyalty, including participation in the military and the purchasing of war bonds.[45] Smith had openly discussed his dilemma at the beginning of 1916 when he expressed a "lack of desire to plead" with Wilson for a greater number of black regiments and a reluctance to see black troops participate in Wilson's war with Mexico. Yet, he noted, if they did participate in that war, he would be proud if they performed well, and he was not inclined to oppose the NAACP's efforts to expand black participation in the army.[46] In fact, the *Gazette* came to accept and support the camp once it was established, calling it "historic" and predicting that it would give each participant a "proud heritage to pass down to one's children's children."[47]

Another initial critic of the camp, the *Baltimore Afro-American*, seemed to take its opposition a step further, comparing the situation of blacks faced with a segregated camp to that of American colonists before the Revolution. "England disfranchised her colonies, so to speak and treated them in much the same way that Uncle Sam treats his colored citizens," the *Afro-American* argued in March. The revolutionary generation had proclaimed: " 'We have no duties where we have no rights, it were cowardly to believe otherwise.' . . . In the spirit of those same patriots, whose children we are, we say the Negro who speaks of duties where he has no rights, places himself in the position where he may deserve the name—a moral coward." Until they obtained their rights, blacks' only duty would be to fight for their own freedom.[48] Like the *Chicago Defender* and the *Cleveland Gazette*, the *Afro-American* predicted that when the nation needed blacks badly enough, it would be forced to give them equal opportunity in the military service.[49] The newspaper seemed to be advocating rebellion, but after the declaration of war, it backed off that radical position, supporting graduates of the camp and dropping its threat to disavow duties not matched by rights. If black officers fought for democracy in France and then returned home to fight for it in the South, an editorial conceded, "then the 'Jim Crow' camp will not have been tolerated in vain." Again, the real problem with the camp had been that blacks and their advocates had asked for it themselves: "Better to be forced into it than to ask for it. The people will accept this sub-citizenship, not because they want to, but because they must."[50]

Similarly, the *Washington Bee*, the *New York News*, the *Appeal*, the *Indianapolis Freeman*, and the *New York Age* objected less to the camp itself than to the fact that blacks themselves or their white friends would advocate segregation. "We do not deem it wise on our part to voluntarily segregate ourselves or permit our white friends to segregate us," the *New York Age* explained. A recent War Department bulletin on military training had said nothing about segregated training and neither should the NAACP, the paper claimed. Those opposed to the camp seemed to fear that if they asked for segregated officer training themselves, they would be helping to legitimize Jim Crow. Black writers responded to the "damnable dilemma" by opposing the camp rhetorically while supporting it in practice, thereby lodging their protest against segregation while maintaining their loyalty to the country.[51]

By May 1917, 470 black college men had applied for admission to the segregated officer-training camp located in Des Moines, Iowa. Prominent black colleges like Hampton Institute and Fisk University cooperated with the call for volunteers, and the camp opened in July with 1,250 candidates.[52] Like the *Baltimore Afro-American,* most opponents seemed to back the camp after it had become a reality. Even Trotter's *Boston Guardian,* which bitterly opposed all segregated institutions, including the camp, proudly announced later in the war that 107 black men, from nearly every state, had received commissions.[53]

Even the camp's biggest promoter praised the black press's dualistic response to the camp. Spingarn said newspapers' "bold and manly" denunciation of the camp was necessary. "I should not want the first reaction to be anything else than what it is," he told Du Bois during the heat of the controversy.[54] The critical response let America in general and the federal government in particular know that blacks did not accept unequal status and opposed the principle of segregation and that the segregated camp was no favor of America to blacks but rather the other way around. In light of this clearly stated opposition, the black press's eventual support of the camp provided an example of self-sacrificing loyalty—the kind demanded by Wilson in his "American Spirit" address of 1916.

IDENTIFYING THE ENEMY AT HOME

At the same time that African American newspapers were displaying blacks' patriotism, they were pointing out ways that lynchers, race rioters, racists, and the unreconstructed South lacked patriotism, loyalty, and enthusiasm for the war effort. During the war, African American writers frequently portrayed their own enemies as unpatriotic or akin to the nation's enemies in Europe. Most of those portrayals—at least in northern newspapers—focused on the South, which could be shown to be an enemy of the nation in at least four ways.

First, the South had once rebelled against the federal government and still opposed federal authority in many instances. The *New York Age* suggested that the "spirit of secession" still reigned in the South, where "fossils of the rebellion" now sought to help the German cause by attacking loyal blacks.[55] The *Chicago Defender* claimed that white southerners hated President Lincoln; the *Baltimore Afro-American* called anti-black politicians "Southern copperheads," a term used in the Civil War to describe Confederate sympathizers in the Union; and the *Cleveland Gazette* repeatedly returned to the theme of the rebel South.[56]

Second, some southern whites seemed not to fully support the war effort. Although southern black newspapers did not emphasize this point, the *Savannah Tribune* lumped southern politicians like Benjamin Tillman Jr., who opposed black recruitment, together with "anti-conscriptionists and anti-draft agitators."[57] Other newspapers highlighted opposition to measures deemed necessary for the war effort. The *Baltimore Afro-American* criticized as "obstructionists" southern congressmen James K. Vardaman, John Sharp Williams, and J. Thomas Heflin when they opposed a measure giving women the vote that President Wilson "regarded as necessary for the quicker winning of the war." "Usually it is the Negro problem in the national Congress that so inflames Southern copperheads that they cease to be patriotic," but this time it was woman suffrage.[58] The *Cleveland Gazette* found southern states' recruitment of soldiers to be lagging behind, and the *Chicago Defender* noted that blacks in many southern towns were enlisting in greater numbers than white southern "loafers."[59]

A third piece of evidence of the South's disloyalty was the fact that southern racial practices interfered with black support of the war effort. African Americans subscribed to the Liberty Loan drive, volunteered for the Red Cross, and enlisted in the armed forces, often at higher rates than white Americans.[60] Not only did southerners sometimes hinder these efforts, but they also threatened to weaken the morale of blacks and turn them against the war effort. Every time a black person was lynched, Jim Crowed, or otherwise discriminated against, it reduced black enthusiasm for the war effort and thus diminished America's fighting force, black editors argued. Even *Birth of a Nation*, created by two southerners, had a "baneful effect upon the enthusiasm, patriotism and loyalty of the Afro-American whom it harms greatly wherever it is exhibited," Smith argued.[61] Thus, antiblack activity was antiwar and anti-American.

White southerners were unpatriotic and certainly discouraged black participation in the war, according to the *Cleveland Gazette*, when they treated black contributors to the Liberty Loan drive and heroes on the battlefield—including Sergeant Henry Johnson, the first American to be awarded the French croix de guerre after almost single-handedly fighting off a German raiding party—as second-class citizens.[62] America's greatest heroes could "cease to be citizens when they cross Mason and Dixon's line going South," the *Gazette* lamented.[63] Not all blacks could be expected to continue to act as patriots under such circumstances, and in fact, the *Chicago Defender* noted, southern blacks were right to remain aloof from the Jim Crow Red Cross there.[64] A *Baltimore Afro-American* article entitled "South Opposes Negro Soldiers" noted that southern congressmen had pledged to "bitterly op-

"Contraband Goods." Satan seeks to deliver to France a box of "contraband goods" made in Dixie. From *Chicago Defender*, February 2, 1918.

pose" including blacks in the armed forces "despite the fact that Uncle Sam will need the services of the colored men, as well as white."[65] Such a stand by the South clearly hampered the country's war effort and highlighted the disloyalty of some white southerners.

Johnson saw treason in South Carolina representative Samuel Nicholls's promise of a war on the home front if the government tried to integrate southern white soldiers and black men from the North.[66] Johnson and another *New York Age* editorialist also argued that the South placed preservation of "'Jim Crow' Democracy" ahead of pro-war measures; that white Houstonians demonstrated the disloyalty of the South when they goaded black soldiers into mutiny; that a southern colonel made "seditious utterances" when he claimed blacks were unfit for military duty and should be drafted solely for manual labor; and that ridicule of black soldiers amounted to German propaganda.[67] Johnson argued that lynching "and other aggravated forms of hatred and prejudice against the Negro" were "nothing less than a certain degree of treason" because such actions caused divisions within the nation's fighting forces and threatened to deny the service of blacks for the war effort.[68]

Black newspapers also accused the South of the unpatriotic use of black labor. The war and the northward migration of blacks had led to a shortage of agricultural laborers, and in some localities, including Memphis, "work or fight" vagrancy laws imposed fines and imprisonment or military service on people without work. Although the laws supposedly applied to both blacks and whites, the black press noted that southerners enforced them only against blacks. When a Baltimore woman tried to use the laws to force black women to work as domestic servants, the *Baltimore Afro-American* charged her with putting "her own convenience ahead of winning the war" and labeled her "a traitor of the rankest kind."[69]

A fourth body of evidence showed the South to be as inhumane and undemocratic as America's European enemies. Black newspapers connected the South to the Central Powers, first, by simply using the same language the nation had employed to dehumanize its enemies on the battlefield. "American 'Huns'" committed violence against blacks in the South. Smith used the terms "southernism" and "Prussianism" interchangeably.[70] The *Chicago Defender* called Jim Crow railroad cars the "Kaiser on wheels" and southern politicians the "Kaisers of America." The "mailed fist and iron heel of crazed southerners have borne down just as mercilessly on our women and children" as the "mailed fist and iron heel of the kaiser," a columnist argued.[71] Several newspapers described southerners as "mobocrats," a play on "autocrats," the term used to denote leaders of the Central Power governments.[72]

Black editorialists cited numerous examples to support their comparison of European and southern "Huns." The South practiced autocracy by denying blacks a say in their own government. Editors borrowed language from both the American Revolution ("taxation without representation") and Wilson (rule without "consent of the governed") to condemn this practice.[73] Southern governments imposed autocratic controls on individuals by mandating racial segregation in public places. And most important, as African Americans had contended before America entered the war, lynching was as bad as any of the alleged atrocities of Germany and its allies.

Statistical evidence released by Tuskegee Institute during the war showed that in spite of African Americans' loyal participation in the war effort, lynchings continued virtually unabated, declining slightly in 1917, then rising dramatically in 1918. A recent study suggests that the number of lynchings in 1917 and 1918—64—declined significantly from the total for the previous two years—89. Statistics released at the time, however, indicated a less significant decline, from 106 to 96, suggesting that more blacks were lynched in 1918 than in any year since 1912.[74] Lynching seemed as bad as ever when Tuskegee released its statistics to the press every six months and newspapers continued to carry accounts of particularly horrifying lynchings. After the Persons lynching in May, two more victims died at the hands of Tennessee mobs, this time tortured with hot pokers before being burned to death: Ligon Scott in Dyersburg on December 2, 1917, and Jim McIlherron in Estill Springs on February 12, 1918. The most disturbing lynchings of the war took place in Brooks and Lowndes Counties, Georgia, where lynchers murdered as many as ten victims, including Mary Turner, a pregnant woman whom they disemboweled. Editorialists used these incidents to condemn both the South and the nation. William Byrd warned that "the downfall of this nation if it comes will be due to southern wickedness," and he advised southern blacks to pack up their belongings and head north.[75]

As part of their appeal to the national government to act to end lynching, black writers increasingly focused on the damage lynching did to the national reputation and denounced the government's failure to do anything about it. "Race prejudice and bias have warped our national conscience," Byrd said, and "America, having learned to be unjust toward colored people with impunity is now ready to follow its habit with other nationalities."[76] The release of annual lynching statistics showing 36 in 1917 moved Johnson to remark that as long as any lynchings took place, "the United States stands as a lawless and barbarous land."[77] A widely circulated open letter to Woodrow Wilson from Kelly Miller, a leading black intellectual and dean of Howard University's College of Arts and Sciences, called lynching an evil that was "national in its range and scope" because northerners and the federal government did nothing to stop it.[78]

The tendency of black newspapers to view violence against blacks as a national crime gained momentum after a race riot broke out in an Illinois city just three months after America entered the war. Yet most black papers refrained from using the race riot in East St. Louis as evidence that northern whites deserved equal blame with southerners.

In May and June 1917, the resentment of white unionized laborers in East St. Louis erupted in scattered violent incidents against the city's black population, which had been growing during the war as rural southerners migrated north, pushed by the declining cotton economy

Virginia's Black Star !

"Virginia's Black Star!" "World opinion" gazes at a star placed within the
outline of the state of Virginia that reads: "One Negro lynched,
Nov. 23, '18." From *Richmond Planet*, December 14, 1918.

of the South and pulled by a boom in northern wartime manufac-
turing. When the Aluminum Ore Company broke a strike in April,
workers blamed blacks for having crossed the picket lines. Although
most of the strikebreakers had been white, black scabs provided easily
recognizable scapegoats. Tensions continued to mount until the early-
morning hours of July 1, when two police officers were shot to death
in their squad car as they drove through a black neighborhood. Local
news reports depicted the shooting as an act of naked aggression by

a crowd of "200 rioting negroes." In fact, a car resembling the squad car had previously driven through the black neighborhood, firing into homes along the way, and those who shot at the police car were acting in self-defense. Parked in front of city hall, the bullet-ridden cruiser served as a rallying point for a crowd of angry white laborers the next morning.[79]

For more than twelve hours that day, bands of marauding rioters attacked, beat, and shot black residents, burning others out of their homes. An estimated 39 blacks and 9 whites (some killed by errant shots from white rioters) died in the rioting; well over 100 were injured. The rioters destroyed 312 buildings, most by fire, and burned 44 freight cars.[80]

Even some white commentators could not help but notice the irony of the riot, coming as it did merely three months after Wilson had launched his war to promote democracy and the rule of law in Europe. A cartoonist for the *New York Evening Mail* asked, "Mr. President, why not make America safe for democracy?," and the *New York Evening Post* saw parallels between the riot and alleged German atrocities.[81] The *Nation* concluded from the affair that Americans must "show that when they say democracy, they mean it."[82]

Black newspapers also sounded this theme. If the federal government did nothing to address the problems revealed by the riot, the *Norfolk Journal and Guide* argued, it "should renounce its purposes for entering the world war and stand convicted among the nations of the earth as the greatest hypocrite of all times."[83] The *Chicago Defender* added: "We sympathize with the Belgians and with the Armenians, then proceed to lynch and burn at the stake one or more of the most loyal citizens the country affords, simply because of color." The paper declined to blame the riot on the immigrants who participated and insisted that they had learned to riot from "real Americans."[84] The *Baltimore Afro-American* called East St. Louis a "Little Belgium," and the *New York Age* warned that unless the government acted against the rioters, lawlessness would spread.[85]

But some editorialists struck a surprisingly optimistic note after the riot. These editors seemed to believe the riot would force white America to confront the contradictions between the war aims and the treatment of black citizens at home. They were bolstered in their optimism when Congress agreed to hold hearings on the riot, Theodore Roosevelt denounced the "brutal infamies imposed on colored people" at a much-publicized meeting in Carnegie Hall, and various mainstream publications recognized the disparity between the riot and the democratic war aims. The *New York Age* proclaimed: "Public sentiment, under the stimulus of the public utterances of Theodore Roosevelt, has been roused as seldom before to the growing spirit of lawlessness in this country. The necessity for the enforcement of law and order at home, while fighting for the democracy of the world abroad, is realized by most thinking people." The *Baltimore Afro-American* praised "thoughtful men" who had come to see that "'America must be made safe for Americans.'"[86]

Alternately, the East St. Louis riot might have led black writers to conclude that northern whites were no better than their southern counterparts. Indeed, the *Richmond Planet* seemed to take that position, seconding the view of a white Jacksonville, Florida, paper, the *Florida Times-Union,* that saw the riot as evidence that blacks who had migrated out of the South were no better off in the North.[87] Paradoxically, John Mitchell did not oppose the northward migration of southern blacks, but the *Norfolk Journal and Guide,* a conservative southern paper that persistently opposed migration, did not see the riot as proof against migration. Illinois, the paper argued in rebutting the arguments of two white Norfolk newspapers, was neither northern nor southern in its "make-up," and the riot was not "'directly traceable to the migration of Negroes from the South.'"[88]

Northern black editors even more forcefully rejected the arguments of white southern newspapers that viewed the riot as evidence of racism in the North and saw it as a reason to halt the migration.[89] Some editors went so far as to blame the catastrophe on the South. Smith said "southern sympathizers" who wanted to discourage "the exodus of our people from the South to this section of the country" had started the riot and recalled that the city had been "strongly pro-southern during the Civil War."[90] The *Chicago Defender* alleged that the riot had been started by a "southern cracker" who taunted a black resident about the Persons lynching.[91] Johnson defended the North and white northerners against an attack by Senator Ben Tillman of South Carolina, who cited the East St. Louis riot as evidence of the unity of all whites—North and South—against blacks. Johnson disagreed, pointing to "the thousands of northern communities in which colored people are not abused" and the "mutual respect and kindly feelings" that had existed between northern whites and southern blacks.[92]

In the face of a bloody pogrom in a northern state, these black editors still saw blacks' problems as originating in the South and looked to the North for solutions. The migration of black workers from the South to the North, for example, was generally seen as a positive solution to southern oppression. Indeed, black writers sometimes over-stated their case, as when the syndicated column "Afro-American Cull-ings" quoted Kelly Miller's comment that the North was "a section of complete public and civil freedom."[93] The *Cleveland Gazette* called on northerners to view Dixie as a foreign enemy. America should make one of its war aims the democratization of the South, William Byrd argued in July 1917, calling the southern white man "America's worst enemy." In a pre-election front-page editorial in the fall of 1918, Byrd cataloged the South's un-American qualities and equated a defeat of the southern-based Democratic Party with a defeat of the European enemy. The South must be repudiated in the election, he argued, be-cause it did not respect the Constitution, was "the most barbarous spot in Christendom," had opposed the administration's war effort, had a poor grasp of governmental and legal matters, and was "unfit to gov-ern a country that is now the ruling nation of the world." America and the South became two separate and opposed entities. "If America defeats the south," Byrd argued, "the world will believe what we are preaching, a world made safe for democracy."[94] Smith made similar arguments, longing for the "happy day . . . when the territory south of Mason and Dixon's line, as well as foreign territory, is made safe for its down-trodden Democracy."[95] Adapting Wilson's words, Smith and Byrd depicted the South—no less than Germany—as foreign territory requiring democratization and defeat.

Other black newspapers similarly placed the South outside the pale of American civilization and equated it with German autocracy. The *Baltimore Afro-American* argued that "real democracy" had existed in the South for only a brief time (presumably during Reconstruction) and that the leadership of individuals from this section in the federal government had created the nation's poor record on race.[96] A *New York Age* editorial argued that the South had "no civilized order of govern-ment," was "ruled by an oligarchy or mob," and "gravitates between a state of autocracy or anarchy."[97] The *Chicago Defender,* perhaps more critical of the South than any other black newspaper, constantly urged black readers to leave the South for the more hospitable North.[98] An editorial called the South "the land of the barbarians" whose great-est contributions to world civilization were " 'Jim Crow,' disfranchise-ment, and lynching."[99]

Southern papers pointed to the ways in which lynching and the East St. Louis riot contradicted the war aims, but they tended not to lay so much of the burden on the South. The *Norfolk Journal and Guide* blamed the riot on recent European immigrants rather than native

"As We Bow Our Heads in Prayer." President Wilson tells a black nurse, "We can use your money—but not your services," while a black soldier lies wounded in France and another black man has been burned to death by a southern lynch mob. From *Chicago Defender,* March 23, 1918.

white Americans—northerners or southerners—living in the city. The lynchings in Dyersburg and Estill Springs, Tennessee, led the *Savannah Tribune* to condemn not just the South but all America: "America has been as harsh and as bloody and as unjust to the Negro as any power on earth ever was to its subjects."[100]

Black editorial writers therefore sought to show how America's poor treatment of African Americans—especially in the South—contradicted President Wilson's stated idealistic war aims. And although they sometimes seemed to let the North off the hook while depicting southern whites as enemies no less vile than the "Huns," they pointedly implicated the whole nation in the crimes of lynching, disfranchisement, and racial discrimination. Yet black writers also seemed to find room for hope in the ideals of America, Wilson's articulation of them upon entering the war, and what seemed to be a growing outrage among whites against wartime lynchings and the East St. Louis riot.

Clearly, some white Americans—including the white northern friends mentioned by Johnson and the "better class" of southern whites, which Mitchell repeatedly invoked—had the will to do something to bring about racial justice. Not only would the parallels with Europe push them in that direction, but so would the continuing example of the almost superhuman loyalty and patience of African American soldiers and citizens in spite of the continued violence and proscription against them.

The *Savannah Tribune*'s editorial on the lynchings in Dyersburg and Estill Springs conjured up a powerful image of loyal black recruits on their way to military training camp who passed "the bloody pyre of a burned Negro" and breathed in the "putrid fumes which rose from the seared flesh" yet nonetheless "went on cheerfully and patriotically to fight for 'Democracy' which to them has been but a mocking fiction."[101] This vision of long-suffering black loyalty as a background to violence and oppression wherever they took place pervaded black newspapers, North and South.

THE HOUSTON MUTINY

In reality, African Americans' patience and patriotism had limits. Before the dust had settled in Illinois, a group of black soldiers, fed up with police brutality and rigidly enforced Jim Crow laws in Houston, Texas, staged a mutiny against their commanding officers and took up arms against local white citizens. This apparent example of black disloyalty would put the black press on the defensive and would challenge its ability to continue to present its message to the nation.

On the evening of August 23, 1917, about 100 black soldiers marched in formation from Camp Logan toward downtown Houston, intent on revenge.[102] Since they had arrived in the city on July 28 to guard the camp during a construction project, the 654 black members of the Third Battalion, Twenty-fourth Infantry, had chafed at the racist epithets hurled by workers at the camp, Jim Crow restrictions in streetcars and other public facilities, and, especially, police brutality. On the afternoon of August 23, a black soldier was badly beaten and arrested after he tried to rescue a black woman from an assault by a notorious police officer, Lee Sparks. When Corporal Charles W. Baltimore, a provost guard and "model soldier," inquired about the arrest, Sparks struck him over the head and then fired his gun as the soldier tried to run away (Sparks denied striking Baltimore and said he had fired into the ground).[103]

The story of the two soldiers' arrests—embellished by rumors that

DAMNABLE DILEMMAS

Baltimore had been killed—quickly filtered back to camp and ignited resentments that had been smoldering for weeks. After Baltimore returned to camp, the officer in charge, Major Kneeland S. Snow, ordered all troops confined to camp until morning. When Snow ordered them to turn in their weapons, some refused, seized ammunition, and began firing in the air. Fearful that a mob of white rioters was approaching, the soldiers fell in line behind Sergeant Vida Henry and marched out of camp.

Unlike the white rioters in East St. Louis a month earlier, the soldiers did not wantonly destroy property but marched deliberately into town with a specific purpose in mind—to take revenge on police officers and streetcar conductors.[104] Before the march finally ended in disarray, the rioters killed several unintended victims, including a teenage boy and 2 white soldiers mistaken for uniformed police officers; 4 police officers, including Sparks's partner, Rufus Daniels; and 2 civilians who were acting as police. In two hours of marching and shooting, the soldiers killed 15 whites and seriously injured 12 others, one of whom, another policeman, later died.[105] When the mutineers disbanded, some slipped back into camp, while others found shelter in black homes or otherwise sought cover. Eventually, authorities rounded up all of the soldiers and sent the entire battalion by train to a camp in Columbus, New Mexico, to await courts-martial.

Some of the soldiers were unrepentant. Anonymous notes dropped from the train on its way to Columbus, picked up by dutiful citizens, and passed on to military authorities expressed righteous satisfaction at having shot up Houston. "We done our part in Houston and are on our way to Columbus, New Mexico," read one note. Another warned: "The people of Houston—Remember the 23rd of August, 1917. At 8:30 the Twenty-fourth Infantry gave Houston their first military blowout. The citizens didn't know what a volley was until that night. They didn't know that a 30 U.S. magazine rifle could shoot so hard. Volley fire! Volley fire!"[106] It is easy to imagine that African Americans throughout the country, accustomed to reading in sickening detail about white attacks on blacks or regularly subjected to the same kinds of insults that Camp Logan soldiers encountered in Houston, might have shared the satisfaction expressed in these notes.

The white American media, however, condemned the soldiers' actions. Even nominal allies of African Americans saw the Houston riot as "one of the most disgraceful mutinies of American troops in our history." The *Outlook*, "Theodore Roosevelt's editorial spokesman," urged that the offending soldiers be executed swiftly so as to obtain the maximum deterrent effect.[107] The journal also advised "Negro leaders" to "visit upon these Negro mutineers the same unanimous condemnation which the white race, North and South, visited upon the white rioters of East St. Louis." If black leaders failed to "vindicate their loyalty," America might decide against entrusting the defense of the nation to black officers and soldiers.[108] Even Oswald Villard's *Nation* asserted that the conduct of local authorities did not justify the Houston mutiny and called for the "severest punishment."[109] Lamenting that "innocent persons were slaughtered," the *New York Times* advised the government to show "no sign of leniency" toward the mutineers. Although the *Times* offered mild criticism of the South for persecuting black soldiers, it recommended avoiding the problem by sending black troops to camps in the North, a solution offered frequently by whites and sometimes by blacks.[110]

In formulating a response to the Houston mutiny, black newspapers encountered one of the most excruciating dilemmas of the war. "It is difficult for one of Negro blood to write of Houston," Du Bois agonized. On the one hand, black soldiers had demonstrated the kind of defiant militancy that many newspapers had advocated in theory. On the other hand, their actions seemed to belie the papers' persistent claim that the loyalty of black citizens in general and black soldiers in particular could be utterly relied upon. Du Bois only obliquely dared to suggest that African Americans might approve of the killings of innocent whites for a change. "Our hands tremble to rise and exult, our lips strive to cry," he wrote. But to exult in the mutiny of a battalion of American soldiers would certainly undermine the image of loyalty Du Bois and others wanted to foster. Thus he added: "And yet our hands are not raised in exultation; and yet our lips are silent."[111]

Most editors in the black press knew that commenting on the mutiny would be for them a dangerous proposition and thus treated it gingerly. After the execution of thirteen of the mutineers in December in San Antonio, Texas, Smith expressed what must have been the sentiment of many African Americans: "We simply dare not start to try to express our feelings and those of our people as a result of that terrible affair."[112] It was a wise choice. When the *Baltimore Afro-American* referred to the soldiers executed in December 1917 as martyrs, the Justice Department forced editor John H. Murphy to promise to "eliminate such stuff hereafter from his paper."[113] The only case of a black publisher jailed under the Espionage Act occurred as a result of an article on the Houston affair. In the November 24, 1917, edition of the *San Antonio Inquirer,* editor G. W. Bouldin published a letter from a black Austin, Texas, woman in support of the soldiers. C. L. Threadgill-Dennis, a student and sometime instructor in domestic science at Til-lotsen College in Austin, urged the soldiers to "rest assured that every [Negro] woman in all this land of ours . . . reveres you, she honors you." The letter continued:

> We would rather see you shot by the highest tribunal of the United States Army because you dared protect a Negro woman from the insult of a southern brute in the form of a policeman, than to have you forced to go to Europe to fight for a liberty you can not enjoy.
>
> Negro women regret that you mutinied, and we are sorry you spilt innocent blood, but we are not sorry that five southern police-men's bones now bleach in the graves of Houston, Tex.
>
> It is far better that you be shot for having tried to protect a Negro woman, than to have you die a natural death in the trenches of Europe, fighting to make the world safe for a democracy that you can't enjoy. On your way to the Training Camps you are jim-crowed. Every insult that can be heaped upon you, you have to take, or be tried by court-martial if you resent it.

The author went on to list a number of recent instances in which blacks were insulted by whites in Austin and could have used the pro-tection of the Twenty-fourth Infantry. She reassured the condemned soldiers that they were dying for "the most sacred thing on earth to any race[,] even the southern white man, his daughter's, his wife's, his mother's[,] his sister's[,] his neighbor's sister's protection from in-sult."[114] Like other blacks who commented on the riot, Threadgill-Dennis expressed regret at the loss of innocent life. Unlike them, how-ever, she ignored Du Bois's warning against exultation. Crossing this boundary proved too much for the authorities. The newspaper's edi-tor, Bouldin, was charged with making "an unlawful attempt to cause insubordination," a violation of Title I, Section 3, of the Espionage Act, and was eventually sentenced to two years in the Leavenworth fed-eral penitentiary. His plight likely served as a warning to other black editors.[115]

For the most part, the black press suppressed the impulse to praise the mutineers or laud their actions. Nor, however, did black writers unanimously condemn the mutineers. Instead, they walked a narrow line between condemning the mutiny and justifying it. Some newspapers, including the *Chicago Broad Ax,* the *Richmond Planet,* and the *Cleveland Gazette,* declined to condemn the mutiny, but most echoed the white press's denunciation of it. As Du Bois put it, "We ask no mitigation of their punishment. They broke the law. They must suffer."[116] The *Chicago Defender,* so eager to praise blacks who fought back against lynchers or rioters, condemned the soldiers' actions and counseled blacks in general to turn the other cheek. "Because a white man stoops to throw mud at us is no reason why we should roll in the mire with them," an editorial advised. Foreshadowing Du Bois's "Close Ranks" editorial, the *Defender* called on blacks to "put our whole heart and soul into the task of aiding our government to crush the enemy."[117] Unlike most of the black press, the *Pittsburgh Courier* did not object to the execution of thirteen of the accused mutineers. "Mutiny and murder are crimes that merit death upon conviction," an editorial proclaimed. "Soldiers who participate in lawlessness must take the consequences."[118] Even the militant socialist *Messenger,* while arguing that "taunts, insults and abuses" had been "unsparingly heaped upon" black soldiers, added: "We do not advocate or condone criminality or lawlessness among Negroes. We condemn it."[119]

But along with their obligatory condemnations of the mutiny, black editors printed explanations of why the soldiers rebelled and tried to reconcile the mutiny with their claims of utter loyalty. Editorialists and reporters sought to show that the soldiers had been pushed to a point at which any normal person would have retaliated. It was "regrettable that the soldiers so far forgot themselves as to spill innocent blood," the *Baltimore Afro-American* conceded, "yet there is another side to the controversy." The participation of so many soldiers illustrated "how great the provocation must have been."[120] A *Cleveland Gazette* reporter felt the need to invent more provocations than actually existed by claiming that the mutiny had been preceded by the killing of a black soldier by a white mob.[121] The *Chicago Defender* speculated that if white soldiers had suffered the same insults as black soldiers in Houston, the response would have been much more "horrible and ghastly." Blacks could tolerate more than most men because they had "a bigger and more generous heart." But despite the *Defender's* attempt to reassert the press's claim of black tolerance and almost superhuman loyalty and patriotism, that paper and several others had to concede that African Americans were "just human" after all and that their national loyalty and tolerance of indignities had limits. "A man," the *New York Age* pointed out, "whether he be black or white, is a human being before he is a soldier."[122]

If black soldiers had been so mercilessly provoked, greater condemnation should be heaped on the provokers than on the soldiers. Black newspapers tried to pin the guilt for the mutiny on racists or poorly trained police. The *Richmond Planet* and the *Norfolk Journal and Guide* argued that Houston police were more to blame than the black soldiers for the violence. The *Planet* absolved the South, saying that "officious police officers" caused trouble "in Northern communities as well as in Southern ones." Editor Mitchell even argued that "the better class of white people" in the South (a group on which he frequently pinned his hopes) did not approve of the "drastic punishment" of the Houston soldiers. As late as September 1918, he continued to argue that the police were "really responsible for the Houston riot."[123]

Black papers in the North, however, tended to blame southerners, who had opposed the calling up of black soldiers and had goaded black troops in a number of places.[124] In a long editorial on the Houston riot, the *Chicago Defender* linked Houston's provocateurs to those in the South who had failed to reconcile themselves to the Union's victory in the Civil War. These southerners were not only hostile to blacks' rights but also lacked loyalty to the federal government. "The true patriots are found in the north; the south has a handful." It was this lack of true patriotism that led southerners to goad into mutiny "one of the most efficient and orderly forces in the regular service."[125] The *Pittsburgh Courier* argued that black soldiers suffered "unbearable abuse" in every southern town in which they were stationed.[126] The *Cleveland Gazette,* one of the least apologetic papers in responding to the riot, blamed it on a "Texas mob of lynch-murderers." Editor Smith even blamed the executions, carried out by the federal government, on the South, which was "determined to drive every bit of loyalty and patriotism from us with all these 'military hangings.'"[127] "Quartering Negro troops in the South is equivalent to sending them into the enemy's country with the difference that they are forbidden to exercise the right of self-protection," the *New York Age* added. Persecution of black soldiers was a result not only of the South's hatred of blacks but also of its lingering hatred, dating back to the Confederacy, of the federal government.

There is no use in seeking to disguise the fact that the United States uniform is not held in high favor in all parts of the South. Despite recent protestations of patriotism there remains a remnant of the spirit of Secession, carefully fostered, which cannot abide the flavor of Federal authority. When that authority is embodied in the black soldier, the combination brings to the surface all the venom and bitterness of the unreconstructed rebel and domineering slave driver of the past assiduously instilled into the present generation.[128]

Clearly, the South had not sacrificed "every interest" to the national good, as Wilson had demanded in the presidential campaign of 1916. Thus, at least for northern black newspapers, Houston became not an attack of black soldiers on American citizens but an attack by the unreconstructed and disloyal South on both the Union and African Americans. As they sought to reinterpret the war to show black loyalty, some black editors sought to reinterpret Houston to show the disloyalty of the South.

SIGNS OF PROGRESS

As racial violence mounted at home and American soldiers began to participate in the war for democracy in Europe, editors and writers in the black press increasingly called on Wilson to apply his lofty ideals to problems at home. In October 1917, the *Savannah Tribune* called on Wilson to condemn lynching, discrimination, and racial prejudice because thousands of black citizens had gone to Europe to fight for liberty and democracy. "In the winning of democracy and freedom for the world, we shall certainly expect to win it for ourselves," the paper added two months later. "We shall accept nothing less than full emancipation from the brutal and humiliating ills of discrimination and proscription."[129] The following April, the *Chicago Defender* argued that America would have to live up to its own "preachments" of democracy if it wanted to win over other nations. In addition, national unity was necessary for the winning of the war, and there could be "no unity without justice to all classes."[130]

Meanwhile, in the summer of 1917, two New York City protests called attention to lynching and the East St. Louis riot. A rally at Harlem's St. Philip's Church attracted over 500 participants in the early summer, and the Silent Protest Parade on July 28 drew nearly 10,000 people and gained national attention. These demonstrations of outrage over violence against blacks were part of the NAACP's evolving antilynching campaign. Early in 1916, the NAACP had established a special committee on lynching and began stepping up efforts to gather information about lynching, promote antilynching publicity, organize whites and blacks especially in the South, establish local committees to identify and prosecute lynchers, and prepare state and fed-

THE DAWN OF A NEW DAY

"The Dawn of a New Day." Uncle Sam pledges to unlock an African American man from the chains of lynching, segregation, and prejudice with a key labeled "WAR." Black editorial pages began to express optimism that the war would lead to progress in racial equality.
From *Richmond Planet,* June 23, 1917.

eral antilynching legislation. The war accelerated the group's organizing efforts, spearheaded by Johnson. Membership mushroomed from 8,700 in 1916 to 44,000 by the end of 1918, emboldening and empowering the group.

On February 19, 1918, Johnson led an NAACP delegation to the Oval Office to appeal for clemency toward the Houston soldiers and request action on lynching. Wilson seemed receptive, asking for further details on the Estill Springs murder and promising to "seek an opportunity" to speak out against lynching.[131] Increasingly, the NAACP and the black press began to demand a federal law against lynching as a war measure. Within a month of the East St. Louis riot, the NAACP had organized a meeting with Wilson's secretary, Joseph Tumulty, to ask that lynching be made a federal crime.[132] In April 1918, Congressmen Leonidas Dyer of Missouri and Merrill Moores of Indiana introduced separate bills to involve the federal government in preventing lynching. Dyer's bill set penalties of five years in prison and $5,000 in fines for any state or local official who failed to prevent a lynching or refused to prosecute lynchers. It also allowed for prosecution of mob members in federal courts and required county governments to pay reparations to families of victims lynched within their jurisdictions.[133] The *Baltimore Afro-American* said Wilson should promote antilynching legislation to save the United States from the "disgrace of crimes for which we are now condemning Germany" and to enhance morale. "Continued mob outrages may affect the morale of the troops in the camps and in France and the patriotism of the colored people at home." At the very least, Wilson should speak out against lynching.[134] In the late spring of 1918, Representative Warren Gard of Ohio agreed to introduce legislation recommending action against lynching as a war measure, and on June 6, the House Judiciary Committee heard testimony from Major Joel Spingarn of army intelligence (who was also chairman of the NAACP) in favor of the measure.

Spingarn used the black press as a key component of his argument to convince the committee, which included several southerners, to approve the bill. In his opening statement, he affirmed the loyalty of most African Americans but said that intelligence had uncovered "evidence of a great deal of bitterness among the colored people as a result of lynching." That bitterness, he added, was being spread primarily by "some 200 colored newspapers." Rather than suppress the newspapers, he argued, Congress should get at the root of it by making lynching a capital federal crime. Such a measure, he argued, would be justified under the war powers clause because lynching interfered with "the success of the United States in the war" when soldiers or potential soldiers were lynched or when they worried about family members who might be lynched. Congress had already passed other legislation, he said, based on "the principle that a soldier can not [*sic*] fight properly or efficiently if he is worrying about the condition of his family at home." Spingarn read several passages from black periodicals that contrasted black service overseas and lynching at home. "We have a great many articles following that general tone," Spingarn added. Three representatives from southern states—including the chairman of the committee—seemed to oppose the measure, suggesting that it violated states' sovereignty. Representative Robert Y. Thomas of Kentucky even argued that lynching was justified "in many cases," including rape. The proposal would never make it past the committee, but at least national leaders were confronting the issue—and on terms defined by black editors.[135]

From the summer of 1917 to the early summer of 1918, in spite of a series of disturbing events, including the East St. Louis riot, the executions of black soldiers convicted in the Houston case, a surge in lynchings during the last year of the war, and "Bulletin 35," a military edict ordering stateside black soldiers not to challenge segregated public accommodations, the optimism of the black press seemed to grow. The *Nashville Globe* declared that "the war had brought to the Negro a better chance for national self-expression than any event in history."[136] A *New York Age* editor thought the Silent Protest Parade showed that "the psychological moment" had arrived "to wake the public conscience." Blacks across the country should organize similar protests, the editor advised, because "the public conscience is uneasy" and it was time to "set it working in the right direction."[137]

Other promising signs appeared. A month after the NAACP met with Tumulty to request antilynching legislation, Boston's mayor, James Michael Curley, sent a bill to Washington that would have made lynching and interference with the northward migration of blacks federal crimes.[138] Although that bill got nowhere, Dyer introduced his just a few months later. In September 1917, Secretary of War Newton Baker appointed Emmett Scott, who had been Booker T. Washington's secretary, as special assistant on race matters, revealing "a more liberal and sympathetic policy on the part of the national administration toward its twelve million loyal Negro citizens," according to the *New York Age*.[139] Evidence also suggests that the migration of blacks out of the South had led whites there to seek greater interracial cooperation to preserve the regional labor force. A study found that the blacks in Nash-

"Real Democracy." Uncle Sam prepares to serve a dish of "real democracy" to a black man already drinking the "wine of prosperity" thanks to "unprecedented industrial opportunities." Also on the table are "678 Negro officers in U.S. Army." From *New York Age*, November 29, 1917.

ville made "noticeable progress during the war"—gains that were not reversed after the Armistice.[140]

Even the *Savannah Tribune*'s gloomy editorial about the black soldiers who saw the burned lynching victim in Tennessee struck a cautiously optimistic note about "America's changing heart" and pointed to a number of encouraging signs, including the admission of black laborers into the American Federation of Labor. Americans would grant justice, if not voluntarily, then because they had no choice. "We believe we see the dawning of a new day on earth," the paper concluded.[141] Other editorialists observed that the war was creating unity between blacks and whites as they worked toward the common goal of victory. The war and the migration had shown southerners that "the colored people are the best friends of the Southern white people," the *Richmond Planet* argued. "The feeling of antipathy toward us has given way to expressions of general sympathy."[142]

In spite of the nation's mounting intolerance of dissenters during the war, black writers saw a growing spirit of democracy. "Strange indeed it will be if a new society does not emerge from this democratic spirit that is being evidenced more and more as the war goes on," the *Chicago Defender* wrote in the early summer of 1918.[143] Even the generally pessimistic *Cleveland Gazette* finally saw reason to hope that Wilson's ideals could be applied at home. Since Wilson had said that every action of the nation must serve the good of man and contribute to social justice, "our people have reason to expect help from him in the way of justice and service to their humanity," Smith wrote.[144]

One of the most hopeful signs was what seemed to be a growing revulsion throughout the country—evident even in the editorials of some southern newspapers—toward lynching among whites who now saw the practice in the light of American war aims. In the spring and summer of 1918, the *Baltimore Afro-American* pointed to antilynching groups formed by white southerners and editorials in white southern papers that argued that lynching did not fit with "our battle cry, 'a world safe for Democracy.'"[145] The *New York Age* even noted an "antilynching movement" among southern newspapers. It was "evident that there has come a change over the spirit of the South," an unsigned editorial commented. Johnson observed that the *Florida Times-Union*'s recent defense of lynching stood out as an exception among southern newspapers, which now were condemning the practice in unqualified terms.[146] A growing chorus supported banning *Birth of a Nation,* a film "worse than poison gas," in order to preserve national unity, according to Smith. The "ready response of the colored men at the time of the call

"The Old Mob and the New Keeper." A black man kneeling on a copy of
"Wilson's speech" is protected by Lady Liberty, who is banishing
segregation, yellow journalism, social privileges, barbarism, and cruelty,
among others. Her newspaper reads: "Freedom for All, Says President.
Democracy Must Rule." Abraham Lincoln's image is visible in the
background. The optimism of the black press grew in the last year of the
war. From *Chicago Defender*, February 16, 1918.

to arms did more to convince the American people of the outrageous
slanders contained in that play than anything else," said Mitchell.[147]

Editors saw that the more the nation needed black help to win the
war and the greater black participation, the more of their demands
could be met. As Mitchell bluntly put it in October 1917, "The longer
the war and the bloodier, the better it will be for the colored folk."[148]
Optimism would continue to grow through the late summer and early
fall of 1918 after the Wilson administration began to respond to a
series of demands presented by a group of black editors in June. Un-

fortunately—from Mitchell's perspective—the war would come to a speedy conclusion only eighteen months after American entry and long before substantive racial progress had been made.

From the beginning of America's entry into the war, the black press sought to maintain a balance between promoting black loyalty and demanding that the government take action to secure that loyalty. In responding to Wilson's war message, reports of German plots among blacks, the segregated officer-training camp, and the Houston riot, black writers had to strike a balance between loyalty and protest. Each writer and each newspaper devised a unique response to each situation, yet the black press as a whole followed a discernible pattern. Most editors pledged to support the war even when they were critical of Wilson's motives; moved toward embracing the war for democracy in spite of being skeptical about it; affirmed the loyalty of blacks while showing that they had every reason to be disloyal and entertain rebellion; resisted segregation by the army but ultimately embraced the Jim Crow officer-training camp and applauded those who signed up; and condemned the Houston mutiny but portrayed those who provoked it as more disloyal than the mutineers themselves. Outside observers might have viewed these responses as either loyal or disloyal. It might have seemed legitimate to invoke Wilsonian ideals in criticizing white supremacists or demand antilynching legislation as a war measure, but doing so might have exacerbated sectional disunity at a time when the nation needed to present a common front or it might have appeared to be placing conditions on black cooperation with the war effort. The black press seemed optimistic about the war and supportive of Wilson's ideals, but then again, it seemed to be measuring success in terms of what the war would do for blacks rather than how the nation as a whole fared.

Different black newspapers balanced protest and accommodation, demands and loyalty, in different ways. Southern papers appear to have been more conciliatory toward the South, but their approach still blended protest and accommodation. The *Norfolk Journal and Guide* placed far greater emphasis on cooperation with the war effort and the loyalty of blacks than on demands for wartime readjustment of race relations, but it still expressed dissatisfaction that the officer-training camp would be segregated, argued that the East St. Louis riot exposed the hypocrisy of Wilson's war aims, and blamed the Houston riot on police brutality. One of the most militant black papers in the North, however, Harry Smith's *Cleveland Gazette*, claimed that blacks were unconditionally loyal to undermine suspicions generated by the "Plan of San Diego," endorsed participation in the officer-training camp, expressed wariness about condemning the execution of Houston mutineers, and accepted the notion that America could lead a war for democracy.

Less important than the fine distinctions among the positions of black newspapers is the way the black press functioned as a link between African Americans and the federal government—as an instrument of political power serving the interests of both the black population and the federal government. The black press displayed the loyalty of blacks to the state while at the same time conveying to blacks the importance of supporting the war effort, including the draft, the Liberty Loan, and in some cases the segregated officer-training camp. It showed the government why Wilsonian ideals had to be applied at home and informed black readers of the ways in which the war was generating racial progress. It sought to explain apparently disloyal actions of blacks like the Houston mutiny or the "Plan of San Diego" while encouraging blacks not to engage in such disloyalty. Most of these links were apparent rather than tangible, but in some cases, the connections between the black press and the state were reinforced by important back channels, as when Johnson met with the president or Spingarn used the advocacy of black newspapers as another reason to enact antilynching legislation in Congress.

Congress's receptiveness to antilynching legislation suggests that by the spring of 1918, the black press's strategy of adapting Wilson's idealistic war aims to its own issues may have begun to work—that progress on race issues might result from the war. Other evidence, however, suggests that the state was successful in making the black press an instrument of control of African Americans during the war. Black newspapers had almost unanimously pledged loyalty to the cause, most embracing Wilson's ideals enthusiastically, all advocating black participation in the military and other war work. Even opponents of the war came to support it, and black writers treaded lightly on the issue of the Houston mutiny, most condemning it in spite of their empathy for the mutinous soldiers. The positive inducements of Wilson's war for democracy and the willingness of black newspapers to accommodate mainstream politics had much to do with the press's determination to support the war effort—but these were not the only factors involved. In addition, the threat of censorship provided an important incentive that must be considered in arriving at an understanding of the black press during World War I.

CHAPTER 4
A FINE PHILOSOPHY OF DEMOCRACY, 1917–1918

When the Richmond, Virginia, postmaster, Hay T. Thornton, picked up a copy of the *Richmond Planet* on Thursday, August 2, 1917, a letter to the editor on the front page caught his attention. The country had been at war for four months, and since mid-June, Thornton and every other postmaster had been instructed to forward to the Postmaster General's Office in Washington any "unsealed matter"—newspapers and other publications with second-class mailing status—that was "calculated . . . to cause insubordination, disloyalty, mutiny, or refusal of duty, or in any other way to embarrass or hamper the Government." Federal law required postal officials to revoke the second-class status of any publication matching this description.

The author of the letter in question, twenty-eight-year-old Howard University graduate Uzziah Miner, said that he would not volunteer for service in the armed forces because the East St. Louis riot showed that the "'World Democracy' which President Wilson preaches" did not apply to blacks. "I fail to see how I can conscientiously volunteer to fight for a 'World Democracy' while I am denied the fruits and blessings of a Democracy at home," Miner wrote.

Thornton decided Miner's letter could be construed as fostering resistance to the war effort or at least as an attempt to embarrass the federal government. He showed the newspaper to Richmond's assistant district attorney, Hiram M. Smith, who deemed Miner's letter "a clear violation" of the Espionage Act, a law Congress had passed that spring to prevent sabotage of the war effort by enemy agents. Thornton forwarded a copy of the paper to Post Office Solicitor William H. Lamar, who would rule from Washington on whether the issue could be delivered. Meanwhile, Thornton said nothing to Mitchell, and eighteen sacks of the *Planet* sat idle in the Richmond Post Office as the August 4 publication date approached.[1]

On Saturday morning, when subscribers should have been receiving their papers, Mitchell finally discovered that something had gone wrong and called the Post Office for an explanation. Angered that his newspapers could be "confiscated . . . without due process of law," he sent a wagon to pick up the undelivered bundles. A clerk refused to release the papers, and Mitchell's driver returned with the news that "they were being held pending further instructions from Washington." Mitchell would have to wait until Monday to resolve the matter. He spent the weekend distributing a press release about the incident, pondering whether the *Planet* had already "been held for such a length of time as to make the entire edition worthless," and worrying that advertisers would demand refunds if the paper was never delivered. On Monday, he drafted two letters pleading for redress, one to Postmaster General Albert S. Burleson and another to Virginia senator Thomas Martin. On stationery of the Merchants Savings Bank, an institution he managed as president from 1902 to 1921, the publisher asserted his loyalty and support for the war, distanced himself from Miner's letter, and decried the unfairness of Thornton's action. "It is needless to say to you that I have done everything to aid the present administration in its present attitude," Mitchell wrote to Martin. "I have published free of charge communications from the Recruiting Service, United States Agricultural Department, War Department and am at present chairman of the local Liberty Bond Committee of the Colored People, which raised approximately $25,000.00 in subscriptions to the Liberty Bonds." He said Miner spoke only for himself and in fact had criticized the *Planet* editor in a letter written "several months ago." Mitchell even appealed to "the southern spirit of fair-play in the upper classes of the people" (Burleson was a Texan). Martin forwarded his letter to the postmaster general without any recommendation.

The next morning, Mitchell boarded a train for Washington, where he hired a lawyer "to look after the interests of the Planet" and visited the U.S. Senate chamber. The following day, Wednesday, he talked by phone with J. Milton Waldron, who offered to bring up his case at a meeting of William Monroe Trotter's National Equal Rights League that night. Finally, on Thursday morning, apparently on orders from Washington, Thornton allowed the August 4 *Planet* to be delivered — almost a full week after it had arrived at his office.[2]

In the following week's newspaper, Mitchell asserted that Miner's letter did not violate the law but added that the young man had demonstrated "more zeal than judgement" in composing it. He also declared that "colored folks are loyal to the national government and will not do anything to embarrass it in its efforts to win a war." Yet he pledged to continue to speak out against racial injustice as long as the nation was not under martial law. In October, he vowed that Americans would never "tamely submit" to the loss of basic constitutional rights. Like Mitchell, the nearby *Norfolk Journal and Guide* believed the *Richmond Planet*'s run-in with the Post Office was no reason to stop agitating for racial justice. In fact, it stated, President Wilson could look forward "from now on" to hearing protests "from millions of Americans, white and black, who believe that this country should set its own house in order before going to fight the battles of civilization 'marching in blood-stained clothes.'"[3]

The story of the August 4 *Richmond Planet* offers striking insight into the ways in which the government handled black newspapers during World War I. In this case as in others, low-level officials found the paper objectionable and believed it violated the law, but higher-ups disagreed and ordered the paper sent out. Censors like Postmaster Thornton thought the "bitter tone" of many newspapers indicated a lack of patriotism, but they—or, more important, their superiors— had to concede in most cases that these newspapers supported the national government and the war effort and that their criticisms were usually "too subtle" to warrant censorship. As one critic of the *Chicago Defender* put it, black newspapers pushed their case right to "the limit," but it was difficult to tell whether they went over it or not. In most instances, officials decided they did not.

At the same time, black editors became aware of the dangers of censorship and sought to moderate their tone, but usually not at the expense of making demands for racial justice. Thus, most black newspapers, including an accommodationist paper like the *Norfolk Journal and Guide,* continued to protest for racial justice during the war yet did not suffer the kind of wholesale repression that put many socialist publications out of business because they neither caved in to government demands for unconditional participation in the war nor refused to accommodate those demands at all. Most black newspapers fell somewhere between capitulation and unequivocal protest. They emphasized the loyalty and patriotism of black folks yet noted the volatility of the black population; they praised American ideals and criticized continuing racial injustice not as a failure of those ideals but as a betrayal of them by unpatriotic, disloyal Americans. Although it offended many white Americans, this approach seems to have succeeded not only in heading off government persecution of African Americans and the black press but also in forcing the nation to take their demands seriously. Worried about the unrest of African Americans, the federal government called a conference of three dozen black editors to give them an opportunity to present their demands and to assure their continued loyalty. The editors interpreted black unrest as a demand for federal action, and the government responded. Although the early end of the war prevented the government from fully carrying out its promises, high-level officials, including Secretary of War Newton Baker and the president himself, accepted the notions that the loyalty of black Americans combined with their unrest required some acts of good faith by the nation and that lynching reduced America's credibility as the self-professed guardian of world democracy. By the fall of 1918, the editors understandably thought their strategy had succeeded.

Thus, in a dangerous time, the black press served as a mediating forum between blacks and the white-controlled government. Black editors and writers used it to present black demands and arguments and to interpret black "unrest" to white America in the ways most likely to be heard and answered positively. At the same time, government officials sought to promote black loyalty to the war by threatening the mailing privileges of black newspapers, delivering verbal and written warnings to black publishers, and calling black publishers to Washington.

The government tried to use the black press as a means of domination during the war, and African Americans sought to use it as a tool of resistance. Although federal officials employed coercive measures to silence a few black publications, most black newspapers avoided persecution and continued their efforts to bend the war to their own purposes. Finally, with the editors' conference of June 1918, the government actually seemed to acquiesce to black demands.

CENSORSHIP DURING THE WAR

All publishers faced the dangers of censorship during the war. Under the Espionage Act, which became law in June 1917, persons convicted of interfering with the conduct of the war could be fined up to $10,000 and sent to prison for up to twenty years. More significantly, those convicted of using the mails for seditious purposes faced fines of up to $5,000 and five years' imprisonment. In addition, Title XII of the law made it illegal to use the mails to send materials "advocating or urging treason, insurrection, or forcible resistance to any law of the

United States." An amendment known as the Sedition Act broadened the scope of governmental powers to enforce loyalty in May 1918. This act prohibited "any disloyal, profane, scurrilous, or abusive language about the form of government of the United States, or the Constitution of the United States, or the flag of the United States, or the uniform of the Army or Navy." Armed with Title XII of the Espionage Act, U.S. Postmaster General Albert Burleson, who had initiated racial segregation in federal offices in 1913, immediately ordered the surveillance of all publications suspected of disloyalty, especially immigrant newspapers, socialist publications, and the black press. Socialist and German-language publications fared the worst at the hands of the censors. In the summer of 1917, the Post Office banned more than a dozen socialist publications from the mails, and of the seventy-five publications that faced government interference of one kind or another during the war, as many as forty-five were socialist organs. German American newspapers probably suffered more from public pressure than from official censorship, but a requirement of the Trading with the Enemy Act of 1917 that German-language newspapers supply the government with an English translation of every issue drove many smaller publications out of business. Between 1917 and 1919, the number of German American publications was cut in half. Neither the German American press nor the socialist movement ever fully recovered after the war.[4]

Meanwhile, although the black press was suspected of disloyalty, few black publications lost second-class mailing privileges, and the publisher of only one minor black periodical received a prison sentence as a result of the Espionage and Sedition Acts. Black newspapers faced several different kinds of censorship. The Justice Department could arrest and prosecute editors for violation of the Espionage or Sedition Act; the federal Post Office Department could revoke second-class mailing privileges, a devastating blow to publications like the *Richmond Planet* that relied on the mails for distribution; local postal officials like Thornton could delay or even prevent the mailing of a publication deemed disloyal; and military, postal, and Justice Department authorities could issue verbal or written warnings to African American editors to try to control the content of their newspapers. Most black newspapers did not encounter censorship directly, yet all knew of the danger of censorship. At the very start of the war, in April, the *Baltimore Afro-American* noted that two blacks had been arrested for expressing "anti-American sentiments" and warned that during the war it would be "necessary that everybody watch his tongue." The

Cleveland Gazette advised against expressing "our feelings" about the executions of the Houston mutineers. Even Mitchell wrote on page 4 of the same issue of the *Richmond Planet* that was withheld by the postmaster that although the law did not prevent individuals from thinking as they pleased, it did penalize "putting your thoughts in a word form. The best way to do is to tell your troubles to God, but go into your closet and shut the door while so doing else some one else than God may hear you and arrest you when you come out."[5]

Only two black publications faced serious legal consequences under the Espionage and Sedition Acts during the war. *San Antonio Inquirer* editor G. W. Bouldin received a jail sentence after the war for printing C. L. Threadgill-Dennis's praise of the Houston mutineers. According to prosecutors, she went too far when she excused the actions of the soldiers, called on other black soldiers to imitate them, and derided the notion that blacks should defend Europe. The Justice Department said her letter "advocated insurrection and forceful resistance to the laws of the United States" while attempting to "cause insubordination, disloyalty, mutiny and refusal of duty in the military forces."[6]

Like many other socialist publications, the *Messenger* forthrightly opposed the war, criticized America's motives, and called for peace. It denounced military spending and war profiteers; printed statistical evidence that blacks opposed conscription; and said that black leaders who supported the war, like W. E. B. Du Bois and Kelly Miller, should sign up for service themselves. "We would rather make Georgia safe for the Negro" than fight for democracy in France, the *Messenger* concluded. Thus, unlike most black editorialists, *Messenger* editors A. Philip Randolph and Chandler Owen opposed the war and supported and encouraged black opposition to it without equivocation.[7] Unlike other black newspapers that embraced the war and connected it to the elimination of racism, Randolph and Owen used racism as a reason for blacks to oppose the war and even questioned the legitimacy of the war machine's methods. Agents broke into the *Messenger*'s Harlem offices, confiscated back issues, and ransacked files. In August 1918, the U.S. Justice Department seized Randolph and Owen in the midst of a speaking tour and charged them with violating a section of the Espionage Act that imposed a twenty-year sentence for inspiring disloyalty or interfering with the military. After they spent two days in jail, a judge threw the case out. When they finished their speaking tour, the army drafted Owen into service, the Post Office revoked the *Messenger*'s second-class mailing privileges, and the journal suspended publication until March 1919. Ultimately, the *Messenger*'s suppression may have had more to do with its being a socialist publication than its being a black publication.[8]

The *Messenger* explicitly opposed black participation in the war effort. But support of the war—the policy of most other black newspapers—did not guarantee immunity from government surveillance and coercion, as several editors found out, most conspicuously W. E. B. Du Bois.

CLOSING RANKS AT THE *CRISIS*

Government attention to Du Bois's *Crisis,* combined with his own patriotic enthusiasm, led him to abandon his defense of protest in June 1918. Du Bois perhaps confronted greater and more persistent pressure to moderate his approach than any other black editor. He faced not only military censors but an NAACP censorship committee as well. His famous "Close Ranks" editorial in the July 1918 *Crisis* advised blacks to stop agitating for their own rights and concentrate on winning the war. "It is necessary in the time of war to be careful of one's utterances," Du Bois confessed to a correspondent that summer. "THE CRISIS will never say anything that it does not believe: but there are a great many things which it does believe which it cannot say just now."[9]

The War Department kept a detailed file of *Crisis* editorials dating back to 1916. The file included material that might have come from any black weekly: criticisms of Wilson administration policies; denunciations of lynching; pleas for equal treatment of blacks during the war; a comparison of Wilson's eloquent denunciations of German atrocities with his silence on lynchings of African Americans in the South. Even after Du Bois published "Close Ranks," the official who assembled the file held the *Crisis* "responsible for a great deal of the present negro unrest and disaffection." The magazine, he concluded, aimed at "exciting the colored races to acts of violence against the whites."[10]

Others also accused the journal of inciting blacks to violence against whites. YMCA officials at Camp Gordon, Georgia, banned the magazine for allegedly inciting a riot between black and white soldiers there in the spring of 1918. A Justice Department investigator in Waco thought the publication had had something to do with the Houston riot the previous year. Assistant U.S. Attorney Earl B. Barnes said he intended to "prevent propaganda" in the magazine that was "calculated to create a feeling of dissatisfaction among colored people" and asked to be sent a complete run of the *Crisis* since the previous April, as well as all future issues.[11] Despite Du Bois's decidedly pro-Allied slant, the chief of the Justice Department's Bureau of Investigation, A. Bruce Bielaski, believed the *Crisis* was a tool of German propagandists.[12]

Pressure on the journal became greatest around the time Du Bois composed "Close Ranks." Both the Department of Justice and the military met with NAACP officials in May 1918, threatening censorship if the rhetoric of *Crisis* editorials was not toned down.[13] Colonel Marlborough Churchill, head of the Military Intelligence Division (sometimes "Branch") (MID) of the army, warned white executive board member Charles H. Studin that the government would "not tolerate carping and bitter utterances likely to foment disaffection and destroy the morale of our people for the winning of the war." NAACP officials agreed to appoint Studin to review each issue before it went to press "to eliminate all matter that may render the paper liable to suppression in the future."[14] "No pains will be spared to make all future issues of this magazine comply with the wishes of the Government," Studin assured Churchill. Helping to win the war had become the *Crisis*'s "paramount purpose."[15] Around the same time, NAACP board chairman Joel Spingarn had offered Du Bois an appointment to work with him in the army intelligence service in the rank of captain. Spingarn and Du Bois believed that in that capacity they would be able to work from within the government to bring about measures for the improvement of racial conditions.

A host of factors converged in the late spring and early summer of 1918 to inspire Du Bois to compose his infamous accommodationist editorial, "Close Ranks," for the July *Crisis*. In addition to pressures from the MID and Studin's committee, Du Bois was subject to all of the same forces leading to optimism among other black editors. The offer of a captaincy in the army was likely a minor inducement since Du Bois seemed to be lukewarm about the prospect of military service. But the fact that he would consider such an offer indicates that he had come to see cooperation with the war effort as the only viable option for blacks during the war. He stated in the editorial:

We of the colored race have no ordinary interest in the outcome. That which the German power represents today spells death to the aspirations of Negroes and all darker races for equality, freedom and democracy. Let us not hesitate. Let us, while this war lasts, forget our special grievances and close our ranks shoulder to shoulder with our white fellow citizens and the allied nations that are fighting for democracy. We make no ordinary sacrifice, but we make it gladly and willingly, with our eyes lifted to the hills.[16]

When the *Crisis* hit the newsstands in late June, Spingarn sent a copy to Churchill as "evidence of the effect of M. I. B. policy." Churchill found it "very satisfactory."[17] The government had managed to effect a change at the *Crisis* without using direct force. A combination of friendly persuasion and implied threats did the trick. In the cases of the *Messenger* and the *Crisis,* government officials silenced black demands that the war be accompanied by fulfillment of black rights. In the former case, they simply arrested or drafted the journal's editors and hampered distribution efforts. In the latter, they convinced the editor, through a combination of threats and enticements, which appealed to his own predilections, that he should stop agitating.[18]

"A LITTLE TOO SUBTLE"

Among black publications, the *Crisis* was unique because of the control of white NAACP executives and Du Bois's close personal relationship to the superpatriot Spingarn. Censorship did not have as much effect on more typical black newspapers, owned and operated by blacks and removed from direct white influence. Most did not, like Du Bois, forget their "special grievances." Instead, they made a case for black rights that was just provocative enough to raise concerns among government officials that blacks might not participate fully in the war yet not quite provocative enough to warrant censorship. Postal, Justice Department, and military officials responded to and argued with what they read in the black press, literally entering a dialogue about race, America, and the patriotic duty of black citizens.[19] This dialogue reveals the nature and size of the gulf separating dominant white conceptions from subordinate black conceptions. What may seem to our eyes like reasonable comments on racism, lynching, and the unreconstructed South seemed "vile, nefarious," and seditious to white censors in 1918.[20] Thus, the black press tested the limits of acceptable racial discourse in America, while at the same time generally avoiding suppression and prosecution.

The Post Office Department's New York Translation Bureau, or Bureau M-1, staffed largely by patriotic volunteers, watched closely over black weekly newspapers, especially the *New York Age* and the *New York News.* Offended by the "unbridled bitterness" of the papers, bureau readers passed along to the local U.S. assistant district attorney and Post Office Solicitor William H. Lamar a series of memos making the case that these two newspapers were disloyal, had violated the Sedition Act, and ought to be "suppressed."[21] But these officials were frustrated in their attempts to find a smoking gun—statements that clearly amounted to sedition and justified censorship. Although one issue of the *News* may have been kept out of the mails, neither it nor the *Age* lost its second-class mailing privileges during the war.[22]

The head of the Translation Bureau, Robert A. Bowen, and his employees seem to have been offended by black newspapers that challenged their own attitudes about race. Bowen objected to a page 1 *Age* article protesting the barring of black soldiers' wives from sleepers on Pullman railroad cars, saying, "The matter boils itself down to the degree of reluctance or its reverse, one may feel in sleeping with and after negroes. *Chacun a son gout!* [everyone to his own taste]." Another New York censor sympathized with those who "do not relish" "contiguity" with African Americans. Comments like these suggest that the New York censors shared the racist assumptions of most white people of the day. Their memoranda on the *Age* and the *News* read like a defense of those assumptions combined with a generally hostile attack on the black press and, by extension, the African American population.

Regardless of whether or not black newspapers violated any laws, Bowen and other censors held a negative opinion of them. "I do not often have the pleasure of reading the negro papers," Bowen wrote with contempt, "and the denial is the greater pleasure."[23] Bowen described the attitude of the black press toward the South as "very offensive" and *Age* editorials on the South as "preposterous" and full of "sweeping assertions."[24] A frequent censor, referred to in documents as L. How or simply "LH," called the *News* "bitter and vicious on the race question" and belittled its advocacy of basic justice and human rights by saying authors of protest articles wanted to be "treated more politely."[25] If the newspapers could not be shown to have violated the law, they could be portrayed as substandard or ridiculous. In one report quoting the *News,* How penciled the letter "u" over an "i" in "insidious," which he had inadvertently spelled correctly on his own typewriter, so the word would be misspelled as "insiduous" as in the article, followed by "[*sic*]."[26] That he would take the time to make this minor adjustment suggests that he was no neutral observer making objective reports but a combatant in hostile dialogue with the black press, using any weapon at his disposal to discredit black newspapers. Yet despite his generally negative view of these newspapers, How referred to the *Age* once as "reasonable enough" and another time as "decidedly patriotic."[27] At least compared with the readers of the *News,* he added in another letter, *Age* readers tended to be "rather decent."[28] Bowen had to admit that he agreed with black newspapers that lynching was "a very lamentable situation."[29] Such statements reflect a tone of reluctant concession, not hearty agreement.

Given their intense hostility, New York censors sought persistently to build a case of sedition against both of these newspapers. One censor accused the *New York News* of sedition for urging the federal government to act against lynching "as a measure for winning the war"—a charge that could have been leveled at almost any black newspaper. The plea implied that blacks would not give their full support to the war "except under certain conditions," the censor wrote. "This is no time for bargains. This is the time for suppressing newspapers that maintain such an attitude."[30] Censors occasionally found what they regarded as veiled encouragement of black retributive violence or rebellion in the *News*. An August 14 editorial observed that on returning from the war, "brave black bayonet fighters" would be ready to fight more boldly for their rights at home. Such "incendiary" statements were deemed "legally objectionable" by How, U.S. Assistant District Attorney George L. Thompson, and others, but no action was taken. A few months later, Bowen told the solicitor's office that two black papers were "deserving of censure if not suppression" because of "their covert threat of violence when the negro soldiers return." He continued: "I know that they [black newspapers] are very influential among their readers, and I wish there might be found some way in which their entirely wrong attitude could be rectified." Yet Bowen did not hold them up in the mails because so much other, more "obnoxious . . . Bolshevik-revolutionary stuff" required immediate action.[31] Bowen's comments reflect the sentiment common among government monitors who were rubbed the wrong way by black newspapers and thought they were disloyal but ultimately did not judge them disloyal enough to suppress.

Usually, complaints about the *News* and the *Age* came down to the vague notion that they were "stirring up race antagonism," which interfered with the war effort. Emphasizing the racial element of news stories tended to perpetuate antagonistic feelings between the races, according to How, as did reprinting racist screeds by white southerners; describing the war for democracy as a two-front campaign in Europe and the South; portraying black people as better than whites; equating southern whites with "Huns"; dwelling on the horrors of lynching; and criticizing "Bulletin 35," in which a general ordered his black troops not to challenge Jim Crow accommodations outside their training camp.[32]

Even in weeks when the *New York News* was "less blatantly objectionable," How wrote, its editors continued "to adopt an attitude which cannot but nourish the [bad] feelings between white races and the colored race." He worried that "some chance white readers of these papers might have their feelings against the colored people vividly stirred up," if by nothing more than the papers' habit of "contemptuously ignoring the white race."[33] A story about a crowd of white onlookers who were unable and unwilling to assist a black man who had collapsed at an elevated train station was "calculated to irritate" because it implied "that the non-colored crowd was both heartless and incapable."[34] How even argued that the newspaper's attacks on lynching, which stirred "feeling[s] of hatred and envy," might "almost directly" have caused the recent rise in lynchings.[35] Even more troubling to How was the black press's potential for arousing black "prejudice" against whites. The New York Age, for example, printed a story on page 1 about a white soldier's attack on a black girl and boy, How said, "purely for the purpose of arousing race prejudice."[36]

In some cases, censors were clearly grasping at straws in searching for reasons to ban the two newspapers. One censor even listed the biennial lynching statistics (a state-by-state accounting with no commentary) released by Robert R. Moton, Booker T. Washington's successor at Tuskegee Institute, as a potentially seditious item, although he did not elaborate.[37] Other censors filed reports on items they admitted did not violate the law but were "of interest."[38] Often, they seemed to suggest that black newspapers were speaking in some kind of code, hiding disloyal sentiments behind patriotic words. How wanted to suppress the March 23, 1918, New York Age on the basis of three objectionable editorials that violated the Espionage Act in spirit, he said, if not in fact. In one of them, James Weldon Johnson said blacks had "never lost faith in . . . the Government of the United States." Its spirit had been "often thwarted and defeated" but could never be destroyed. Nevertheless, "our faith in the spirit of the country will not deter us from pointing the accusing finger at those individuals and groups of individuals who are striving to defeat and destroy that spirit," Johnson continued. No one should doubt the African American's loyalty during the present crisis, Johnson said, but everyone should know that he would do "his duty with his eyes wide open; and when that duty is done he will demand that this nation live up to the protestations of democracy that it is now making." How quoted the last sentence disapprovingly but had to admit that Johnson's editorials were "a little too subtle perhaps to object to."[39]

Comments of the censors about the Chicago Defender and some other black newspapers reveal still more ambivalence. Army intelligence officer Roy F. Britton described a May 3, 1918, editorial in the *St. Louis Argus* as "insidious and dangerous propaganda" because it sowed "seeds of discontent" and "coupled" the buying of liberty bonds with support for a federal antilynching bill. But Britton had to admit that the editorial advocated the use of only "legitimate, legal and patriotic means" of protest. Britton visited *Argus* city editor Herbert Meadows and "warned him about saying anything in his paper that would make the negroes discontented or make them want to avoid service." Meadows asserted the *Argus*'s "loyalty and patriotism" and assured Britton "that his paper was behind the government."[40] Britton may have been persuaded by the arguments that appeared in the newspaper. In June, he responded to an article about a black draftee ejected from a train in Arkansas by suggesting to his supervisor that the incident be investigated.[41]

Government officials called the *Chicago Defender* "the most dangerous of all Negro Journals," yet they could not agree on whether it needed to be censored.[42] Distribution of the first mass circulation black newspaper reached deep into the South, and some believed it had caused the migration of hundreds of thousands of blacks from South to North during the war. According to government estimates, Robert Abbott sold 92,000 issues in Chicago each week by mid-1918 and thousands more throughout the country, including 2,000 in New Orleans alone.[43] Abbott may have been somewhat less vulnerable to threats of lost mailing privileges because he distributed many of his newspapers through a network of black Pullman porters who dropped off bundles of papers at railroad stations for local agents.

Most of the critiques of Abbott's paper came not from postal censors in Chicago but from southerners who accused the *Defender* of stirring up trouble in their neighborhoods. M. E. Nash, postmaster of Belcher, Louisiana, wrote the Post Office solicitor in Washington that every issue of the *Defender* "contains a libel on the South. . . . The sentiments expressed in it were unknown in this section previous to its appearance" and threatened to "inflame" a "heretofore peaceful section" where "the negroes have always been well and equitably treated." Just as the black press portrayed southern racism as unpatriotic, these white southerners portrayed the black press as hindering the war effort. The newspaper's advocacy of migration threatened to deplete the South's supply of agricultural labor, Nash wrote, and "anything that interferes with the agriculture of the South is a menace to the whole Nation and such influences should be closely watched."[44]

Whites from Denison, Texas; Tucson, Arizona; Little Rock and Pine Bluff, Arkansas; New Orleans; Jacksonville, Florida; Memphis, Tennessee; and Mobile, Alabama, argued that the *Defender* had threatened wartime national unity by poisoning otherwise harmonious race relations.[45] The Denison postmaster tried to convince the solicitor that the *Defender* inspired "rank race hatred," was involved in a "German conspiracy," and showed signs of "anti-Americanism." Beyond that, the rural postmaster took issue with the newspaper's interpretation of racial violence. "Inhumanities," he wrote, did not occur "only between the white race and the negro race" but among people of the same race as well. Thus, "the occurrence of trouble occasionally between the two races is no special sign of exclusive inhumanity from one or the other."[46]

Government officials were sympathetic to southerners' view of reality and in agreement with their opinions of black newspapers like the *Defender*. A federal postal official agreed with Nash that the June 1 and 22, 1918, issues of the paper should be barred from the mails because they interfered with the supply of southern labor and intensified "racial prejudices and animosities."[47] Colonel Ralph H. Van Deman, Churchill's predecessor as head of the MID, regarded the *Defender* as "undoubtedly disloyal in most of its utterances" because it contained "repeated attacks on the Government" and tended to encourage "disloyal acts" among blacks. Yet he did not recommend any particular actions against the paper.[48]

Most other officials concluded that the *Defender*, however objectionable, had done nothing illegal, and like Van Deman, they could find no particular reason to censor it during the war. The Post Office ruled that the page 1 story, "Southern Stunts Surpass Hun," which the Denison postmaster had criticized, did not warrant suppression, although it did tend to "stir up race hatred and race prejudice" and encourage mob violence.[49] The Justice Department investigated charges that Germans were conspiring to distribute the newspapers to all African Americans in Tucson and concluded late in 1917 that "since the war began, [the *Defender*] has been loyal to the core. There is nowhere connected with it the slightest evidence of German influence."[50]

Even two southerners who hoped to silence the journal had to admit that it generally stayed within (or at least did not go far beyond) the bounds of acceptable discourse. Bolton Smith, a white Tennessee banker who had formed the prowar, antilynching Law and Order League in his state, said the *Defender* should be suppressed because it stirred up "violence and strife" but acknowledged that the newspaper probably did "no harm." He could not decide whether it stayed within or went "a little beyond the limit."[51] Mississippi's segregationist senator, John Sharp Williams, conceded that his quarrel with the *Defender* sprang from conflicting views of the truth. He complained to Postmaster General Burleson that the *Defender*'s "lies [were] all intended to create race disturbance and trouble. . . . If there is any provision of law whereby you can exclude a paper from the mail on the ground that it is a liar, of course, you can exclude this one, but I don't know of any such provision."[52]

Although the government did not take official action against the *Defender,* agents from three different branches met with Abbott between April 1917 and the summer of 1918. The publisher assured Justice Department agents just after the start of the war that he was actively supporting the war effort and that "the colored people throughout the country" would be loyal.[53] An employee of the postal solicitor's office warned Abbott to avoid printing material that tended to "cause friction between the two races" or suggested that blacks had "no part in the struggle against the Imperial German Government."[54] He also, however, expressed "no doubt as to the loyalty of" the *Defender* and certainty that Abbott would perform his patriotic duties in the prescribed manner.

Major Walter H. Loving, a black MID agent, met with Abbott to inform him "officially that the eye of the government is centered upon his paper" and that "he would be held strictly accountable."[55] In a remarkable reply to Loving, Abbott cast himself as absolutely loyal to the federal government and supportive of the war effort and explained that the *Defender* had been outspoken only "from a southerner's point of view." Abbott pointed out that he had vigorously supported the war by subscribing to the Liberty Loan to the tune of $12,000, speaking for the Committee on Public Information, and contributing a regimental flag to the 365th Infantry Division. Additionally, "in exposing the injustices done our race in" the South, the *Defender* had tried "in every case . . . to avoid placing our criticism on the national administration." Abbott said he had "more than once advised my staff writers to refrain from expressing their views on problems that would precipitate national strife, or inculcate in the heart of any member of my race the spirit of revolt against the laws of the national or state governments." Clearly, Abbott concluded, his enemies were "taking undue advantage" of his delicate wartime position.[56]

Abbott's strategy generally followed that of many other black editors and publishers from the beginning of the war. Although the pressure of censorship may have reduced the *Defender's* criticism of the federal government, his staunch and active support for the war was a natural and uncoerced response. Meanwhile, he continued to equate the South with the enemy, demand civil rights for African Americans, and advocate blacks' migration out of the South. Government officials who actually read the *Defender* and other black newspapers may not have agreed with them, but they found little basis for suppression. Indeed, a few seem to have been swayed ever so slightly by black newspapers' arguments. More important, their reports on black newspapers reached the highest levels of government, where officials were persuaded to respond not with censorship but by addressing black demands partly out of concern over the unrest among the black population and partly as an acknowledgment of the legitimacy of those demands.

WASHINGTON CONFERENCE OF BLACK EDITORS

On May 28, 1918, Loving wrote *Argus* publisher J. E. Mitchell that "the officials at Washington are being daily acquainted with facts of the real grievances of the American negro through the colored press, private letters and such a great journal as the New York World." [57] The war, it seemed, had created an opportunity for black concerns to be heard by major media outlets and in the halls of power, and the key channel was the black press. Eight days after Loving penned his letter to Mitchell, Joel Spingarn and Emmett Scott met to plan a conference of black editors in Washington to impress on them the importance of leading "Negro public opinion . . . along helpful lines rather than along lines that make for discontentment and unrest." But this statement, made in a letter to George Creel, chairman of the federal wartime propaganda agency, the Committee on Public Information, did not reveal the whole purpose of the conference. Scott and Spingarn, both advocates of African American equality, hoped not to silence the black press but to give it a hearing with the federal government. They hoped the conference would make black editors better boosters of the war effort, but they also hoped it would lead the federal government to alter its policies on race. Spingarn explained to the new head of the MID, Colonel Marlborough Churchill, that "constant complaints from Intelligence Officers and others" had indicated "that the colored press was spreading disaffection among negroes." The conference would modify the "bitter tone" of the newspapers while at the same time stimulating "negro morale." It would also provide "information [from the editors] in regard to the negro situation and the means of improving it."[58] Had black newspapers been militant enough to warrant outright censorship or accommodationist enough to avoid close scrutiny, the conference would not have been necessary and Spingarn and Scott would never have opened this channel of communication between African Americans and the federal government.

The government paid the travel expenses of between twenty-seven and thirty-three editors and ten other black leaders from all over the country to gather at the Interior Building at 18th and F Streets from June 19 to 21, 1918, for three private four-hour sessions. Participants included publisher Fred Moore and editor W. E. King of the *New York Age,* John Murphy of the *Baltimore Afro-American,* Harry Smith of the *Cleveland Gazette,* Robert Abbott of the *Chicago Defender,* W. E. B. Du Bois of the *Crisis,* George Knox of the *Indianapolis Freeman,* Calvin Chase of the *Washington Bee,* Robert Vann of the *Pittsburgh Courier,* George Harris of the *New York News,* John Mitchell Jr. of the *Richmond Planet,* J. E. Mitchell of the *St. Louis Argus,* P. B. Young of the *Norfolk Journal and Guide,* and Henry Allen Boyd of the *Nashville Globe.* William Monroe Trotter was invited but did not attend, and the publishers of the *Savannah Tribune,* the *California Eagle,* and the *Chicago Broad Ax* were not invited.[59] The editors listened to speeches by Secretary of War Newton Baker, Committee of Public Information chairman George Creel, Assistant Secretary of the Navy Franklin D. Roosevelt, a general and two majors from the French army, and representatives of the Shipping Board and the Food Administration. Clearly, the government succeeded in scoring propaganda points with the editors. Simply holding the conference and giving the editors a chance to " 'let off steam,' " as Spingarn put it, may have siphoned off some of their anger. Baker presented evidence to disprove rumors that black soldiers were being sacrificed to save white soldiers in France. The presentation by the French officers on the treatment of African troops by their country "made a very deep impression" and generated "enthusiasm" among the editors. Spingarn concluded that the conference "conformed" to the military's "original plan," noted that the demands of the editors required no "fundamental social readjustments," and predicted "an excellent effect on the colored press."[60]

A "Liberty Congress" held later that week by Trotter, Hubert Harrison, radical publisher of the *Negro Voice,* and other mavericks scorned the government-sponsored conference as an attempt to buy off the black press. Editors were "wined and dined at the government's expense for the sole purpose of muzzling them," said one Liberty Congress speaker.[61] But the more conciliatory editors' conference un-

About forty-one African American leaders—most of them newspaper editors—met with government officials in Washington in June 1918. Depicted in the front row, from left to right, are P. B. S. Pinchback, Charles W. Anderson, Emmett J. Scott (flanked by two French officers), R. R. Moton, Robert H. Terrell (with Robert S. Abbott over his left shoulder), W. E. B. Du Bois, Joel Spingarn (in uniform), *Philadelphia Tribune* editor Christopher J. Perry, and an unidentified man. Harry C. Smith is wearing a black bow tie, directly above the French officer to the right of Scott. Courtesy Special Collections and Archives, W. E. B. Du Bois Library, University of Massachusetts, Amherst.

doubtedly accomplished more than the militant Liberty Congress. In spite of his sympathy for the aims and methods of the Liberty Congress participants, Harry Smith argued that there was "no possibility of comparison" between the two in terms of results.[62]

The editors' conference participants were not acting as merely subjects of government manipulation. Their pledge of national loyalty and support for the war did not contradict their long-standing positions, and they presented their case as well as listening to presentations from government and military officials. A defining moment of the conference, which made a strong impression on Secretary of War Baker, occurred when Moton argued that unrest among African Americans was the result of "the apparently increasing frequency of lynchings of brutal and barbarous character" and "every negro at the conference" agreed. "Several conferees" shrewdly suggested that German agents might have incited recent lynchings as a way of "producing a dangerous feeling among the colored people of the country."[63]

In Spingarn's and Churchill's reports to their superiors, the conference's official declaration, and press accounts, the editors' wartime themes surfaced: African Americans were loyal and patriotic citizens, but the failure of the government to address their legitimate grievances, particularly over lynching, could prevent them from giving their best effort. A statement drafted by Du Bois and endorsed by the editors masterfully walked the line between declaring loyalty and making demands. The statement began by expressing the "belief that the defeat of the German government . . . is of paramount purpose" and recalling African Americans' "untarnished record" of national loyalty. Their goal at the conference, the editors said, was to find a way to keep black patriotism "at the highest pitch, not simply of passive loyalty, but of active, enthusiastic and self-sacrificing participation in the war." The editors deftly affirmed black patriotism while at the same time illustrating the need for the government to address black grievances. They continued: "We believe today that justifiable grievances of the colored people are producing not disloyalty, but an amount of unrest and bitterness which even the best efforts of their leaders may not be able always to guide unless they can have the active and sympathetic cooperation of the National and State governments." "German propaganda among us is powerless," the editors continued, making a telling point, "but the apparent indifference of our own Government may be dangerous."

The statement then enumerated three ongoing problems the editors asked the federal government to address. "First and foremost," they wanted "a strong, clear word on lynching from the President of the United States" and legislation that would allow the federal government to use its war powers "to stamp out this custom which is not only holding our Nation up to just criticism, but is seriously affecting the morale of 12,000,000 Americans." Second, the editors called for an end to discrimination against blacks who offered their services to the nation as Red Cross nurses and physicians, stenographers and clerks in the federal government, and seamen in the navy. Third, they sought an end to Jim Crow travel restrictions on railroads, which were now controlled by the government. All of the demands were important, but the plea for action against lynching stood out, mirroring the editorial emphasis of black newspapers.[64]

The head of military intelligence, Churchill, got the message. After the conference, he concluded in a memorandum to the army chief of staff that "the leaders of the race are intensely loyal, but feel keenly their inability to carry the great mass of their race with them in active support of the war unless certain grievances receive immediate attention. The most important of these is lynching." Churchill also sent along to the chief of staff a "Bill of Particulars," including fourteen demands adopted by the conference. Attention to them "would stimulate negro morale to an extraordinary degree," Churchill wrote. The bill was "to be submitted privately to bureau heads in Washington." [65] It listed the following demands:

1. National legislation on lynching
2. Colored Red Cross nurses
3. Colored able seamen
4. Colored volunteer soldiers to the extent of their volunteering
5. Colored physicians for colored troops
6. Training of larger number of colored officers
7. Unlimited promotion of colored officers according to proven efficiency
8. Utilizing the services of Colonel Charles Young (retired)
9. An attempt to equalize among black and white troops the proportion of draftees assigned to stevedore regiments, service battalions, etc.
10. Systematic getting and dissemination of news of Negro troops at home and abroad
11. Systematic attempt to correct ridiculous and [sic] misrepresentation of the Negro and omissions of his achievement in the white press
12. The consideration of a Government loan to the Negro Republic of Liberia, now actively aligned with the Allies
13. Executive clemency for the Negro soldiers recently tried and sentenced at Fort Sam Houston, Texas
14. Condition of travel among colored people [66]

News of the conference finally reached President Wilson. Creel had told the chief executive about the conference of "loyal and enthusiastic" editors beforehand.[67] Recalling "several delegations of negroes" who went away dissatisfied from meetings with him (Trotter, no doubt, among them), Wilson declined Creel's invitation to meet informally with the editors. The program, he said, should go on without him until he could "act in a way that would satisfy them." [68] After the conference,

Wilson received letters from Creel and Scott. Scott enclosed the conference resolution and asked for "a word from you . . . addressed to colored Americans."[69] Around the same time, Baker told Wilson of his growing "anxiety" over what he considered unprecedented unrest among the black population. He passed along the judgment of editors' conference participants that the cause of the unrest was the increase in frequency and barbarity of lynchings. He then asked Wilson to take action. Two weeks later, Baker again prodded Wilson to act on the matter, at least by replying to Scott.[70]

In the wake of the conference, black editors were guardedly optimistic. Not since Reconstruction had the federal government devoted so much attention to blacks' concerns. Since war had proved to be a catalyst for black progress, it seemed reasonable to assume that another major advance might accompany this war.[71] *Chicago Defender* columnist Ben Baker called the conference "one of the greatest events in the history of the Race" and believed it marked "an epoch in Race progress."[72]

The editors' optimism became a little less guarded a month after the conference as some of their demands began to be met. The *Baltimore Afro-American* reported that the Department of War had ordered the employment of black nurses by the Red Cross and was about to reinstate Colonel Charles Young, the highest-ranking black officer in the army, who had been discharged because of an alleged health problem at the beginning of the war. "Given the continuation of the war every possible avenue for the rending of service will be opened to all Americans white or black," the paper predicted.[73]

Hope surged after Wilson issued a long-awaited statement on lynching on July 26, which was published in major newspapers across the country the following day. Although Wilson's statement has been linked to the lynching of German American Robert Prager in Collinsville, Illinois, on April 5 and the president did not mention blacks specifically or single out the South for special condemnation (in fact, he took care not to blame "any single region"), Wilson followed black editors' practice of comparing lynching to lawlessness in Germany and depicting it as a threat to "the honor of the Nation" and a contradiction of the principles America was fighting for in Europe:[74]

We are at this very moment fighting lawless passion. Germany has outlawed herself among the nations because she has disregarded the sacred obligations of law and has made lynchers of her armies. Lynchers emulate her disgraceful example. . . . We proudly claim to be the champions of democracy. If we really are, in deed and in truth, let us see to it that we do not discredit our own. I say plainly that every American who takes part in the action of a mob or gives it any sort of countenance is no true son of this great Democracy, but its betrayer. . . . How shall we commend democracy to the acceptance of other peoples, if we disgrace our own by proving that it is, after all, no protection to the weak? Every mob contributes to German lies about the United States what her most gifted liars cannot improve upon by the way of calumny. They can at least say that such things cannot happen in Germany except in times of revolutions, when law is swept away.

Had a black editor made this statement, Translation Bureau readers or Post Office monitors might well have classified it as seditious because it likened the United States to Germany. Wilson went on to "earnestly and solemnly beg" governors, local law enforcement officials, and all Americans to work "to make an end of this disgraceful evil."[75]

It is not clear how much Wilson's statement was influenced, directly or indirectly, by the black press and the editors' conference. But in a letter written a week after the speech, he said he had been impressed by the "fine philosophy of democracy" expressed by the editors at the conference and conceded that the problems they enumerated were "grave and weighty" and deserved the "frank and calm consideration" of the American people.[76] A week later, he told a white correspondent that he hoped his "colored fellow citizens" were "beginning to believe" that he was glad to "serve" them.[77]

At the end of August, Wilson made another move aimed at winning the loyalty of African Americans. He commuted ten of the Houston soldiers' death sentences to prison terms in "recognition of the splendid loyalty of the race to which these soldiers belong and [as] an inspiration to the people of that race to further zeal and service to the country."[78] Although disappointed that Wilson had allowed the execution of six other black soldiers to go forward, the *Richmond Planet* thought "something has been gained in the way of recognition on the part of the colored people, when this great statesman, in the midst of manifold and momentous duties, stops to assign reasons for his actions and to say a word of commendation of the brave colored men who are fighting and dying for this country on the other side of the Atlantic."[79] On October 1, Wilson met face-to-face with a delegation of blacks to accept a memorial from the National Race Congress signed by publisher Calvin Chase, among others. Although Wilson counseled patience, he promised the group that "everything that I can do will be accomplished." According to the *Planet,* Wilson was moved to tears by the group's plea.[80] It seemed the president had been won over by the ambiguous assertions of the black press that African Americans were loyal but that the government had to meet their demands to assure their full cooperation in the war effort.

Some black editors were convinced that their efforts had moved Wilson to speak out against lynching. The *Baltimore Afro-American* reported that his statement had "grown directly out of the recent conference of editors." Columnist William H. Weaver assumed a connection. "If the conference had effected no more than this, it would have" done enough to "justify its assembling," he wrote.[81] In the *Cleveland Gazette,* Harry Smith observed that Wilson had not simply condemned the lynching of opponents of the war or the lynching of Prager (as the Associated Press had predicted he would) but had denounced "mob action of all sorts." Thus, Smith asserted, the statement must have pertained to and been inspired by blacks. Smith marveled that "a southern Democratic president, surrounded in the two other coordinated branches of government by men of the same political faith and place of residence [the South]," could make such a statement. It surprised "even the most sanguine members of that great Race Conference that brought it about."[82]

Writers in the *New York Age* and the *Chicago Defender* thought Wilson had been persuaded by them to speak out. Just seven weeks earlier, the *Defender* had printed on page 1 an open letter from a black soldier asking Wilson to make a statement against lynching.[83] "The Chicago Defender deserves the conscientious thanks of all liberty-loving members of our Race for its continual and unceasing fight to secure an expression from the chief magistrate of the nation against mob violence," wrote reporter A. N. Fields. "Embodied in the President's appeal to the country can be found the principles enunciated by this paper for the past twelve months." The *Defender,* Fields said, had consistently "laid down one fundamental principle" (which Wilson now accepted) — that to carry democracy to other nations, "we must cease to burn men and women at the stake."[84]

The *New York Age* also saw Wilson's statement as a reflection of its editorial policy. The *Age* had "taken this position ever since the war began and has sought to open the eyes of those in authority to this view of the case," an editor wrote.[85] Johnson reiterated this point a week later. "For the past year The Age has been pointing out that the torturing and lynching of black Americans by Americans laid the country liable to the charge of hypocrisy in its pronouncements about democracy; and here President Wilson has said the same things."[86] These comments by Fields, Johnson, and the other *Age* editorialist reveal a conception of the black press not simply as an arena for communication among blacks but as a way "to open the eyes of those in authority." In this case, with the help of an important back channel, the conference, and well-placed allies behind the scenes, including Spingarn, Scott, Moton, and, perhaps, Loving, it worked.[87]

Wilson's speech led to a peak in the wartime optimism of black editors, which had begun to mount shortly after the declaration of war in 1917. After all, the *St. Louis Argus* editorialized, Americans had "responded nobly" to every other request Wilson had made of them during the war. Surely they would respond to this plea, too.[88] Even before Wilson's statement, some southerners had spoken out against lynching. Tennessee Law and Order League secretary, Bolton Smith, a self-proclaimed liberal from Memphis and reader of the *Chicago Defender*, publicly stated that lynching could prolong the war effort and that his fellow southerners should exhibit "self-control" by allowing accused blacks to be tried in court.[89] Similarly, the Conference on Charities and Corrections, the *Atlanta Constitution*, the *Houston Post*, the *Little Rock Gazette*, the *Christian Science Monitor*, *Outlook* magazine, and the University Commission on Southern Race Relations had all recently condemned lynching. The *Little Rock Gazette* had said that barbaric lynchings in the South did not "fit" with "our battle cry 'A World Safe for Democracy.'" The *Baltimore Afro-American* quoted this article at length. "This is just what almost every Negro newspaper in the country has been saying all the time," it commented. "When the editor of an Arkansas newspaper comes to the same conclusion we look forward in hope that . . . our Southern white friends will be able to see the error of their ways and repent."[90]

After the president's message, more white newspapers began to come out against lynching. Wilson had "awaken[ed] the conscience" of the *Chicago Tribune*, said Fields.[91] Johnson noted that the *Florida Times-Union*, which had defended lynching a few weeks earlier, now praised and supported Wilson's statement.[92] By the end of the year, even white Mississippians had formed a group, the Mississippi Welfare League, that opposed lynching.[93] The combination of the president's statement and the fulfillment of a few of the demands listed in the Bill of Particulars, including the appointment of a black war correspondent, Ralph W. Tyler, in September, along with the perception of a groundswell of mainstream antilynching sentiment, understandably fed the hopes of black editors, reporters, and publishers. "Perhaps after all," the *Chicago Defender* dared hope, "we are on the eve of true democracy. Who knows?"[94]

Such feelings naturally led to a greater willingness to cooperate with the war effort, although still not completely at the expense of blacks' special grievances. The *Richmond Planet* defended Du Bois's "Close Ranks" editorial. "Conditions are improving," the paper explained, "and the attitude of Southern white men towards us recently has been so gratifying that we feel disposed to do everything in our power to aid them in particular and the country in general." Yet the *Planet* thought Du Bois might have " 'leaned a little too far backward.' " Wartime, in fact, was the best time to make demands. Emancipation had been accomplished as a war measure and now woman suffrage, prohibition, and better wages were coming about because of war. Mitchell proposed revising "Close Ranks" to read: "Let us while this war lasts, forget our special personal prejudices and innate antipathy to the Negroes, and close our ranks shoulder to shoulder with our black fellow citizens and the allied nations that are fighting for democracy."[95]

At that moment, in the late summer and early fall of 1918, the war seemed to be evolving in the way that black leaders had hoped it would. Although lynchings and other extralegal violent acts against black individuals were rising significantly in 1918, the federal government was beginning to act in the interests of black Americans, and it seemed that public opinion might finally turn against lynching. Most important, African Americans had apparently convinced the man with the greatest access to the American public to speak out against lynching. They had won all this not through passive accommodation or extreme militancy but with a measured approach combining militant demands with accommodating assurances. In short, they wielded what power they had but not heedless of the dangers they faced. "All things come to him who will but wait," the *Baltimore Afro-American*'s publisher, John Murphy, concluded after Wilson's statement. But Smith corrected him and in so doing encapsulated the approach of the black press to World War I: "Yes, wait, but only because you have to, and be sure to contend in a proper way for what you are entitled to while you wait."[96]

Wilson's war for democracy had come full circle. Black editors had seized his rationale for war and applied it to the situation of blacks, particularly in the American South. Now the president himself had been forced to admit that his own principles were unfulfilled at home.

Although he did not single out the South as the perpetrator or African Americans as the victims, his statement certainly encompassed within its view the lynching of blacks in the South. Prodded by top advisers, Wilson had come to see the need to recognize black loyalty and undermine black unrest. The black press did not bring this about single-handedly. Leaders like Scott, Spingarn, and Moton also had significant influence within the government and, in the cases of Scott and Moton, directly on Wilson.[97] More important, however, the black population acted in ways that worried officials in charge of mobilizing for war. The Houston riot was only the most extreme example of black soldiers lashing out against racism. In several other cases, black soldiers retaliated against white soldiers and civilians who were trampling on their rights.[98] Southern blacks began rebelling against restrictions in the South by standing up to white oppressors, migrating to the North, and joining militant organizations. Some black men resisted conscription.[99]

The black press did not create this wave of "unrest," as government officials thought, but rather interpreted and placed it in the context of the loyal actions of African Americans. When Creel and Baker sought to understand black unrest, they monitored black newspapers and then called black editors to Washington. The black press became a channel through which black America communicated with the highest levels of authority. It portrayed African Americans in a favorable light, announced their demands, and made a convincing case that those demands had to be met sooner rather than later. Although many white readers resisted the black press's approach, top federal officials became convinced that lynching was to blame for black unrest. In actuality, lynching had been going on for decades. It had declined from 1916 to 1917, and the statistics that showed an increase for 1918 would not be made public until after the Armistice. Clearly, other factors—such as black participation in the war effort and expanded opportunities in wartime industry—played a greater role in generating unrest. But by convincing Wilson that lynching was the main cause and that African Americans were fundamentally loyal, the black press persuaded him to make his statement of condemnation, in which he endorsed the notion that lynching contradicted the nation's war aims.

Ultimately, Wilson's statement on lynching stopped far short of fulfilling African Americans' highest hopes. He never supported federal antilynching legislation, and in the following year, the number of lynchings would rise dramatically, making it the worst year for lynchings since 1908. In addition, with the end of the war in November, the government's willingness to address the demands listed in the Bill of Particulars, most of which had to do with the war anyway, evaporated.[100] Yet the antilynching sentiment that had begun to emerge in the South during the war did not vanish. Public opinion— even in the South—now sustained organized opposition to lynching. The first major organization of the white South to oppose lynching— the Southern Commission on Interracial Cooperation—was formed in 1919, and during the 1920s, the annual number of lynchings declined significantly.[101] But the end of the war by no means meant the end of lynching, interracial conflict, or white interest in the black press. In fact, during the tumultuous year following the war, all three intensified.

THE NEW NEGRO'S MESSAGE TO AMERICA, 1918–1920

While riding in a racially segregated streetcar in Memphis, Tennessee, one day during the war, Bolton Smith was alarmed to see an elderly black couple walk by and sit in two of the seats in front of him—in the white section of the car. Just a week earlier, Smith, a white investment banker who had formed an antilynching league but supported disfranchisement of blacks and separation of the races, had read a newspaper account of the killing of a black man after a similar incident in the city. He decided to prevent the same climax in this case by offering to trade places with the couple.

The two streetcar episodes troubled Smith because they seemed part of a larger disturbing pattern. During a recent visit to New York City, Smith had stopped on a street corner to listen to a black orator who stood on a stepladder condemning racial injustice and declaring that "every white man is an enemy of the Negro." These incidents and other stories relayed by friends and acquaintances convinced Smith that the war had brought a change over African Americans. "The Negro is not as jolly, care-free, and good-natured as he once was," Smith concluded. "His leaders—especially of the North through the Northern Negro press—are shaming him into a new attitude."

As the war came to an end in the fall of 1918 and in the following turbulent year, an increasing number of white Americans would notice the change in blacks' attitudes and would frequently blame it on the black press. But these observers probably exaggerated the role of black newspapers in creating the phenomenon that would become known as the "New Negro," an African American consciousness characterized by confidence, assertiveness, and militancy that seemed to emerge after World War I. Although black newspapers may have had a hand in shaping this new consciousness, the northward migration and participation in the war effort probably had a greater impact. Smith, too, noted that "the war has shown the Negro that he has some power."[1]

Rather than serving as the creator of the New Negro, the black press acted as its publicist—announcing its arrival, explaining its origins, and shaping the public's perception of it. Black writers and activists like James Weldon Johnson thought that even more important than the impact of the war on black Americans was its effect on whites like Bolton Smith who had become more aware of black concerns. "Mr. Smith now notices some things to which he has hitherto been blind," Johnson wrote.[2] While white Americans were paying greater attention to race, Johnson and his colleagues in the black press took the opportunity to educate them. In the year after the end of the war, black newspapers sought to present the New Negro to white America in a particular way. If the emphasis during the war had been on loyalty and cooperation with the war effort, militant demands now overshadowed reaffirmations of patriotism and denunciations of radicalism.

In the year or so after the end of the war, white Americans were eager to listen to these messages. Federal government surveillance did not end with the cessation of hostilities but expanded, and it was matched by increasing interest among white citizens, ranging from a former president to white residents of numerous rural southern communities. Following the war, the black press became the subject of a speech on the floor of Congress and a book by a professor of English in Virginia. Major dailies commented on the threat of "radical" black publications, and local and state law enforcement officials joined at least four federal agencies in watching over black periodicals. The rise of interest in the black press coincided with one of the most turbulent years in American history, marked by the signing of a controversial peace treaty in Europe, growing fear of radicalism at home and abroad, a devastating influenza epidemic, a dramatic rise in lynchings, and a series of bloody race riots in twenty-five American cities and towns. Although the increasing scrutiny of black newspapers presented significant dangers at a time when mob violence was on the rise and the government was cracking down on dissenters, publishers welcomed the opportunity to educate white America concerning the moral implications of racism for the nation and to plead with enlightened whites to align themselves with justice, democracy, and American ideals rather than the undemocratic ways of white supremacists. In addition to reiterating these themes from the war years, black journalists conveyed new messages about how blacks had helped the war effort, blacks' rising self-respect and willingness to stand up for their

"Wake Up Uncle or You Are Going to Fall." Blacks who fought in the war were now more insistent on demanding their rights, according to this cartoonist. From *Baltimore Afro-American*, August 8, 1919.

own rights, and the dangers white hooligans faced when they initiated violence against the New Negro. All this and more, they believed, "America must be told."

AMERICA ENCOUNTERS A NEW NEGRO

In spite of the end of hostilities in Europe on Armistice Day in November 1918, the war would not officially end until 1921, and federal officials would continue to enforce the Espionage and Sedition Acts and monitor black publications even after 1921. Officials feared that African Americans were particularly susceptible to the radicalism that seemed to threaten every Western nation after the devastation of world war and the Bolshevik revolution in Russia in 1917. In America, workers organized 3,630 strikes in 1919, including a general strike in Seattle and a police strike in Boston, and terrorists sent mail bombs to a U.S. senator and the attorney general. Government and corporate leaders retaliated by brutally suppressing strikes, deporting Russian aliens, and harassing radical organizations like the Industrial Workers of the World (IWW) and the Socialist Party. Repression culminated in the so-called Palmer raids of January 2, 1920, when federal marshals and local police raided the headquarters of allegedly radical organizations in 32 cities, arresting 4,000 people, of whom 550 were eventually deported.

Officials in the government often lumped African Americans with IWW members, socialists, anarchists, and labor agitators as dangerously prone to radicalism. Woodrow Wilson himself believed African Americans would be the "greatest medium in conveying bolshevism to America." [3] Even Walter Loving, the black military intelligence agent, reported that African Americans were "the most radical of all radicals" and blamed a race riot in Chicago on "vicious and well-financed propaganda" in the black press. [4] Officials were especially concerned about New York City's new crop of militant journals, including the *Messenger;* Marcus Garvey's mass circulation daily, the *Negro World;* and two short-lived incendiary monthlies, the *Challenge* and the *Crusader,* and they directed much of their energies toward investigating and harassing the publishers of these periodicals. But officials often grouped genuinely radical journals with generally conservative weeklies like the *New York Age* or the *Chicago Defender,* which either opposed or ignored radical ideologies while focusing on racial issues. Although the *Baltimore Afro-American,* the *Richmond Planet,* the *St. Louis Argus,* and the *Pittsburgh Courier* escaped close scrutiny after the war, agents continued to monitor and occasionally interfere with the *Boston Guardian,* the *New York News,* the *New York Age,* the *New York Amsterdam News,* the *Chicago Whip,* the *Chicago Broad-Ax,* and especially the *Chicago Defender* and the *Crisis.*

Again, the federal agencies investigating these mainstream black newspapers imposed no serious negative sanctions against them, and most of the publishers were probably unaware of the extent of government scrutiny. Post Office Solicitor William Lamar repeatedly ruled against subordinates who recommended banning these black newspapers from the mails. The *Crisis* suffered the most serious consequence of postwar militancy among these more conservative journals when the Post Office Translation Bureau chief, Robert Bowen, held the May issue at the New York Post Office because of an editorial he deemed "seditious" and "insolently abusive of the country." In "Returning Soldiers," W. E. B. Du Bois seemed to be making up for his "Close Ranks" editorial. Calling America a "shameful land" for lynching, disfranchising, and otherwise abusing African Americans, he urged blacks to "return fighting" from Europe "against the forces of hell in our own land." Although Lamar thought the editorial "unquestionably violent," he conceded that it was directed against "deplorable conditions" rather than the "constitutional authority of the United States government." After a delay of six days, the Post Office released 100,000 copies of the magazine.[5]

Throughout 1919 and into the next decade, government reports continued to question the patriotism of even conservative black newspapers and to charge them with encouraging racial conflict. The most influential report on the black press, produced by Bowen on July 2, 1919, singled out the *New York Age* while warning that the black press "increasingly employed the tone of menace and the threat of violent resistance" and had become aligned "with the most destructive forces of our political life today."[6] A passage from Bowen's "Radicalism and Sedition among the Negroes" quoted by the Chicago Commission on Race Relations claimed that characteristics common to many black periodicals made the black press a "persistent source of a radical opposition to the government, and to the established rule of law." These included advocacy of retaliation against mob violence; demands for social equality; strong opposition to the Wilson administration, the South, and the League of Nations; and an emphasis on "race consciousness." A fifth characteristic, identification with radical organizations and bolshevism, applied only to a minority of black publications. The Justice Department submitted Bowen's report to the Senate in November 1919 and to the House of Representatives in May of the following year.[7]

One of the most spirited attacks against the black press in 1919 came in late August, when Representative James F. Byrnes of South Carolina interrupted a debate on teacher pensions in the House of Representatives to blame the recent race riots on "incendiary utterances of the would-be leaders of the [black] race now being circulated through negro newspapers and magazines." Although Byrnes, who would later serve as Harry Truman's secretary of state, quoted mostly William Monroe Trotter and articles from the *Crisis* and the *Messenger*, he repeatedly denounced the "negro press" as a whole, and indeed, the sentiments he found so objectionable—like advocacy and praise of armed self-defense—could be found in many black weekly newspapers. Byrnes read excerpts from black publications on the floor of Congress to warn "the white men of America . . . of the efforts that are being made to induce the negro to resort to violence." He attributed immense power to black newspapers, saying they were stirring up an otherwise contented black population, inciting them to violence and rebellion. In addition to warning whites, he hoped to convince black leaders to "tell their people that in seeking political and social equality they are cherishing false hopes that are doomed to disappointment." He also refuted the black press's claim to pure Americanism. Byrnes thought criticism of white supremacy in the South amounted to criticism of the government, the flag, the nation as a whole, and "the white man of the North and of the South." He presented militant statements of black soldiers as evidence of the disloyalty and lack of fitness for military duty of African Americans and warned that the "Bolsheviki of Russia" might be "using the negro press of America to further their nefarious purposes." Byrnes sought to dash black people's hopes that they might find racial justice in the North or obtain it from the national government. He asserted that blacks were doing better in the South than in the North, quoted Abraham Lincoln's opposition to social equality of the races, and predicted that now that so many blacks had moved North, all whites would unite in opposition to racial equality. For these reasons, he said, black people must know that violence would not further their cause. They must "realize that there are in this country 90,000,000 white people determined not to extend political and social equality to the 10,000,000 negroes, and a resort to violence must inevitably bring to the negro greater suffering."[8] This flew in the face of a growing optimism in the black press that armed self-defense and war-bred assertiveness would reduce violence against blacks and increase their political influence.

Byrnes accused the black press of driving black readers to interracial violence. Yet in the one case in which a black newspaper directly provoked a riot in 1919—in Longview, Texas—the paper stimulated *white* readers to initiate violence. A July 5 *Chicago Defender* article claimed that a married white woman had declared that she loved and wanted to marry Lemuel Walters, a black man, before he was lynched on June 17 in Longview. On July 10, three white Longview men confronted S. L. Jones, the *Defender*'s local agent, accused him of authoring the article, and beat him with a wrench. Jones escaped, but later that night, a mob marched to his house intent on lynching him or driving him out of town. In an ensuing riot, whites killed one black man and burned several homes and stores. The sheriff destroyed copies of the *Defender* and banned its future circulation. After Jones and some of his allies fled the state and order was restored, leading white citizens condemned the *Defender*'s "scurrilous article" and pledged they would never again "permit the negroes of this community and country to in any way interfere with our social affairs or to write or circulate articles about the white people of our city or country."[9] To these whites, the black press mattered not merely for the way it affected black readers but also for what it said about whites.

Longview was not the only community where whites kept their eyes on black publications. White readers from across the South complained to federal authorities about the *Defender* and other black newspapers. Five hundred citizens of Atlanta unanimously approved a resolution denouncing the *Defender* and the *Atlanta Independent*, another black newspaper, for "abuse of our citizens, civilization and its institutions" and for "engender[ing] bad feelings and an evil spirit in the hearts and minds of the Colored People of this City toward their White neighbors."[10] Again, they felt a need to set the record on white people straight. Whites from Pine Bluff, Monticello, and Helena, Arkansas; Greenville, North Carolina; Macon, Missouri; Marks, Mississippi; and Baldwin, Louisiana, among others, asked the Post Office Department to ban from the mails the *Chicago Defender,* the *Pittsburgh Courier,* the *New York Age,* the *Boston Guardian,* and the *Indianapolis Freeman*.[11] A Justice Department agent in Memphis reported that he heard a "good deal of criticism" of the *Chicago Defender* in the South during the summer of 1919.[12] Letter writers accused the black press of printing "wild and exaggerated" accounts of whites' crimes against blacks.[13] Two of the *Defender*'s southern agents were killed, according to Robert Abbott's biographer, and more than a dozen others were driven from their homes. The state of Mississippi made it a misdemeanor "to print or circulate or publish appeals or presentations or arguments or suggestions favoring equality or marriage between the white and Negro race," and one county in that state banned the *Defender* altogether. Some communities reportedly charged prohibitively excessive licensing fees to distributors of black newspapers; in Birmingham, Alabama, the Ku Klux Klan warned the black *Baptist Leader* to stop criticizing the Klan; in Houston, the Klan allegedly stole the circulation list of the black *Houston Informer;* a correspondent for a black newspaper was lynched in Athens, Georgia; and across the South, according to the

New York Age, white authorities scanned black newspapers "with a critical eye."[14]

White Arkansans, including Governor Charles H. Brough and the *Arkansas Gazette,* based in Little Rock, claimed that black newspapers had incited blacks in Phillips County to plot a massacre of local white plantation owners. As it turned out, whites in Phillips County would massacre perhaps hundreds of poor blacks that fall. On October 1, a posse rounded up and killed members of the Progressive Farmers and Household Union of America, recently formed by poor black tenant farmers and sharecroppers to demand fair treatment from landowners. In a letter to Postmaster General Albert Burleson, Governor Brough claimed the posse had thwarted a plot incited by the *Chicago Defender.* He said the paper had molded "the sentiment out of which this recent conspiracy" emerged. The *Defender,* the *Crisis,* "and all other similar publications should be suppressed" in order to preserve racial harmony, he concluded.

In a second letter, this time to the new postal solicitor, H. L. Donnelly, Brough attempted to further prove the "incendiary and misleading character" of the *Defender.* He enclosed a copy of the November 1 issue, which published NAACP investigator Walter White's report on the Arkansas riot. After conducting his own investigation in Phillips County, White had formulated a version of events totally at odds with the account given by Brough, the *Arkansas Gazette,* and the Committee of Seven (white citizens who had investigated the riot). White's report, which also appeared in several northern dailies, described the exploitative plantation system that kept black farmers in a state of virtual peonage by forcing them to purchase supplies from plantation stores, denying them itemized account statements, and paying them well below fair market prices for their crops. Sixty-five black farmers had contacted a sympathetic local attorney, O. S. Bratton, about challenging elements of this peonage system in the courts, and others were planning to refuse to harvest cotton unless the landowners agreed to pay market prices. White found "no basis" for claims that the farmers had planned a massacre of plantation owners and argued that the two white men who were shot by blacks in the incident that precipitated the riot had first fired into a black church without provocation.

According to Brough, Arkansas had no peonage system, black farmers were treated fairly, and the union's demands were unreasonable. Further, the governor claimed to possess "documentary evidence" of a plot to massacre white planters. Investigators had found "twenty-one highpowered rifles and several thousand rounds of ammunition" in the office of a black dentist thought to be a leader of the conspiracy, and the two white men had not shot into the church, he claimed. Brough went beyond refuting White's story, however, and attempted to counter the black press's portrayal of African Americans as discontented and increasingly militant. Except for the unionists, black Arkansans were peaceful, law-abiding, and "thrifty." He praised their "splendid patriotic services to our government" and cited a resolution that some black citizens presented to him after the riot "deploring the attitude of the rioters of their race" and asserting that "the Governor of Arkansas and the white people generally, are giving them a square deal."[15]

Given the content of the *Defender* and the fact that no massacre of whites ever took place, Brough's claim that the newspaper incited blacks to plan a bloody attack seems unlikely to say the least. But the *Defender* and other black publications probably did contribute to the emergence of a more militant attitude among black readers in Phillips County, thus nurturing activism and encouraging armed self-defense. At the same time, assertive black newspapers may have spurred whites to launch their massacre of African Americans.[16] The organization of black tenant farmers and the inflammatory rhetoric in black newspapers, of which white Arkansans were apparently aware, might well have added to escalating fears of rebellion in a county where blacks outnumbered whites by three to one. One white reader from the county warned the *Defender* that its rhetoric led whites to kill blacks. "You are agitating a proposition through your paper which is causing some of your good Bur heads to be killed and the end is not in sight yet, but you have not got sense enough to see it," the letter writer explained. "You think you have won but the price is being paid still, and will continue so long as you Bur heads keep this . . . propaganda up."[17]

At least one white southerner took a more positive view of the black press. Between July and November, Robert T. Kerlin, a professor of English at the Virginia Military Institute, read black newspapers in a diligent effort to understand African Americans. He published a compilation of editorials and articles from eighty black publications early in 1920 under the title *Voice of the Negro, 1919*. Kerlin hoped to understand the black view of the year's race riots and "present it to the white public, if that public would accept it." The book includes chapters entitled "The New Era," "The Negro's Reactions to the World War," "The Negro's Grievances and Demands," "Riots," "Lynchings," "The South," and "Labor Unionism and Bolshevism." Unlike Representative James Byrnes of South Carolina and Robert Bowen of the

Post Office, Kerlin recognized the importance of examining a wide sampling of papers rather than a few of the most radical ones. African Americans, he said, had a "right to be heard in the court of the world," and he believed that helping to bring such a hearing about "would be a service to the country." *Chicago Broad Ax* editor Julius Taylor thought Kerlin's book was "calculated to have a tremendous effect in creating a better understanding of the Negro's problem of adjustment."[18] Clearly, though, Kerlin was outnumbered by those in the South who would do whatever it took to keep African Americans in their place, including censorship—or when that didn't work, intimidation—of black newspapers like the *Chicago Defender.* Still, even committed white supremacists like Brough sometimes had to engage in dialogue with northern black editors whom they could not destroy through force.

White readers in the North seemed more open-minded to the arguments they read in black newspapers but still offered more criticism than praise of the black press and worried about its inciting effect. The Chicago Commission on Race Relations identified the sensationalism of the reporting of interracial clashes in local black newspapers as one factor precipitating the July race riot in Chicago.[19] A committee of the New York legislature claimed in the summer of 1919 that documents seized from the socialist Rand School of Social Science proved that radicals hoped to rouse the black population to rebellion by subsidizing black orators and newspapers and exaggerating racial injustice. Although these charges turned out to be baseless, the Lusk Committee concluded that radical propaganda addressed to blacks fell on soil made fertile by racial oppression, a point some black editors had made.[20]

The *New York Tribune* blamed the Washington race riot on "dangerous propaganda" printed in black newspapers and devoted almost a full page to the problem, quoting the *New York Age,* the *Crisis,* the *Boston Guardian,* the *Washington Bee,* the *Richmond Planet,* and others.[21] White soldiers who participated in that same riot apparently agreed. They seized a bundle of forty copies of the *Baltimore Afro-American* from a distributor they accused of pedaling "propaganda."[22] Former president William H. Taft also assumed the black press had something to do with the riots and asked editors to "cease publishing articles, however true, having inciting effect."[23]

In Cleveland, Police Chief Frank W. Smith called Harry Smith to his office to discuss an August 2 *Cleveland Gazette* editorial advising blacks to keep "a U.S. Army Riot Gun in your home" as protection against white rioters. "Cleveland may be the next riot-storm center. Who knows?," Smith had written. According to the white daily, the *Cleveland News,* Chief Smith accused the *Gazette* editor of trying to stir up trouble and threatened to charge him with murder if anyone died in a race riot in Cleveland. Another local daily, the *Cleveland News-Leader,* however, reported that Chief Smith denied the remarks. Editor Smith described his one-hour meeting with the police chief as a "pleasant chat." He said the two men discussed the editorial, recent riots, lynching, and mob violence in general. In the next *Gazette,* Smith reiterated his endorsement of armed self-defense, while noting his longterm opposition to mob violence. "*The Gazette,*" he asserted, "stands for law and order!"[24]

To all of these white readers, what appeared in black newspapers mattered. It mattered because they believed black newspapers had a major impact on the consciousness and actions of African Americans, whom they hoped to control. But sometimes their responses to the black press suggest that their concerns went beyond a desire to control the flow of information to black people. The *Chicago Defender'*s suggestion that a white woman could fall in love with a black man, for example, contradicted the lynching and rape myths so deeply embedded in southern white consciousness. Longview rioters who responded to this were not simply defending the honor of one white woman; they were defending their particular view of reality and way of life. Other readers, particularly northerners and Robert Kerlin, showed a more open-minded curiosity about the black press, a willingness to listen to it and learn from it. On such individuals, the editors, publishers, and writers of the black press pinned their hopes for a more just society.

THE NEW NEGRO IN THE BLACK PRESS

Black editors seem to have been aware of the rising interest in the black press and hoped to seize the opportunity to convey their ideas about African Americans and race relations in the United States to the American public. They commented on editorial notices in major dailies, government monitoring of the black press, the remarks of Representative Byrnes, and the Lusk Committee's discussion of blacks. Indeed, their comments suggest an eagerness to use the press to influence white public opinion—to counter the "insidious and dangerous propaganda" constantly issuing from "Negro-hating southerners" or anyone who sought "to poison public sentiment all over the country."[25] The *Cleveland Gazette,* for instance, asked black readers to call whites' attention to an article in the paper on a French general's praise of

African Americans' performance in battle during the war.[26] The *Chicago Defender* reprinted a racist editorial from a Mississippi newspaper "to show government officials it is in their plain duty to suppress such trouble-breeding sheets as this."[27]

The editor in chief of the Associated Negro Press, Nahum Daniel Brascher, expressed black journalists' interest in reaching white readers most clearly. He told the Chicago Commission on Race Relations that "most of us are proud to have them [colored newspapers] seen in the hands of our white friends and it is only through them that they can really get our viewpoint. . . . I am very much interested in having the editorial feeling of the newspaper get to the white people."[28] In a June 7 column in the *Chicago Defender,* Brascher revealed his hopes that the black press would have an effect on white America. "America must be told . . . the truth, and the whole truth, about our condition and our aspirations and our demands," he wrote. Blacks must fund "the necessary propaganda to get and maintain the rights of freedom." In the face of such a "NATIONAL, UNCEASING CAMPAIGN OF PUBLICITY IN ALL FIELDS AND DEPARTMENTS, PREJUDICE AND ITS KINDRED IMPS WILL RUN LIKE A SCARED HOUND," Brascher proclaimed.[29]

Not coincidentally, as white interest in the black press reached its peak in 1919, the black press's efforts to create and describe a new image of African Americans escalated. To be sure, this "New Negro" was grounded in social reality. The migration of hundreds of thousands of blacks from the politically and socially repressive rural South to the more prosperous and less restrictive urban North, the recent service of 370,000 black men in the military (about half of whom went to Europe), the contributions of blacks at home to a war to make the world safe for democracy, and the self-assertion of ethnic groups throughout Europe made many African Americans aware of new possibilities, eager for greater freedoms, and optimistic about the efficacy of social activism. Membership in protest groups like the NAACP and Garvey's nationalistic Universal Negro Improvement Association soared.[30]

But African American newspapers did not simply present the New Negro to white America. At a time when white Americans were looking to the black press in an effort to understand African Americans, the black press emphasized a version of the New Negro calculated to affect public opinion, black and white, in particular ways.[31] The black press's image of the New Negro was designed to persuade America that black people deserved full citizenship and were willing and able to fight for it and that they would no longer passively submit to mob violence.

News stories called readers' attention to the praise from French generals and other Europeans of the performance of African American soldiers, asserting that it " 'gives the lie to any who may have declared that Negroes were not fighters.' "[32] The *Chicago Defender* told returning soldiers that they were "bigger and better men than when you left us," and "the country that commands your service in times of war owes you protection of life and property in times of peace." The "fighting spirit" displayed by these men in France was not likely to allow them to accept second-class citizenship in America. "WE ARE LOATH TO BELIEVE that the spirit which 'took no prisoners' will tamely and meekly submit to a program of lynching, burning and social ostracism as has obtained in the past. With your help and experience we shall look forward to a new tomorrow, not of subservience, not of meek and humble obeisance to any class, but with a determination to demand what is our due at all times and in all places."[33] Other black newspapers highlighted the words and deeds of returned black soldiers who stood up for their rights. Letters from militant soldiers who loved their "race better than life itself" became a regular feature.[34] "My appeal is for that which we claim to have been fighting for, to establish a true and everlasting Democracy," Sergeant James P. Webb wrote in the *Baltimore Afro-American*.[35] The *Cleveland Gazette* reported that when Sergeant James G. Ellis, a decorated black war hero who had made friends with white soldiers in military hospitals and on the boat ride home from France, arrived in Newport News and boarded a local ferry, a white southerner tried to prevent him from accompanying his friends. The man said that " 'niggers' had to go upstairs." Ellis threatened the man with a Colt 45 and was urged to use it by his comrades. Had a black minister not intervened, "there certainly would have been another 'cracker' gone to heaven."[36]

Black newspapers in the South, where black soldiers in uniform were lynched throughout 1919, sometimes chose to soft-pedal the militancy of returning servicemen. The *Savannah Tribune* denied that wearing a uniform made black soldiers "forget 'their places.' " The " 'uppishness' " of blacks, an editorial argued, "is imagined, rather than real." In fact, black soldiers had come back from the war "more mannerly, of better personal appearance and health, better trained, of maturer judgment and more refined." A greater source of disorder had been "mischief-making" by returned white soldiers.

But the *Tribune* did not deny that the war had made African Americans in general more militant. It reprinted an Associated Negro Press story about a mass meeting in Philadelphia that concluded that "since

"Will Uncle Sam Stand For This Cross?" The South pins the "croix de lynch" medal on black soldiers while winking at Uncle Sam.
From *Chicago Defender*, April 5, 1919.

the Negro has shown his fighting strength in the World War, he is going to see that he gets the justice due him in this country." Blacks emerged from the war "self-conscious" and "bitter" and were determined to make demands. A year later, the paper editorialized: "We have with us a new Negro, and it will be well for the nation at large to realize it and undertake to adjust conditions at the South and the North to meet this new order of things."[37] The *Richmond Planet* also argued that the country would have to deal with blacks who had been transformed and made more assertive by the war.[38]

Northern newspapers made this point even more forcefully. "We take this opportunity to say to America that neither in France nor America will colored men suffer indignities from southern white brutes whether they are in the uniform of the United States or in citizen's garb," William Byrd warned in the *Cleveland Gazette*.[39] The experience of the war, according to Johnson, had "worked a great change" in the consciousness of all 12 million African Americans, and they would no longer "tamely submit" to treatment they had "hitherto received."[40] "This is not a time for our Race to be unassuming," a letter writer told the *Chicago Defender*.[41]

These black writers—North and South—used black participation in the war as a rationale for whites to give them their rights—first, because they had earned and deserved them and, second, because they were now capable of fighting for them. No doubt much of this writing was directed at African Americans to encourage them to seize the propitious moment soon after their patriotic contribution. But writers frequently aimed their remarks directly at white Americans or the nation as a whole. They reminded white people of what blacks deserved and what would happen if they did not get it. In practice, whites in Phillips County, Arkansas, seem to have taken the *Defender*'s threats at face value, but sadly, instead of reacting by making concessions, they launched a preemptive strike, massacring unionizing sharecroppers who they feared had read the paper.

It is unclear whether the black press contributed to the outbreak of the other two dozen race riots of 1919, but that year marked a dramatic shift in the pattern of such disturbances. Previously, what historians refer to as "race riots" bore a greater resemblance to pogroms, in which vengeful whites descended on black neighborhoods, killing, maiming, and burning. From 1919 on, black residents met violence with almost equal force, inflicting comparable losses on whites. "It is plainly evident that the slaughtering of unarmed and helpless colored people without its accompanying killing of white people will never take place in this country again," John Mitchell's *Richmond Planet* pointed out.[42] From April to October 1919, an estimated 120 people died in race riots in twenty-five cities, North and South. The largest riots occurred in Charleston, South Carolina; Longview, Texas; Washington; Chicago; Omaha, Nebraska; and Phillips County. With the exception, perhaps, of Phillips County, the worst riot occurred in Chicago, where 500 people were injured and 38 killed. Were it not for the police, who killed 7 blacks, the death toll would have been nearly even in Chicago: 16 blacks and 15 whites.

Black editors and journalists—North and South—generally condemned the lawlessness but applauded blacks who fought back with force. Reports on the riots resembled accounts of sporting events, with writers tallying up the casualties on each side of the color line. The *Savannah Tribune* estimated that blacks on Chicago's Southside possessed "two thousand Springfield rifles with considerable ammunition" and claimed that a majority of those injured in the initial rioting were white. The *New York Age* agreed and added that blacks in Washington had also defended themselves "with a grim determination to exact a life for a life," with the help of machine guns, hand grenades, and homemade bombs.[43] The *Cleveland Gazette* claimed that white newspapers were "hiding the truth" about the high number of whites killed in the Washington riot "to keep Afro-Americans afraid to strike back." The *Baltimore Afro-American* opened its story on the Washington riot with an itemized list of casualties on both sides:

COLORED CASUALTIES
3 killed—6 wounded—8 beaten
WHITE CASUALTIES
4 killed—22 wounded—12 beaten

Like a box score, the graphic told the tale at a glance: "The colored population was well armed and able to take care of itself."[44]

Although it is impossible to know for sure, it is not unreasonable to assume that black editors intended to encourage black readers to defend themselves and to dissuade whites from attacking them in the future. "White boys and men in the South should know the havoc wrought among their race so that they will shrink from committing a similar offense," the *Cleveland Gazette* warned. "The truth will end this thing sooner than anything else." Smith's editorial, which advised readers to arm themselves with U.S. Army riot guns, got him into trouble with the local police. The title of the editorial, "The Mob!: A Warning," suggests that it was aimed as much at white would-be attackers as at potential black victims. Both the chief of the Cleveland police and the local newspapers got the message.[45] The *Savannah Tribune* took a less aggressive posture but still presented a message that could have been meant to persuade white southerners to stop attacking blacks. Blacks were fighting back and migrating out of the South, the paper warned, because "Negro blood is running down the streets of many cities" and "nothing is being done by the national and local governments to prevent it."[46]

In the midst of the Chicago riot, the *Chicago Defender* began to move away from its previous encouragement of black self-defense, urging black readers "to do your part to restore quiet and order." "This," a headline proclaimed, "is no time to solve the race question!" Roi Ottley, Abbott's biographer, argues that the publisher wanted to help restore order by urging caution on his *black* readers. Yet Abbott still wanted to drive the lesson of the rioting home to white Americans who might read or hear about his paper. In an editorial in the same issue that advised caution, the *Defender* said that America was "reaping the whirlwind" for having so long lynched and mobbed blacks with impunity. "The black worm has turned," the editorial added; "a Race that has furnished hundreds of thousands of the best soldiers that the world has ever seen is no longer content to turn the left cheek when smitten upon the right."[47] In a similar vein, the *New York Age* said that blacks' militant self-defense in the riots "proclaimed to the country" (in case the country had missed the point) that "the Negro will no longer allow himself to be mobbed free of cost. Those who indulge in mobbing him now and hereafter have got to pay the cost, and pay it in lives."[48] The *Richmond Planet* agreed—white-cappers, the Ku Klux Klan, and lynchers would hesitate before attacking blacks now that blacks were determined to assert their fundamental right of self-defense.[49]

These editorialists never took such warnings as far as they could have—as far as Richard Wright would in his famous novel, *Native Son,* in which he suggested that African Americans had been driven to indiscriminate and horrible retribution by poverty, oppression, and injustice. On the contrary, in all of these warnings, black writers were careful to point out that African Americans never initiated the riots but were provoked and acted in "pure defense." Some northern newspapers painted a picture of the New Negro as respectable, rational, and aligned with the forces of order, justice, and enlightenment against the forces of disorder, injustice, and darkness, especially in the South.[50] Mitchell, while maintaining blacks' right to defend them-

THE WORM TURNS

"The Worm Turns." "Boys, we've each been wounded. The blacks fought
back. We've got to go," a lyncher says to a rioter and an agitator.
From *Richmond Planet,* August 9, 1919.

---

selves, denounced the "lawless elements of both races" who may have
caused the riots and called on the "better classes" of blacks and whites
to unite against them.[51]

Other aspects of the New Negro were his political assertiveness and
susceptibility to radical ideologies. Black weeklies embraced and made
much of blacks' political assertiveness but were ambivalent about radi-

calism. Only a few black publications, like the *Messenger*, the *Challenge*, and the *Crusader*, all published in New York City, professed the radical ideologies the government feared most: bolshevism, socialism, anarchism, and syndicalism. With the exception of Garvey's daily *Negro World*, which espoused a doctrine of radical black nationalism, radical black journals had small circulations, and all of them were short-lived. Most black weekly newspapers used great care in presenting this aspect of the New Negro to white America. The *Richmond Planet* minimized black radicalism, saying in response to the "Radicalism and Sedition among the Negroes" report by the "Department of Injustice" that "radicalism is reflected in our publications, but not sedition."[52] The *Chicago Defender* went further, denouncing radical doctrines and arguing that it was southern whites, not northern blacks, who were radical. An editorial said bolshevism sounded the "death knell of law and order" and endorsed federal raids on anarchists and other radical "snakes in the grass."[53] Elsewhere, the *Defender* equated southern opponents of black rights with Bolshevists and referred to the Omaha riot as a "fit of semi-bolshevism."[54] The *Cleveland Gazette* and the *New York Age* tended to oppose bolshevism, too, the *Age* associating it with lawlessness and thus "the white lynchers of the South." But they also noted that they could see why disfranchised blacks, in their "depth of desperation," might grab onto a radical doctrine.[55] "If Negroes feel that they are justified in being Bolsheviki there is nobody in America to condemn them for it," Byrd wrote. "The greatest Reds and I. W. W. in this country are the men in power who are exploiting the people for their pockets."[56] Johnson's editorials, unlike the unsigned editorials in the *Age*, expressed some sympathy for radicalism, although he ultimately rejected it as a viable political strategy. He asserted that most blacks could not be classified as radicals since they were contending for rights most people took for granted. But he warned that "the treatment they are getting will eventually" force them "into the ranks of the radicals." Thus, Johnson warned of the possibility of black radicalism while attempting to "combat the propaganda that the Negro is a 'dangerous radical' because he is demanding the common fundamental rights of all other citizens of the country."[57]

The *Baltimore Afro-American* came close to endorsing radical views, stopping just short of supporting the Socialist Party. Carl Murphy, son of the publisher, joined the editorial staff in 1918, and his socialist and pacifist views soon made an imprint on the journal's editorials.[58] During 1919, the *Afro-American* quoted the socialist *Messenger* sympathetically; defended the Rand School, a socialist institution raided by

THE AMERICAN OUTLAW

"The American Outlaw." "I am not a savage, a wild-man, not a heathen.
I am an *American,* a *thug,* a *Red flag,* a *Bolshevist,* a *lyncher.*"
From *Richmond Planet,* April 12, 1919.

the government in July; and predicted rising black support for the Socialist Party. But ultimately the editors maintained a stand of political independence.[59] In August, the *Afro-American* noted with satisfaction that the Washington and Chicago riots had "opened the eyes of the country to the fact that the urban Negro will fight back when he has to" and had led the *New York World* to see that continued oppression of African Americans would drive them into the clutches of radical political organizations. Increasing radicalism among African Ameri-

"—And Take These with You!" Uncle Sam prepares to throw "the lyncher" and "race prejudice" off a pier onto a boat with "the Reds," who are being deported to "anywhere outside America." From *Chicago Defender*, January 10, 1920.

cans would lead the government to do more to bring about racial justice, a later *Afro-American* editorial asserted: "If white people are more willing to listen to reason on the color question today than ten years ago, we have to thank the growing radicalism among colored people."[60] Although radical ideas appealed to Murphy, he seems to have valued them most for their ability to force white people to "listen to reason on the color question."

THE BLACK PRESS AND THE REDEMPTION OF AMERICA

Parallel to and inseparable from the black press's projection of a New Negro—at least among northern newspapers—was its ongoing portrayal of the old, corrupt, uncivilized South. The two were sometimes depicted as locked in battle with each other for the soul of America. In the aftermath of World War I, the nation was at an important crossroads, facing a choice between the path represented by the racist, disorderly, uncivilized South or the humanitarian soul of the nation exemplified by the Declaration of Independence, northern abolitionists, Abraham Lincoln, and the New Negro. An editorial cartoon in the *Chicago Defender* depicted a cloud of black smoke emanating from the scene of a lynching and enshrouding the Statue of Liberty, with the caption "Stifling Liberty!"[61] The riots and lynchings of 1919 suggested that southern violence was in danger of contaminating the entire nation. But the moment also held extraordinary promise for the redemption of America.

Rather than taking the urban rioting in northern cities as evidence that racism was a national rather than primarily a southern problem, black newspapers could blame it, as they had the East St. Louis riot, on the influx of southern "crackers" and the proliferation of "dirty, criminal southern propaganda."[62] "No attention has been paid to the large numbers of 'crackers' who came from the South in the past three years to work" in northern factories, the *Cleveland Gazette* editorialized. Their arrival "explains the great increase in prejudice and friction between the races in this city." Smith went on to assert that these southerners caused the Chicago and Washington riots and "tried to start a riot in Cleveland last Monday." He called on his "brethren of the race press" to make this point clear to the "whites of your respective communities."[63]

In addition to migrating "crackers," the antiblack propaganda spread by the "bourbon press" also caused the riots. A *Chicago Defender* editorial listed antiblack propaganda, originating in the South, as the "primary" cause of the Chicago riot. The propaganda alleged that blacks had to be kept in their place through lynching and mob violence or whites in the South would be subject to "Negro domination. The result is the inculcation of a disregard of law and order in both races." This view and the resulting disorder could not be confined to the South and were in danger of infecting the whole nation and creating a wave of disorder.[64]

Despite these dangers, some thought the riots indicated that conditions were not as bad in the North as they were in the South. They showed that northern blacks had been less cowed than southern blacks, who generally did not fight back. If southern blacks would learn how to "meet violence with violence" like blacks in Washington and Chicago had, the *Baltimore Afro-American* reasoned, "there would be a riot after every Southern lynching."[65] The southern black man had less chance to defend himself when he was attacked by a southern mob, Johnson pointed out, because the whole community attacked him. In the North, he had more chance for a "fair fight. He does not feel that he has the force of the whole community, the whole county, the whole state, and the whole section of the country against him."[66] Even a southern newspaper, the *Savannah Tribune,* could agree that blacks had "at least a fighting chance to survive the mob" in northern cities.[67] Some editors also argued that blacks involved in rioting in the North had a chance of getting a fair trial. After indicting fifty blacks on riot-related charges, Johnson noted, a Chicago grand jury had refused to indict more blacks until they heard evidence against white rioters. "Such an action on the part of a grand jury in a Southern community is inconceivable," he concluded.[68]

Black authors sometimes invested an exaggerated faith in American ideals and institutions. The Constitution drew no color line, a speaker quoted in the *New York Age* asserted, overlooking that document's original endorsement of slavery.[69] Other editorialists argued that African Americans needed no new legislation to ensure their rights, just enforcement of the Constitution.[70] Another defined racial divisions as unpatriotic and un-American.[71] And newspapers like the *Cleveland Gazette,* the *Savannah Tribune,* and the *Chicago Defender* that continued to recommend northward migration downplayed some of the difficulties of life for blacks in northern cities.[72]

The ways of the "southern 'Hun'" threatened to undermine core American values. The "one great sin of America" was its "weak and vacillating policy . . . in dealing with southern lawlessness," Byrd argued.[73] Failure to meet the southern threat endangered the very existence of American values and institutions. "THE SOUTH is a part of the body

A TIP FROM ONE WHO KNOWS

"A Tip from One Who Knows." The defeated ex-Kaiser warns the American South that white supremacy "doesn't pay." The black press frequently compared the white South to America's enemies in World War I. From *Chicago Defender,* December 13, 1919.

"The Mark of the American Hun—Blot It Out." "Two Lynchings Last Week. The records of history will show that the United States fought valiantly for Democracy *in Europe.*" From *Baltimore Afro-American,* January 24, 1919.

politic of this country," the *Chicago Defender* warned. "If poison is injected into any part of the human system and the same is not arrested and eradicated, it will eventually infect the whole system and may result in death."[74] The South threatened the nation's spiritual health in a number of ways. It spread lawlessness, undermined democratic values, and promoted the values of the enemy—whether they be autocratic Germans or Russian Bolsheviks.[75] Byrd saw in the summer's riots a calculated plan by southerners to make the rest of America like the South—a white man's country—by spreading violence against blacks to all corners of the nation.

Byrd and the *Cleveland Gazette* took this view of the South as dangerous to American values and institutions about as far as any other editorialist or newspaper. They also presented a grand vision of what blacks could do to preserve those values and defeat America's dark side. America could save itself by following the example of militant blacks in Washington and Chicago who had made those cities "decent places to live" by standing up to southern-influenced ruffians, Byrd argued. And since the federal government seemed unwilling to do this, African Americans would have to lead the fight against the "southern 'Hun' who sought to destroy the Union and is now seeking to endanger it by his savage traits."[76]

Southern black newspapers never made such dramatic claims or drew such sharp distinctions between North and South, but they sometimes portrayed the South as a threat to democratic principles and placed their hopes for progress in the North. The *Savannah Tribune,* for instance, classified news of southern lynchings, which appeared at the same time as news of the Armistice, as "pro-Germanism and disloyalty" committed "by a species of Huns (made in America) running wild throughout the Southland, defying law, dominating public opinion, and shedding innocent blood."[77] In spite of the newspaper's location in a state that was exceeded only by Mississippi in violence against blacks, the *Tribune* portrayed the South as a threat to America's reputation. "Georgia's fame for lynching and burning is familiar and common knowledge throughout the nation, and now since the war, with wider communication between this country and Europe, this fame is spreading over Europe and attaining international proportions."[78] Another southern paper, the *Richmond Planet,* sometimes expressed faith in a North capable of living up to democratic principles and imposing them on the South. In August, a mob led by a county judge and a local constable attacked and seriously injured NAACP executive secretary John R. Shillady in Austin, Texas. After Governor William Hobby condoned the attack, Mitchell wrote an editorial that indicted the South and invested hopes for racial progress solely in northerners.[79] At other times, though, Mitchell's paper viewed racial problems as national in scope, especially in light of the recent rioting in northern cities. Just a week after the Shillady editorial, Mitchell argued that Smith's run-in with the Cleveland Police Department proved that "the condition of the colored peo[ple] now seems to be about the same in one section of the country as it is in the other." He also continued to praise the "better class" of southern whites and held up the local authorities' response to a race riot in Knoxville, Tennessee, as a model for all to follow.[80]

By the late summer of 1919, African Americans seemed to have lost a good deal of the optimism of a year earlier, when many thought the idealistic crusade in Europe might lead directly to the "dawn of real democracy" in America and a returning black soldier could write with eager sincerity: "I truly believe that this democracy will not be denied us."[81] The signing of the Armistice on November 11, 1918, was bittersweet for African Americans. Mitchell had shrewdly surmised that the longer the war went on, the more race reform it would bring. All of the measures realized since the editors' conference had been undertaken as war measures, most of which evaporated after the Armistice. The following year's riots in Washington and Chicago and a dramatic increase in lynching—including the killings of some returned black soldiers in uniform—made it clear to most that the federal government would not follow through on Wilson's statement against lynching and that the South would not be made safe for democracy any time soon.

In fact, the attacks on black radicals and periodicals after the war showed that the federal government could not be relied on to bring about justice for African Americans. Federal policy may have reached a nadir in January 1920 when the House and Senate passed different versions of a peacetime sedition law that would have allowed the Post Office Department to ban any publication that made an "appeal" to "racial prejudice" and would thus "cause rioting or the resort to force and violence within the United States." Du Bois predicted that, by this standard, officials could rule something as innocuous as a "list of lynchings" a violation of law.[82] Indeed, one postal censor had made just such a case during the war. Smith thought the law would wipe the black press "out of existence," and a *Chicago Defender* cartoonist depicted the black press facing the "lynching," "mob law," "concubinage," and "hatred" of the South with its hands tied by the sedition law.[83] As public opinion turned against the government's persecution of political dissidents in the late winter and spring of 1920, however, peacetime sedition legislation lost momentum and the House and Senate never agreed on a compromise version.[84] As Mitchell had put it back in December, "The persistent effort to discredit the Negroes of this country has dismally failed and our place in history has been forever established."[85]

Meanwhile, in spite of signs that the country had pulled back from the reform impulses stimulated by the war, black newspapers did not stop prodding America to live up to its ideals and did not completely lose hope that someday it would. Most black writers continued to believe that the North, once the home of abolition and the underground railroad, could provide a haven—however flawed—for persecuted

"Helpless!" Black newspapers' hands are tied by the "Graham Sedition Bill."
From *Chicago Defender*, February 7, 1920.

blacks fleeing the South. They continued to hold fast to America's founding ideals and institutions—a set of principles that, if adhered to, would guarantee their just treatment. They continued to trust that many white men of goodwill believed in fairness and justice without regard to race and that many would support black rights if only they were better informed. They assumed that if the black press kept on "in the same old uncompromising way, asking the white man to live up to his constitution and laws . . . the so-called 'Race Problem,' which flies so ghostly before his eyes, will be no more."[86] Such consistent prodding would do more than benefit African Americans; it would redeem the republic itself—make it, as one black soldier wrote, "the greatest on the face of the earth."[87] In the middle of the red summer of 1919, Reverend W. Sampson Brooks encouraged and instructed the black press during a conference on the race riots: "The fundamental principles upon which this nation was founded must be ever kept aloft by the colored press, and when it achieves their universal acceptance for all, it will have made the greatest contribution to American ideals and government."[88] Although that day was still a distant dream, black journalists kept believing in its inevitability and in the possibility that they could help bring it about.

CONCLUSION

TOWARD A WAR FOR ALL THE PEOPLE, 1919–1945

Students of World War I and the Red Scare usually come away from their topic with a sense of pessimism about the prospects for democracy and freedom of expression in America. The ease with which government propagandists manipulated public opinion during the war led journalist Walter Lippmann and others to conclude that the people could not be relied on to comprehend the complexities of modern mass society and to call for intelligent and knowledgeable leaders to guide public opinion in the interests of order and prosperity, even at the cost of truly democratic decision making.[1] Media critics have subsequently lost faith in the reliability of facts and the possibility that the public sphere could serve as a neutral ground on which citizens have access to the state and exercise some power over it. The media, they point out, is not truly open to all views, and the press's posture of political neutrality gives an unfair advantage to those with the power and resources to disseminate ideas and manipulate symbols. Indeed, they could point out that the mainstream media supported World War I and passed along government propaganda uncritically while offering superficial and fragmented coverage of important underlying issues like the rise of racially motivated violence in 1918 and 1919.[2]

Moreover, studies of government repression during the war and the Red Scare point to the ways that the crackdown on sedition limited civil liberties, destroyed radical organizations, and paved the way for later and more substantial abuses, especially during the Cold War.[3] Studies that focus directly on government repression of the black press suggest that the campaign succeeded in cowing editors into submission at the same time that antiradical campaigns stimulated the rise of reactionary forces that generated racial violence across the country in the months after the war.[4]

But although the experience of the black press in World War I demonstrates the fragility of democracy and free expression, it also offers some cause for optimism. In a nation founded on democratic ideals, President Wilson found it necessary to articulate a democratic rationale for going to war, and some activists managed to convince him, in turn, that the same ideals should be applied to oppressed individuals at home. For example, Wilson acknowledged that lynching made a mockery of his humanitarian war aims and declared in June 1918 that giving women the vote was "an essential psychological element in the conduct of the war for democracy."[5] Further, the black press did not act as a passive transmitter of government propaganda during the war. Whereas the mainstream press had been generally uncritical of the war effort and government propaganda, the black press offered significant criticism. Editorials usually did not oppose the war or its basic aims, but they continually pointed out the ways in which African Americans were being discriminated against by the war machine or how persecution of blacks at home contradicted Wilson's ideals.

To some extent, African Americans soft-pedaled their criticisms, especially after the enforcement of the Espionage and Sedition Acts began. But their wartime moderation should not be judged simply as a response to the threat of physical force wielded by the government or uncritical acceptance of prowar propaganda. The threat of repression certainly played a role in shaping the black newspapers' response to the war, but black editors did not dramatically alter their tone after the antisedition machinery gathered steam in 1918. Even historian Theodore Kornweibel Jr., who argues that federal agents achieved their goal of moderating the *Chicago Defender* and other black newspapers during the war, points out that Robert Abbott's newspaper continued to promote black migration and condemn lynching and the government's racist policies through the end of the war.[6] Like the *Defender,* most black newspapers exercised greater caution in the months just before the Armistice, but they did not change the basic thrust of their message. After the end of the war, militancy increased again even though government scrutiny continued.

So a number of factors, including coercion, prowar propaganda, public opinion, local conditions, and the expectations of African American readers, helped to shape the responses of black newspapers to the war. But although black journalists could not ignore these factors or act as if they were free of their social context, their actions were not wholly determined. Black writers were not passively manipulated by government policies, majority opinions, and patterns of discourse, although they were affected by them. Rather, they took account of existing circumstances while devising responses that helped to shape events in ways that, for the most part, served black interests well.

Another factor that may have altered the tone of black newspapers and that contradicts historians' pessimism was the apparent success of their efforts. After the government met with black editors, listened to their demands, and then began acting on them, it seemed that the war might actually advance the interests of African Americans. Editors who believed the war was serving their interests accordingly became more supportive of the federal government. There is no reason to believe that their optimism was misplaced. Although the government was acting out of necessity rather than moral conviction—as some black editors observed—the measures it took were real and seemed to signal a reversal of its long-standing inattention to African Americans. Had the war lasted longer, the gains might have been more substantial.

Another sign of success was the growth of an antilynching movement and, in the 1920s and 1930s, a dramatic decline in the number of people lynched each year. A number of southern organizations began to campaign against lynching during the war, and a congressman from Missouri introduced a bill to make lynching a federal crime. If, as sociologists Stewart E. Tolnay and E. M. Beck argue, white southerners came to oppose lynching because they thought it was driving away their labor force, then the black press can be said to have reinforced this trend by urging blacks to migrate and publicizing the theory that lynching caused migration of blacks from the South.[7]

Even without achieving substantial tangible results, the black press succeeded in its mission in important ways during World War I, at least considering what was within its control. Not only did it manage to avoid wholesale and persistent suppression, but it also overcame its exclusion from the mainstream marketplace of ideas, injecting black demands and beliefs into the public sphere and, most important, conveying them to the national government's highest officials. Although most of the mainstream media remained closed to dissident or minority views and concerns, the experience of the black press suggests that alternative media can circumvent that limitation and allow disfranchised citizens access to the state.

Of course, the black press was not completely successful. In the final analysis, little lasting progress toward racial justice came about as a direct result of the war. In addition, the effort to avoid prosecution and accommodate wartime political ideas led to some ambiguity and inconsistency in editorial policies. The most glaring example was the

support of preparedness and the war by editors who saw no compel-
ling reason to be fighting in Europe. Although the fighting seemed
pointless to them, they advised other African Americans to put their
lives on the line. Others simultaneously criticized and embraced Wilson's idealistic war aims or supported the campaign for Americanism
and condemned the divided loyalties of "hyphenates" while seeking
to make the war a vehicle for their own group demands and calling for
black unity and solidarity in the face of racism. Many editors seemed to
be offering unconditional support of the war at the same time that they
were setting conditions for blacks' participation. Some opposed segregation in the army yet accepted a separate training camp for black
officers. Advocates of militant protest sometimes played down or condemned evidence of black rebelliousness during the war. Editors who
saw the reasons for the Houston mutiny denounced the mutineers or
even endorsed their punishment. Even the most militant of the black
newspapers followed a path that combined protest and accommodation and mixed demands for reparations with pledges of loyalty. But
none of the papers were either purely militant or purely accommodating. Although southern black newspapers often treated evidence
of southern racism more gingerly than their northern counterparts
or placed more faith in the goodwill of the "better class" of southern
whites, they did not abstain from criticizing southern racial practices
or making comparisons between the enemy in Europe and lynchers
in the South. Although northern black newspapers made more scathing condemnations of the South and southern whites, they also exhibited accommodation in important ways with their strong support of
the war.

Looking back, militants have found too much accommodation in
the black press during the war. Protest ideology, however, ought to be
judged on the basis of its effectiveness, not an arbitrary standard of
ideological purity. Militancy should not be considered an end in itself
but rather a means to bringing about greater human rights. Moreover, African Americans were not alone in struggling with ideological
contradictions in relation to World War I. All over the world, individuals attempted to reconcile the desire to promote democracy with
nationalistic feelings. No one exhibited this tension more than the
American president, who pledged to make the world safe for democracy while signing and enforcing legislation that sent dissenters to jail.

Although black editors' strategies may have fallen short during
World War I, they set the pattern for World War II, when the black
press seemed to present its demands with greater persistence and suc-

cess. Yet while the "Close Ranks" editorial has been used to characterize the accommodationist response of the black press to World War I,
the *Pittsburgh Courier*'s Double V campaign has been seen as emblem-
atic of its militancy in World War II. While fighting against the evils of
Nazism abroad, the *Courier* argued—and other black newspapers came
to agree—blacks should fight against similar evils at home. As the
Michigan Chronicle put it, "We are determined to make this a people's
war and we mean all the people." Meanwhile, black journalists, including the editor of the *Crisis*, explicitly pledged not to repeat the "Close
Ranks" mistake of the previous war.[8] As shorthand for the black press's
positions during the two world wars, however, "Close Ranks" and the
Double V campaign distort reality by exaggerating the differences in
the two cases. During World War I, most black newspapers—including the *Crisis* until the last six months of the war—followed a Double V
strategy, pointing out parallels between the misdeeds of enemies and
the persecution of blacks at home and calling on the government to
act on their behalf as part of the war effort. Even after W. E. B. Du
Bois had penned "Close Ranks," the *Crisis*'s parent organization, the
NAACP, was working through back channels to promote antilynching
legislation as a war measure. And in spite of black journalists' pledges
not to back down during World War II, as they believed their prede-
cessors had done two decades earlier, reports of government monitors
suggest that the black press moderated its tone significantly by June
1942, again apparently in response to a combination of threats and
concessions from the government.[9]

If black newspapers did present a more militant front or win more
concessions from the government during World War II, it likely had
more to do with factors other than the tactical choices of black editors.[10] Government monitors of the black press in World War II were
less hostile, and the Roosevelt administration was generally less zealous in attacking seditious utterances than the Wilson administration
had been, thanks in large part to Attorney General Francis Biddle's
commitment to civil liberties.[11] In World War I, the Wilsonian rhetoric
of self-determination and democracy lent itself to black purposes, but
World War II, a war against the ultimate racist doctrine, was even more
adaptable to the cause of black equality. Moreover, the fighting lasted
nearly four years in the later war, whereas America's involvement in
World War I concluded after less than two years, just when the federal
government was beginning to address some black demands.

In both wars, most black publishers proceeded resolutely but cautiously in forwarding black demands during a time of national crisis.

They did so with a realistic understanding of both the possibilities and the dangers they faced and devised their strategies accordingly. This conclusion does not diminish the significance of black journalists' agency. Although they adjusted their protests to fit their circumstances, they kept protesting and actively shaped history, often in creative and courageous ways. Like all individuals, they did not make history just as they liked but from existing conditions. From 1914 to 1920, black journalists contributed to the shaping of American history under circumstances only partly amenable to their purposes.

NOTES

INTRODUCTION

1. Quoted in Bella Gross, *"Freedom's Journal* and the *Rights of All," Journal of Negro History* 17 (July 1932): 241.
2. *Chicago Broad Ax,* Dec. 18, 1915. For an example of a letter writer who characterized the *New York Age* as "defender of the race," see J. Williams, "Leading Paper of the Race," *New York Age,* Feb. 22, 1917, p. 4. Among letters "commending the *Age,"* most writers complimented the newspaper for educating black readers. Some, however, commented on its role as a representative or defender of the race. A North Carolina reader said the *Age* was pleading the race's case "as a consummate diplomat both to the heart and the head of this great nation" (ibid., Mar. 1, 1917, p. 4).
3. *California Eagle,* Sept. 29, 1917. Without the "united and strong support" of the entire black community of Los Angeles, however, the *Eagle* could defend the race only selectively, the editor added by way of explaining the paper's failing.
4. On the exclusion of African Americans from the mainstream media, see Lauren Kessler, *The Dissident Press: Alternative Journalism in American History* (Beverly Hills: Sage Publications, 1984), 21–47. On the treatment of blacks in the media, see Marian J. Moore, "The Advertising Images of Black Americans, 1880–1920 and 1968–1979: A Thematic and Interpretive Approach" (Ph.D. diss., Bowling Green State University, 1986); Carolyn Martindale, *The White Press and Black America* (New York: Greenwood Press, 1986), 79–109; Clint C. Wilson II and Felix Gutierrez, *Race, Multiculturalism, and the Media: From Mass to Class Communication,* 2d ed. (Thousand Oaks, Calif.: Sage Publications, 1995), 152–58; and Roi Ottley, *The Lonely Warrior: The Life and Times of Robert S. Abbott* (Chicago: Henry Regnery, 1955), 127–28.
5. I. Garland Penn, *The Afro-American Press and Its Editors* (1891; reprint, New York: Arno Press and New York Times, 1969), 13; Frederick G. Detweiler, *The Negro Press in the United States* (Chicago: University of Chicago Press, 1922), 131–32, 136, 144, 151–52, 204, 268; Gunnar Myrdal, *An American Dilemma: The Negro Problem and Modern Democracy* (1944; reprint, New York: Harper and Row, 1962), 908, 910, 912; Vishnu V. Oak, *The Negro Newspaper* (Yellow Springs, Ohio: Antioch Press, 1948), 20–21, 35–37; Charles A. Simmons, *The African American Press: A History of News Coverage during National Crises, with Special Reference to Four Black Newspapers, 1827–1965* (Jefferson, N.C.: McFarland, 1998). See also Roland E. Wolseley, *The Black Press, U.S.A.* (Ames: Iowa State University Press, 1971), 4; Henry Lewis Suggs, "Preface," in *The Black Press in the South, 1865–1979* (West-

port, Conn.: Greenwood Press, 1983), viii, x; Ottley, *Lonely Warrior*, 128; and Benjamin Quarles, *Black Abolitionists* (New York: Oxford University Press, 1969), 89. Although she focuses on the antebellum black press's role within the black community, Frankie Hutton also argues that it fought for vindication and acceptance from white America (*The Early Black Press in America, 1827–1860* [Westport, Conn.: Greenwood Press, 1993], ix).

6. Oak, for example, examines the press's impact on black opinion, exploring the way it crystallized black thought and action against oppression and sometimes diffused black anger and despair with fiery rhetoric (*Negro Newspaper*, 26, 133). Simmons in *African American Press* spends a great deal of time studying the way black newspapers fostered black unity or affected blacks in other ways. His chapter on the *Chicago Defender*, for example, is mostly concerned with showing how that newspaper influenced the migration of southern blacks to the North.

7. Suggs, "Preface," x; Myrdal, *American Dilemma*, 910.

8. See Myrdal, *American Dilemma*, 908–24. In his biography of *Chicago Defender* publisher Robert Abbott, Ottley calls his subject a warrior and says that "Negroes looked more and more to their own press to fight their news battles, even, indeed, to apologize [for] and defend their wrongdoing." Yet Ottley does not elaborate on the way such battles were fought, and his portrait of the *Defender* emphasizes its role within the black community. See Ottley, *Lonely Warrior*, esp. 128.

9. Detweiler, *Negro Press in the United States*, 204, 31; Myrdal, *American Dilemma*, 911.

10. E. Franklin Frazier's wholly negative account gives little credit to editors' attacks on racism and oppression because they were not, he argues, part of a coherent and consistent oppositional ideology that rejected industrial capitalism. Like many Marxist scholars, Frazier finds the lack of left-wing ideology among his subjects to be a dysfunctional adaptation requiring some explanation. See E. Franklin Frazier, *Black Bourgeoisie* (New York: Free Press, 1957), chap. 8. For a critique of radical historians' search for radical consciousness among the working class, see Aileen S. Kraditor, *The Radical Persuasion, 1890–1917: Aspects of the Intellectual History and the Historiography of Three American Radical Organizations* (Baton Rouge: Louisiana State University Press, 1981). For a defense of radical history, see Robert Westbrook, "Good-bye to All That: Aileen Kraditor and Radical History," *Radical History Review*, 28–30 (1984): 69–89.

11. Albert Lee Kreiling, "The Making of Racial Identities in the Black Press: A Cultural Analysis of Race Journalism in Chicago, 1878–1929" (Ph.D. diss., University of Illinois at Urbana, 1973). For another account that emphasizes the black press as an agent of identity formation, see Martin E. Dann, ed., *The Black Press, 1827–1890: The Quest for National Identity* (New York: G. P. Putnam's Sons, 1971).

12. On the public sphere, see Jurgen Habermas, *The Structural Transformation of the Public Sphere: An Inquiry into a Category of Bourgeois Society*, trans. Fred-

erick Lawrence (Cambridge: MIT Press, 1995). On parallel public spheres or "parallel discursive arenas," see Susan Herbst, *Politics at the Margin: Historical Studies of Public Expression outside the Mainstream* (New York: Cambridge University Press, 1994), and Kessler, *Dissident Press.*

13. Another piece of evidence that whites read the black press of which the editors would not have been aware is that some whites saved clippings from black newspapers in their private papers. See Suggs, "Preface," viii.

14. Linguist M. M. Bakhtin argues that the act of speaking or writing involves an effort to break through the "alien conceptual horizon of the listener" and make sense in the context of the listener's "apperceptive background" (*The Dialogic Imagination: Four Essays,* trans. Caryl Emerson and Michael Holquist; ed. Michael Holquist [Austin: University of Texas Press, 1981], 282). According to Terry Eagleton, "Literature may appear to be describing the world, and sometimes actually does so, but its real function is performative: it uses language within certain conventions in order to bring about certain effects in a reader. It achieves something in the saying: it is language as a kind of material practice in itself, discourse as social action" (*Literary Theory: An Introduction* [Minneapolis: University of Minnesota Press, 1983], 118). On speech act theory, which emphasizes the way language produces effects rather than how it transmits information, see J. L. Austin, *How to Do Things with Words,* 2d ed., ed. J. O. Urmson and Marina Sbisa (Cambridge: Harvard University Press, 1975).

15. The idea that power is exercised through discursive practices as well as coercive force is discussed in Michel Foucault, *The History of Sexuality,* vol. 1, *An Introduction,* trans. Robert Hurley (New York: Vantage Books, 1990), 92–102.

16. On the exclusion of deviant views from the news media, see Lance Bennett, *News: The Politics of Illusion,* 2d ed. (New York: Longman, 1988), 51–52.

17. As Bakhtin puts it, "Many words stubbornly resist, others remain alien, sound foreign in the mouth of the one who appropriated them and who now speaks them" (*Dialogic Imagination,* 293–94).

18. On making the South "safe for the Negroes," see *Boston Guardian* clipping, circa October 1918, folder 91, box 5, William Monroe Trotter Papers, Mugar Library, Boston University, Boston, Massachusetts. As another newspaper put it two years after the war, "Let us make America safe for Americans" ("The Price of a Life," *Chicago Defender,* Sept. 4, 1920, p. 12). On southern atrocities, see *Savannah Tribune,* Nov. 16, 1916, p. 4, and William A. Byrd, "Things Must Change," *Cleveland Gazette,* June 2, 1917, p. 2.

19. On violence against the black press, primarily in the South, see John Nerone, *Violence against the Press: Policing the Public Sphere in U.S. History* (New York: Oxford University Press, 1994), 128–59.

20. A theory of how ideology and physical force are used in combination to control subordinate groups can be found in Antonio Gramsci, *Selections*

from the Prison Notebooks, ed. and trans. Quintin Hoare and Geoffrey Nowell Smith (New York: International Publishers, 1971). For a model of how to apply Gramsci's theories to modern American cultural history that emphasizes the interaction of physical coercion and ideological control and leaves open the possibility of successful resistance to authority, see T. J. Jackson Lears, "The Concept of Cultural Hegemony: Problems and Possibilities," *American Historical Review* 90 (June 1985): 567–93.

21. The best example of this interpretation is in Arthur E. Barbeau and Florette Henri, *The Unknown Soldiers: Black American Troops in World War I* (Philadelphia: Temple University Press, 1974), 10–14. A more nuanced view, which mentions "deeply-felt patriotism," can be found in Jane Lang Scheiber and Harry N. Scheiber, "The Wilson Administration and the Wartime Mobilization of Black Americans, 1917–18," *Labor History* 10 (Summer 1967): 452. See also David M. Kennedy, *Over Here: The First World War and American Society* (New York: Oxford University Press, 1980), 279–80. For the argument that blacks followed Du Bois's advice to "close ranks" because they thought it would win democratic reform after the war and that their disappointment concerning these expectations led to greater postwar militancy, see William M. Tuttle Jr., *Race Riot: Chicago in the Red Summer of 1919* (New York: Atheneum, 1970), 216–17. For the claim that the *Chicago Defender* was the main exception to the black press's acquiescence to Du Bois's "Close Ranks" editorial, see Simmons, *African American Press,* 39. Patrick S. Washburn, in *A Question of Sedition: The Federal Government's Investigation of the Black Press during World War II* (New York: Oxford University Press, 1986), 4, 11–29, argues that the black press was "cowed by government pressure" from 1917 to 1919. Another book argues that federal harassment of the black press during and after World War I "played an important role in aborting the most militant period of African American history" (Theodore Kornweibel Jr., *"Seeing Red": Federal Campaigns against Black Militancy, 1919–1925* [Bloomington: Indiana University Press, 1998], xii).

22. Theodore Kornweibel Jr., in "Apathy and Dissent: Black America's Negative Responses to World War I," *South Atlantic Quarterly* 80 (Summer 1981): 322–38, estimates that 40 to 50 percent of African Americans opposed the war. Kornweibel and others argue that accounts that emphasize black support of the war shortchange militancy by relying too heavily on elite sources and ignoring the actions of the masses. See, for example, Steven A. Reich, "Soldiers of Democracy: Black Texans and the Fight for Citizenship, 1917–1921," *Journal of American History* 82 (Mar. 1996): 1478–1504. Mark Ellis, in "W. E. B. Du Bois and the Formation of Black Opinion in World War I: A Commentary on 'The Damnable Dilemma,'" *Journal of American History* 81 (Mar. 1995): 1584–90, sees significant opposition to the war and traces the division in the black community to the Du Bois/Washington dichotomy. For the view that the war led to militant labor organizing among blacks in the Mississippi Delta, see Nan Elizabeth Woodruff, "African-American Struggles for Citizenship in the Arkansas

and Mississippi Deltas in the Age of Jim Crow," *Radical History Review* 55 (Winter 1993): 33–51.

23. Barbeau and Henri, for example, say that, unlike Du Bois, "not all black leaders could so totally swallow their bitterness. . . . But most black people went along with Du Bois's 'Close Ranks position'" (*Unknown Soldiers*, 11–12).

24. Ellis makes this point explicitly, saying that "the question of whether to agitate for reform during the war divided them in ways that perpetuated the long-standing rift between Booker T. Washington and W. E. B. Du Bois" ("W. E. B. Du Bois and the Formation of Black Opinion," 1585).

25. This approach to intellectual history is discussed in Dominick LaCapra, *Rethinking Intellectual History: Texts, Contexts, Language* (Ithaca: Cornell University Press, 1983), 30–34. See also John E. Toews, "Intellectual History after the Linguistic Turn: The Autonomy of Meaning and the Irreducibility of Experience," *American Historical Review* 92 (Oct. 1987): 879–907, esp. 891–92.

26. The *Crisis* sold 100,000 copies in May 1919, but this was a onetime high.

CHAPTER ONE

1. Unless otherwise noted, the following account is based on Christine Lunardini, ed., "Standing Firm: William Monroe Trotter's Meetings with Woodrow Wilson, 1913–1914," *Journal of Negro History* 64 (Summer 1979): 255–62.

2. "Mr. Trotter and Mr. Wilson," *Crisis* 9 (Jan. 1915): 120.

3. Stephen R. Fox, *The Guardian of Boston: William Monroe Trotter* (New York: Atheneum, 1970), 181–87.

4. Lunardini, "Standing Firm," 263 (n. 5).

5. Joseph Patrick Tumulty to Woodrow Wilson, Apr. 24, 1915, and Woodrow Wilson to Joseph Patrick Tumulty, Apr. 24, 1915, in Woodrow Wilson, *The Papers of Woodrow Wilson*, ed. Arthur S. Link (Princeton: Princeton University Press, 1980), 33:68.

6. On politically marginal groups' use of "back channels" of communication, see Susan Herbst, *Politics at the Margin: Historical Studies of Public Expression outside the Mainstream* (New York: Cambridge University Press, 1994), 28–30.

7. Some would question whether Du Bois belongs in this group. Unlike most black periodicals, the *Crisis* was published monthly instead of weekly and was not fully controlled by blacks. The journal is included here, however, because Du Bois was largely independent in his editorial judgment (aside from some important exceptions), because the *Crisis* participated so significantly in the discourse of the black press, and because government officials lumped the *Crisis* with other black-owned publications.

8. Quoted in Bella Gross, "*Freedom's Journal* and the *Rights of All*," *Journal of Negro History* 17 (July 1932): 242–43, 284–85. See also Charles A. Sim-

mons, *The African American Press: A History of News Coverage during National Crises, with Special Reference to Four Black Newspapers, 1827–1965* (Jefferson, N.C.: McFarland, 1998), 9–10.

9. Clint C. Wilson II, *Black Journalists in Paradox: Historical Perspectives and Current Dilemmas* (New York: Greenwood Press, 1991), 25, 32.

10. I. Garland Penn, *The Afro-American Press and Its Editors* (1891; reprint, New York: Arno Press and New York Times, 1969), 61–63.

11. Frederick Douglass, *The Life and Times of Frederick Douglass* (1892; reprint, New York: Collier, 1962), 259.

12. Quoted in Gross, *"Freedom's Journal and the Rights of All,"* 284–85. See also ibid., 258, 259–60, 272, 284.

13. See ibid., 249. Douglass also considered it his duty as editor to promote the "moral and intellectual improvement of the colored people," to make blacks aware of "their own latent powers" to fight prejudice, and to provide blacks with hope for the future. See Roland E. Wolseley, *The Black Press, U.S.A.* (Ames: Iowa State University Press, 1971), 20, 22. On the nationalism of the antebellum black press, see Frankie Hutton, *The Early Black Press in America, 1827–1860* (Westport, Conn.: Greenwood Press, 1993), xii.

14. On racial attitudes in the antebellum period, see George M. Fredrickson, *The Black Image in the White Mind: The Debate on Afro-American Character and Destiny, 1817–1914* (1971; reprint, Middletown, Conn.: Wesleyan University Press, 1987), chaps. 1–5, and Thomas F. Gossett, *Race: The History of an Idea in America* (1963; reprint, New York: Shocken Books, 1965). Fredrickson argues that Lincoln acknowledged the humanity of blacks while denying them equality with whites and favoring colonization to Africa. See George M. Fredrickson, "A Man, but Not a Brother: Abraham Lincoln and Racial Equality," in *The Arrogance of Race: Historical Perspectives on Slavery, Racism, and Social Inequality* (Hanover, N.H.: Wesleyan University Press, 1988), 54–72. On Victorianism and race, see Stanley Coben, *Rebellion against Victorianism: The Impetus for Cultural Change in 1920s America* (New York: Oxford University Press, 1991), 69–90.

15. Hutton, *Early Black Press in America*, 74, 39–43, 66. For the interpretation that the antebellum black press sought to "attract white readers, thus furnishing an evidence of Negro abilities as well as an exposure to his viewpoints," see Benjamin Quarles, *Black Abolitionists* (New York: Oxford University Press, 1969), 84–89.

16. Thomas J. Davis, "Louisiana," in Henry Louis Suggs, ed., *The Black Press in the South, 1865–1979* (Westport, Conn.: Greenwood Press, 1983), 151–76.

17. Few of these journals survived more than a decade; most collapsed after a few years. Circulations rarely exceeded 1,000. The *Montgomery Sentinel* of Alabama printed 1,000 copies weekly in 1872, and three South Carolina newspapers had circulations of 280, 480, and 1,000 in 1873. See Allen Woodrow Jones, "Alabama," in Suggs, *Black Press in the South*, 25, and Theodore Hemmingway, "South Carolina," in ibid., 293. Although these numbers seem extremely small by today's standards, even major urban

newspapers' circulations were generally low in the mid-nineteenth century. The *New York Sun,* a leading daily in the nation's largest city, for example, had a circulation of just 43,000 in 1868. And "country weeklies" in small towns usually sold less than 1,000 copies a week—often less than 500. See Frank Luther Mott, *American Journalism: A History of Newspapers in the United States through 250 Years, 1690–1940* (New York: Macmillan, 1941), 374, 396, and John Cameron Sim, *The Grass Roots Press: America's Community Newspapers* (Ames: Iowa State University Press, 1969), 29.

18. Emma Lou Thornbrough, "American Negro Newspapers, 1880–1914," *Business History Review* 40 (Winter 1966): 467–90.

19. For a critique of uplift ideology, see Kevin K. Gaines, *Uplifting the Race: Black Leadership, Politics, and Culture in the Twentieth Century* (Chapel Hill: University of North Carolina Press, 1996).

20. August Meier, *Negro Thought in America, 1880–1915: Racial Ideologies in the Age of Booker T. Washington* (1963; reprint, Ann Arbor: University of Michigan Press, 1988), 88–89.

21. *Selma Advocate,* 1915, quoted in Jones, "Alabama," 39. According to Jones, although black papers in Alabama "continued to protest racial violence, segregation, white supremacy, and disfranchisement, . . . the editors were less militant. Booker T. Washington's influence upon black editors in Alabama became evident by the mid-1890s, and his ideas of racial survival were reflected more each year in the black newspapers" (ibid., 36).

22. Clarence E. Walker, "The American Negro as Historical Outsider, 1836–1935," *Canadian Review of American Studies* 17 (Summer 1986): 147.

23. Quoted in Penn, *Afro-American Press and Its Editors,* 173.

24. Albert Lee Kreiling, "The Making of Racial Identities in the Black Press: A Cultural Analysis of Race Journalism in Chicago, 1878–1929" (Ph.D. diss., University of Illinois at Urbana, 1973), 464.

25. *Savannah Tribune,* Jan. 1, 1876, quoted in Alton Hornsby Jr., "Georgia," in Suggs, *Black Press in the South,* 120.

26. Lester C. Lamon, *Black Tennesseans, 1900–1930* (Knoxville: University of Tennessee Press, 1977), 16; *Nashville Globe,* Aug. 28, 1908, quoted in Samuel Shannon, "Tennessee," in Suggs, *Black Press in the South,* 332.

27. Duke, quoted in Jones, "Alabama," 30.

28. Ibid., 31–33; Benjamin, quoted in ibid., 33.

29. Mildred I. Thompson, *Ida B. Wells-Barnett: An Exploratory Study of an American Black Woman, 1893–1930,* Black Women in United States History, ed. Darlene Clark Hine et al., vol. 4 (Brooklyn: Carlson, 1990), 15, 16, 29–30; Emma Lou Thornbrough, *T. Thomas Fortune: Militant Journalist* (Chicago: University of Chicago Press, 1972), 123–24; Rodger Streitmatter, *Raising Her Voice: African-American Women Journalists Who Changed History* (Lexington: University Press of Kentucky, 1994), 50–54.

30. Joel Williamson, *The Crucible of Race: Black-White Relations in the American South since Emancipation* (New York: Oxford University Press, 1984), 195–201; Henry Louis Suggs and Bernadine Moses Duncan, "North Carolina," in Suggs, *Black Press in the South,* 266–67.

31. According to newspaperman George Schuyler, black newspapers in Mississippi avoided "nine-tenths of the real news and practically all of the possible topics crying for comment" (quoted in Julius E. Thompson, *The Black Press in Mississippi, 1865–1985* [Gainesville: University Press of Florida, 1993], 20). On the Mississippi black press, see ibid., 11–12, 13, 17, 20; Julius Eric Thompson, "Mississippi," in Suggs, *Black Press in the South*, 180–82; and Neil R. McMillen, *Dark Journey: Black Mississippians in the Age of Jim Crow* (Urbana: University of Illinois Press, 1989), 172–77.

32. Jones, "Alabama," 33–34.

33. Yollette Trigg Jones, "The Black Community, Politics, and Race Relations in the 'Iris City': Nashville, Tennessee, 1870–1954" (Ph.D. diss., Duke University, 1985), 104–8.

34. W. Fitzhugh Brundage, " 'To Howl Loudly': John Mitchell Jr. and His Campaign against Lynching in Virginia," *Canadian Review of American Studies* 22 (Winter 1991): 325–41.

35. Some southern black newspapers like the *Dallas Express*, the *Nashville Globe*, and most notably the *Norfolk Journal and Guide* prospered after the turn of the century, but these were the exceptions. In Alabama, the black press "declined rapidly" after 1915, in both the number of papers published and overall circulation. See Jones, "Alabama," 36, 37, 39–40, 42, and *Selma Advocate*, quoted in ibid., 39. The years from 1914 to 1920 marked a "departure point in the affairs of Florida blacks" that had the effect of making the state's African American press "much less dynamic and more static" and "more difficult to establish and maintain," with the result that many readers now turned to northern papers for race news. See Jerrell H. Shofner, "Florida," in Suggs, *Black Press in the South*, 99–100, 105, 106. On the decline of the black press in other states, see Calvin Smith, "Arkansas," in ibid., 73; Hemmingway, "South Carolina," 296, 299–300, 302; and James Smallwood, "Texas," in Suggs, *Black Press in the South*, 361.

36. Thornbrough, *T. Thomas Fortune*, 110.

37. Quoted in Kreiling, "Making of Racial Identities in the Black Press," 200.

38. Quoted in Meier, *Negro Thought in America*, 30.

39. On the political independence of Taylor, see Kreiling, "Making of Racial Identities in the Black Press," 187, 193–94. On Smith, see Kenneth L. Kusmer, *A Ghetto Takes Shape: Black Cleveland, 1870–1930* (Urbana: University of Illinois Press, 1976), 133–34. On Fortune, see Thornbrough, *T. Thomas Fortune*, 86–93, and Meier, *Negro Thought in America*, 31.

40. Kreiling, "Making of Racial Identities in the Black Press," 166; William Jordan, "Tyler, Ralph Waldo," in John A. Garraty and Mark C. Carnes, eds., *American National Biography* (New York: Oxford University Press, 1999), 22:81–82.

41. On the *Chicago Conservator*'s endorsement of retaliatory violence, see Kreiling, "Making of Racial Identities in the Black Press," 140.

42. Quoted in Thornbrough, *T. Thomas Fortune*, 279. See also ibid., 183.

43. Ibid., 200.

44. See, for example, *Appeal*, Mar. 6, 1915, p. 2; "Census Segregation," ibid.,

June 5, 1915, p. 2; and Kenneth L. Kusmer, "Smith, Harry C[lay]," in Rayford Logan, ed., *Dictionary of American Negro Biography* (New York: W. W. Norton, 1982), 564. Fortune thought the best course for the future of mankind would be the mixing of races, and he promoted the term "Afro-American" because he believed the use of a proper noun would force white Americans to assert the humanity of blacks. See Thornbrough, *T. Thomas Fortune*, 133–34, 145–46.

45. Thornbrough, *T. Thomas Fortune*, 54–55, 157–58. See also Kreiling, "Making of Racial Identities in the Black Press," chaps. 4, 5; David Howard-Pitney, "Calvin Chase's *Washington Bee* and Black Middle-Class Ideology, 1882–1900," *Journalism Quarterly* 63 (Spring 1986): 89–97. On Chase's support of economic uplift and industrial education, see Meier, *Negro Thought in America*, 45, 92. On the support of Smith's *Cleveland Gazette* and Taylor's *Chicago Broad Ax* for industrial education, see Thomas Kirkman Jones, "The Debate over African-American Industrial Education, 1901–1914: A Post-Revisionist Historical Case Study" (Ph.D. diss., University of Tennessee, 1993).

46. The *Indianapolis Freeman* claimed a circulation of 16,000 in 1903 and 20,000 in 1913. See Willard B. Gatewood Jr., "Introduction," in Willard B. Gatewood Jr., ed., *Slave and Freeman: The Autobiography of George L. Knox* (Lexington: University Press of Kentucky, 1979), 32. For an account that suggests these figures are probably exaggerated, see Thornbrough, "American Negro Newspapers," 475. See also Gatewood, *Slave and Freeman*, 3–4.

47. Quoted in Gatewood, *Slave and Freeman*, 35.

48. Ibid., 17, 36, 27, 34.

49. Also, like some Agitators, Knox accepted financial assistance from Tuskegee. See ibid., 34.

50. For an assessment of Knox's balance of accommodation and protest, see ibid., 35.

51. Kreiling, "Making of Racial Identities in the Black Press," 186.

52. Washington bought the shares through his personal secretary, Emmett J. Scott. See Thornbrough, *T. Thomas Fortune*, 296–308. See also Emma Lou Thornbrough, "More Light on Booker T. Washington and the *New York Age*," *Journal of Negro History* 43 (Jan. 1958): 34–49.

53. Louis R. Harlan, "The Secret Life of Booker T. Washington," *Journal of Southern History* 37 (Aug. 1971): 393–416; Meier, *Negro Thought in America*, 224–36. On Washington's control of the black press, see August Meier, "Booker T. Washington and the Negro Press, with Special Reference to the *Colored American Magazine*," *Journal of Negro History* 38 (Jan. 1953): 67–90; Thornbrough, "More Light on Booker T. Washington," 34–49; and Fox, *Guardian of Boston*, 70–71.

54. Meier argues that Washington's patronage did not eliminate militancy from the black press and may not even have significantly altered its political content. It is impossible to know what impact his financial contributions had, but it is possible that they reduced militancy even if they did not eliminate it. See Meier, *Negro Thought in America*, 224–36.

55. For one theory on the role of the black press in black America, see Kreiling, "Making of Racial Identities in the Black Press," 10–13, 110, 117–20, 464–65.
56. Ida B. Wells, *Crusader for Justice: The Autobiography of Ida B. Wells* (Chicago: University of Chicago Press, 1970), 63.
57. Thornbrough, *T. Thomas Fortune*, 48–50, 108–9, 199. Ida Wells reported that "the *Age* was on the exchange list of many of the white periodicals of the North" (*Crusader for Justice*, 78).
58. On the concept of invisibility, see Ralph Ellison, *Invisible Man* (New York: Random House, 1952). On the veil metaphor, see W. E. B. Du Bois, *The Souls of Black Folk* (New York: Vintage Books, 1990), 8.
59. Fox, *Guardian of Boston*, 4–12, 16–19, 21–28, 29–30.
60. William Monroe Trotter, "Why Be Silent?," in August Meier, Elliott Rudwick, and Francis L. Broderick, eds., *Black Protest Thought in the Twentieth Century* (Indianapolis: Bobbs Merrill, 1971), 35.
61. Fox, *Guardian of Boston*, 58.
62. Meier, *Negro Thought in America*, 176–81; Fox, *Guardian of Boston*, 60–66.
63. On the Niagara Movement, see W. E. B. Du Bois, "A Brief Resume of the Massachusetts Trouble in the Niagara Movement" (1907), 1–13, W. E. B. Du Bois Papers, W. E. B. Du Bois Library, University of Massachusetts, Amherst, Massachusetts; Elliott Rudwick, "The Niagara Movement," *Journal of Negro History* 42 (July 1957): 177–200; Fox, *Guardian of Boston*, 101–10, 112–14; and David Levering Lewis, *W. E. B. Du Bois: Biography of a Race, 1868–1919* (New York: Henry Holt, 1993), 376–77. For more on Trotter, see Meier, *Negro Thought in America*, 174, 224, 232, and W. E. B. Du Bois, "William Monroe Trotter," *Crisis* 41 (May 1934): 134.
64. "Wilson vs. Trotter," *Cleveland Gazette*, Nov. 21, 1914, p. 2.
65. Meier, *Negro Thought in America*, 245–47, 256–78. For a nuanced view of the way conservative and radical ideology came together in the New Negro, see Kreiling, "Making of Racial Identities in the Black Press," chap. 9.
66. William Jordan, "'The Damnable Dilemma': African-American Accommodation and Protest during World War I," *Journal of American History* 81 (Mar. 1995): 1568–69.
67. W. E. B. Du Bois to Joel E. Spingarn, Oct. 28, 1914, in W. E. B. Du Bois, *The Correspondence of W. E. B. Du Bois*, ed. Herbert Aptheker (Amherst: University of Massachusetts Press, 1973), 1:206–7.
68. Du Bois and Spingarn battled for control of the *Crisis* in 1914 and 1915. In 1919, Ovington disciplined the editor for failing to submit his editorials to a committee for approval. On efforts to control Du Bois, see Joel E. Spingarn et al. to NAACP board of directors, Dec. 6, 1915, Du Bois Papers; Charles Flint Kellogg, *NAACP: A History of the National Association for the Advancement of Colored People* (Baltimore: Johns Hopkins University Press, 1967), 92–115; Elliott M. Rudwick, *W. E. B. Du Bois: Propagandist of the Negro Protest*, 2d ed. (Philadelphia: University of Pennsylvania Press, 1968), 165–78; and Lewis, *W. E. B. Du Bois*, 468–500.

69. Joel E. Spingarn to W. E. B. Du Bois, Oct. 24, 1914, in Du Bois, *Correspondence*, 200–202.

70. Mary White Ovington, "The National Association for the Advancement of Colored People," *Journal of Negro History* 9 (Apr. 1924): 112; Mary White Ovington to W. E. B. Du Bois, Apr. 11, 1914, Du Bois Papers; Kellogg, *NAACP*, 101.

71. Quoted in Rudwick, *W. E. B. Du Bois*, 125.

72. On Washington, see Booker T. Washington to Thomas T. Fortune, Jan. 20, 1911, in Booker T. Washington, *The Booker T. Washington Papers*, ed. Louis R. Harlan and Raymond W. Smock (Chicago: University of Chicago Press, 1979), 10:55–56, and Booker T. Washington to Emmett J. Scott, Jan. 16, 1914, in ibid., 12:417. On Trotter, see Fox, *Guardian of Boston*, 140–44, 202, 223. On Garvey, see Elliott M. Rudwick, "Du Bois versus Garvey: Race Propagandists at War," *Journal of Negro Education* 28 (Fall 1959): 421–30.

73. Lewis, *W. E. B. Du Bois*, 500.

74. Francis L. Broderick, *W. E. B. Du Bois: Negro Leader in a Time of Crisis* (Stanford, Calif.: Stanford University Press, 1959), 92.

75. Moore's mismanagement led Washington to seize control of the paper in 1908. The paper was operating at a weekly deficit of $200, and the succession of journalists Moore hired to write editorials brought the paper more in line with Tuskegee principles. See Thornbrough, *T. Thomas Fortune*, 255, 333, 331, 334, 314.

76. Eugene Levy, *James Weldon Johnson: Black Leader, Black Voice* (Chicago: University of Chicago Press, 1973), 54, 151–60; *New York Age*, quoted in ibid., 154.

77. James Weldon Johnson, *Along This Way: The Autobiography of James Weldon Johnson* (New York: Viking Press, 1933), 323–26. The meeting occurred on February 19, 1918, according to Robert L. Zangrando, *The NAACP Crusade against Lynching, 1909–1950* (Philadelphia: Temple University Press, 1980), 39.

78. Thornbrough, "American Negro Newspapers," 475.

79. Roi Ottley, *The Lonely Warrior: The Life and Times of Robert S. Abbott* (Chicago: Henry Regnery, 1955), 139.

80. The discussion of Abbott and the *Chicago Defender* is based on ibid. On the newspaper's early years, see ibid., pp. 87–139.

81. Ibid., 105. On the masthead suit, see ibid., 140–41.

82. On the *Chicago Defender*'s conservative stands, see Mary E. Stovall, "The *Chicago Defender* in the Progressive Era," *Illinois Historical Journal* 83 (Autumn 1990): 159–72.

83. On the *Chicago Defender*'s advocacy of migration, see Katherine A. Bitner, "The Role of the *Chicago Defender* in the Great Migration of 1916–1918," *Negro History Bulletin* 48 (Apr.–June 1985): 20–26; James R. Grossman, *Land of Hope: Chicago, Black Southerners, and the Great Migration* (Chicago: University of Chicago Press, 1989), 82–88; Kreiling, "Making of Racial

Identities in the Black Press," 372; and Alan Douglas Desantis, "Selling the American Dream: The *Chicago Defender* and the Great Migration of 1915–1919" (Ph.D. diss., Indiana University, 1993). An estimated 700,000 to 1 million blacks left the South between 1917 and 1920 (Joe W. Trotter Jr., "Migration/population," in Jack Salzman et al., eds., *Encyclopedia of African-American Culture and History* [New York: Simon and Schuster Macmillan, 1996], 4:1779–85).

84. Kathleen Thompson, "Charlotta Spears Bass (1880–1969)," in Darlene Clark Hine, ed., *Black Women in America* (Brooklyn: Carlson, 1993), 1:93; Charlotta A. Bass, *Forty Years: Memoirs from the Pages of a Newspaper* (Los Angeles: Charlotta A. Bass, 1960), 30–31, 33.

85. Hayward Farrar, *The "Baltimore Afro-American," 1892–1950* (Westport, Conn.: Greenwood Press, 1998), 7–9.

CHAPTER TWO

1. "The European War and Its Horrors," *New York Age,* Aug. 13, 1914, p. 4; "Black Troops' Bravery," *Richmond Planet,* Aug. 29, 1914, p. 4; "The Opportunity of the Dark Races," ibid., Sept. 5, 1914, p. 4; *Baltimore Afro-American Ledger,* Sept. 5, 1941, p. 4.

2. "Address to the Country," *Richmond Planet,* Sept. 26, 1914, p. 1.

3. "The Opportunity of the Dark Races," ibid., Sept. 5, 1914, p. 4.

4. On African American opposition to the war, see Theodore Kornweibel Jr., "Apathy and Dissent: Black America's Negative Responses to World War I," *South Atlantic Quarterly* 80 (Summer 1981): 322–38.

5. Quoted in *Nation,* May 20, 1915, pp. 554–55.

6. "German Atrocities," *New York Times,* May 13, 1915, p. 14; "The Cup of Bitterness" and "The Bryce Report," *Nation,* May 20, 1915, pp. 553–55. On the American response to the Belgium invasion, see Patrick Devlin, *Too Proud to Fight: Woodrow Wilson's Neutrality* (New York: Oxford University Press, 1975), 139, 408, 564. On Belgium, Reims, and the Bryce report, see Frederic L. Paxson, *Pre-War Years, 1913–1917,* vol. 1 of *American Democracy and the World War* (Boston: Houghton Mifflin, 1936), and M. L. Sanders and Philip M. Taylor, *British Propaganda during the First World War, 1914–1918* (London: MacMillan, 1982), 143–45. On the Armenian massacres, see Stephen Pope and Elizabeth-Anne Wheal, *Dictionary of the First World War* (New York: St. Martin's Press, 1995), s.v. "Armenian Massacres," 34–35. On the Bryce report, see *The United States in the First World War: An Encyclopedia,* ed. Anne Cipriano Venzon (New York: Garland, 1995), s.v. "Propaganda: British Propaganda in the United States," 476–78.

7. James W. Johnson, "Not Quite the Same," *New York Age,* Jan. 11, 1917, p. 4.

8. "Has America Anything to Lose?," *Norfolk Journal and Guide,* July 14, 1917, p. 4.

9. James W. Johnson, "Not Quite the Same," *New York Age,* Jan. 11, 1917, p. 4.

10. "World War and the Color Line," *Crisis* 9 (Nov. 1914).

11. "The Belgians," *Washington Bee,* Mar. 3, 1917, p. 4.
12. Two notable exceptions included the *Crisis,* as already mentioned, and the *Norfolk Journal and Guide,* which agreed with Du Bois that Germany must be defeated. See "Progress of the Horrible War in Europe," *Norfolk Journal and Guide,* Feb. 17, 1917, p. 4.
13. *Savannah Tribune,* Dec. 4, 1915, p. 4. See also ibid., Feb. 20, 1915, p. 4, and "Getting Us Told," *Chicago Defender,* Aug. 7, 1915, p. 8.
14. "President Wilson," *Washington Bee,* Feb. 17, 1917, p. 4.
15. James W. Johnson, "Not Quite the Same," *New York Age,* Jan. 11, 1917, p. 4.
16. James W. Johnson, "The United States and Germany," ibid., June 3, 1915, p. 4. For a description of the sinking as an atrocity, see "The Larger Effects," *Nation,* May 20, 1915, p. 553.
17. "The Sinking of the *Lusitania,*" *Richmond Planet,* May 15, 1915, p. 4. For an editorial that depicts the summary execution of a Jew in Russia as "another bit of evidence to show how nearly similar is the position of the Jew in Russia and the Negro in America," see untitled editorial, *Baltimore Afro-American,* Oct. 2, 1915, p. 4. For the observation that the overthrow of the czar should serve as a warning to white southerners who believed in the divine right of one group to rule over another, see ibid., Apr. 28, 1917, p. 4. For another editorial comparing Russian Jews with American blacks, see James W. Johnson, "Russian Democracy and the Jews," *New York Age,* Mar. 22, 1917, p. 4.
18. "How Much Longer," *Chicago Defender,* Feb. 12, 1916, p. 8.
19. "Ruthlessness," *Baltimore Afro-American,* Feb. 10, 1917, p. 4.
20. James W. Johnson, "Well Worth Thinking About," *New York Age,* Feb. 15, 1917, p. 4.
21. See Stewart E. Tolnay and E. M. Beck, *A Festival of Violence: An Analysis of Southern Lynchings, 1882–1930* (Urbana: University of Illinois Press, 1995), appendix C-3, and Robert L. Zangrando, *The NAACP Crusade against Lynching, 1909–1950* (Philadelphia: Temple University Press, 1980), 9–10. Statistical evidence of lynching is sketchy, even after the *Chicago Tribune* initiated an effort to compile statistics in 1882. Even statistics after that time are considered conservative estimates since some lynchings were never reported. On the early history of lynching, see W. Fitzhugh Brundage, *Lynching in the New South: Georgia and Virginia, 1880–1930* (Urbana: University of Illinois Press, 1993), 5–6. On problems with statistics, see ibid., 292–93.
22. For the view that lynching was a means to preserve the caste structure of southern life, see Gunnar Myrdal, *An American Dilemma: The Negro Problem and Modern Democracy* (1944; reprint, New York: Harper and Row, 1962), 563. For an account that emphasizes lynching's importance in maintaining the sexual status quo of the Victorian Era, see Jacquelyn Dowd Hall, *Revolt against Chivalry: Jesse Daniel Ames and the Women's Campaign against Lynching* (New York: Columbia University Press, 1979), 145–49. On lynching as a by-product of the South's struggle to develop a racial system that balanced white separation with control of the black population, see

George M. Fredrickson, *The Black Image in the White Mind: The Debate on Afro-American Character and Destiny, 1817–1914* (1971; reprint, Middletown, Conn.: Wesleyan University Press, 1987), 275. For an account that finds the roots of lynching in the social psychology of the generation of white southerners who grew up during the turbulence and disruption of the Civil War and Reconstruction, see Joel Williamson, *A Rage for Order: Black-White Relations in the American South since Emancipation* (New York: Oxford University Press, 1986), 117–20. Brundage, in *Lynching in the New South*, 13–14, emphasizes the relationship between lynching and the New South's economic structure, especially its rural labor system.

23. "Ruthlessness," *Baltimore Afro-American*, Feb. 10, 1917, p. 4.

24. "Concerns Not Even the Sheriff," *New York Age*, Aug. 5, 1915, p. 4.

25. "German Intrigues and War Progress," *Norfolk Journal and Guide*, Mar. 17, 1917, p. 4.

26. "Down in Georgia," *Pittsburgh Courier*, Aug. 2, 1912, p. 4.

27. See Gail Bederman, " 'Civilization,' the Decline of Middle-Class Manliness, and Ida B. Wells's Antilynching Campaign, 1892–94," *Radical History Review* 52 (Winter 1992): 5–30.

28. Zangrando, *NAACP Crusade against Lynching*, 29–30.

29. Tolnay and Beck, *Festival of Violence*, 271.

30. "Haiti Cutting Up," *Chicago Defender*, Aug. 14, 1915, p. 8. A guest columnist opposed U.S. involvement in Haiti. See Reverdly C. Ransom, "Toussaint L'Ouverture's Rusty Sword," ibid., Nov. 6, 1915, p. 8. The *New York Age* supported the American intervention in Haiti but warned that the government must take care to find officials free of race prejudice to direct it. See James W. Johnson, "The Haitian Situation," *New York Age*, Aug. 12, 1915, p. 4, and "The Haitian Situation," ibid., Sept. 2, 1915, p. 4.

31. Untitled editorial, *Baltimore Afro-American*, Aug. 7, 1915, p. 4. See also "Bullying Haiti," ibid., Aug. 28, 1915, p. 4. For the argument that America had little reason to invade Haiti and the Dominican Republic, see untitled editorial, *Savannah Tribune*, Aug. 28, 1915, p. 4; Oct. 21, 1916, p. 4; untitled editorial, *Cleveland Gazette*, Mar. 3, 1917, p. 2; and James W. Johnson, "Words vs. Acts," *New York Age*, June 8, 1916, p. 4.

32. "Haiti," *Washington Bee*, Oct. 16, 1915, p. 4.

33. "Southern White Gentlemen Burn Race Boy at Stake," *Chicago Defender*, May 20, 1916, p. 1.

34. James W. Johnson, "Chance for Humanity," *New York Age*, May 25, 1916, p. 4. The *Age* contrasted the nation's role as "protector of human rights before the world" and its toleration of lynching within its own borders in 1915. See ibid., Aug. 5, 1915, p. 4. See also "Civilization," *Chicago Defender*, May 19, 1916, p. 8; "To the Presidential Nominee," ibid., June 10, 1916, p. 8; and untitled editorial, *Savannah Tribune*, Jan. 29, 1916, p. 4. On the black press's reaction to a previous U.S. adventure in Latin America, see David J. Hellwig, "The Afro-American Press and United States Involvement in Cuba, 1902–1912," *Mid-America* 71 (Apr.–July 1990): 135–45.

35. "The Question of Lynching," *Richmond Planet*, Jan. 8, 1916, p. 4.

36. James W. Johnson, "Is This Civilization?," *New York Age,* Jan. 21, 1915, p. 4.
37. "Distance Lends Enchantment," *Chicago Defender,* May 8, 1915, p. 8.
38. "Our Own House in Order," ibid., Aug. 28, 1915, p. 8. See also "Civilization," ibid., May 20, 1916, p. 8.
39. Untitled editorial, *Savannah Tribune,* Oct. 16, 1915, p. 4.
40. "Getting Us Told," *Chicago Defender,* Aug. 7, 1915, p. 8.
41. James W. Johnson, "Concerns Not Even the Sheriff," *New York Age,* Aug. 5, 1915, p. 4, and "Bryan Talks," ibid., June 15, 1916, p. 4.
42. "Lynching and 'Civilization,'" *Richmond Planet,* Oct. 17, 1914, p. 8.
43. "How Long," *Baltimore Afro-American,* Jan. 23, 1915, p. 4; "Prominent Men Score Lynching," ibid., June 3, 1916, p. 1.
44. Arthur S. Link, *Wilson: The Struggle for Neutrality, 1914–1915* (Princeton: Princeton University Press, 1960), 68–69; "Ruthlessness," *Baltimore Afro-American,* Feb. 10, 1917, p. 4.
45. "Think It Over Mr. Wilson," *Chicago Defender,* Aug. 5, 1916, p. 12.
46. "To the Presidential Nominee," ibid., June 10, 1916, p. 8.
47. Quoted in "Texas Mob Burns Human Being in Public Square," ibid., Aug. 7, 1915, p. 1. See also *Cleveland Gazette,* Sept. 4, 1915, p. 2.
48. Quoted in "Lynching and 'Civilization,'" *Richmond Planet,* Oct. 17, 1914, p. 8. The *Milwaukee Free Press* said: "Americans have gazed askance at the bloody immorality of Serbia. But Serbia is a paradise of civilization compared with the state of Georgia." See "The South at the Bar," *Milwaukee Free Press,* in *New York Age,* Sept. 2, 1915, p. 4, also printed in *Cleveland Gazette,* Aug. 28, 1915, p. 2. For an example of the *New York World*'s opposition to lynching, see *New York Age,* Jan. 21, 1915, p. 1, and *Savannah Tribune,* May 20, 1916, p. 4.
49. James W. Johnson, "An Interesting Parallel," *New York Age,* June 15, 1916, p. 4.
50. Untitled editorial, *Savannah Tribune,* Jan. 1, 1916, p. 4. See also ibid., Jan. 29, 1916, p. 4.
51. Leon F. Litwack, "The Birth of a Nation," in *Past Imperfect: History according to the Movies,* ed. Mark C. Carnes et al. (New York: Henry Holt, 1995), 138; Thomas Cripps, *Slow Fade to Black: The Negro in American Film, 1900–1942* (New York: Oxford University Press, 1977), 44, 46.
52. Quoted in Cripps, *Slow Fade to Black,* 51.
53. David Levering Lewis, *W. E. B. Du Bois: Biography of a Race, 1868–1919* (New York: Henry Holt, 1993), 507.
54. Quoted in Jack Beatty, *The Rascal King: The Life and Times of James Michael Curley, 1874–1958* (Reading, Mass.: Addison-Wesley, 1992), 182.
55. D. W. Griffith, *Birth of a Nation* (1915), distributed by Republic Video. See also Litwack, "Birth of a Nation," 139–40.
56. Quoted in *Cleveland Gazette,* June 5, 1915, p. 2.
57. Cripps, in *Slow Fade to Black,* 52, and Litwack, in "Birth of a Nation," 136, for example, use the quote. According to the only attributed firsthand account of the White House preview, "Wilson seemed lost in thought during the showing, and . . . walked out of the room without saying a word

when the movie was over." Wilson's alleged quote first appeared, without attribution, in a 1937 magazine article. See Woodrow Wilson, *The Papers of Woodrow Wilson*, ed. Arthur S. Link (Princeton: Princeton University Press, 1985), 32:267 (n. 1). Although Wilson asked that Dixon and Griffith not mention to the press that he viewed the film, the filmmakers used the White House preview and the Supreme Court chief justice's viewing in their arguments against censorship in New York and Boston. See Arthur S. Link, *Wilson: The New Freedom* (Princeton: Princeton University Press, 1956), 253. Supreme Court Chief Justice Edward White and Margaret Blaine Damrosch informed the White House of rumors that Wilson and White had "sanctioned" the film. Wilson told his personal secretary, Joseph Tumulty, to "please say I have expressed no opinion about it." See Warren Forman Johnson to Woodrow Wilson, Mar. 29, 1915, in Wilson, *Papers*, 32:454–55; Edward Douglass White to Joseph Patrick Tumulty, Apr. 5, 1915, in ibid., 32:486; and Woodrow Wilson to Joseph Patrick Tumulty, Apr. 28, 1915, in ibid., 33:86.

58. Michael Rogin, *Ronald Reagan, the Movie, and Other Episodes in Political Demonology* (Berkeley: University of California Press, 1987), 195.

59. Wilson, quoted in ibid., 193. See also Florette Henri, *Black Migration: Movement North, 1900–1920* (Garden City, N.Y.: Anchor Press/Doubleday, 1975), 229.

60. Rogin, *Ronald Reagan, the Movie*, 197.

61. Cripps, *Slow Fade to Black*, 57.

62. Quoted in Henri, *Black Migration*, 227.

63. Beatty, *Rascal King*, 181; Lewis, *W. E. B. Du Bois*, 507. On the influence of *Birth of a Nation* on the reestablishment of the Ku Klux Klan in 1915, see David M. Chalmers, *Hooded Americanism: The History of the Ku Klux Klan* (Durham: Duke University Press, 1987), 22–32, and Bill Stanton, *Klanwatch: Bringing the Ku Klux Klan to Justice* (New York: Grove Weidenfeld, 1991), 83. On the Klan's later use of the film as a recruiting tool, see Leonard J. Moore, *Citizen Klansmen: The Ku Klux Klan in Indiana, 1921–1928* (Chapel Hill: University of North Carolina Press, 1991), 3.

64. Rogin, *Ronald Reagan, the Movie*, 192.

65. *California Eagle*, Jan. 30, Feb. 6, 13, 1915.

66. Ibid., Sept. 4, 1915, p. 3.

67. Cripps, *Slow Fade to Black*, 55–57.

68. Stephen R. Fox, *The Guardian of Boston: William Monroe Trotter* (New York: Atheneum, 1970), 191–97; Cripps, *Slow Fade to Black*, 59–61; Beatty, *Rascal King*, 180–85.

69. See Cripps, *Slow Fade to Black*, 63; Lewis, *W. E. B. Du Bois*, 507–8; Fox, *Guardian of Boston*, 197; Henri, *Black Migration*, 231; "Wilmington Bars Photo-Play," *Baltimore Afro-American Ledger*, June 5, 1915, p. 1; "*Birth of a Nation* Barred," *Norfolk Journal and Guide*, Jan. 1, 1917, p. 1; and Zangrando, *NAACP Crusade against Lynching*, 34. Henri claims that the film was banned in Cleveland but not in the rest of Ohio. Evidence from the *Cleveland Gazette*, however, indicates that the film was banned in the state for at least

a year. See also David A. Gerber, *Black Ohio and the Color Line, 1860–1915* (Urbana: University of Illinois Press, 1976), 467.

70. Kenneth L. Kusmer, *A Ghetto Takes Shape: Black Cleveland, 1870–1930* (Urbana: University of Illinois Press, 1976), 130–34. On his 1920 campaign, see *Cleveland Gazette*, Sept. 4, 1920, p. 1. See also Summer E. Stevens and Owen V. Johnson, "From Black Politics to Black Community: Harry C. Smith and the *Cleveland Gazette*," *Journalism Quarterly* 67 (Winter 1990): 1090–1102, and Kenneth L. Kusmer, "Smith, Harry Clay," in John A. Garraty and Mark C. Carnes, eds., *American National Biography* (New York: Oxford University Press, 1999), 20:196–98.

71. This discussion is based on a content analysis of twelve editorial pages, one randomly selected from each month of 1915. Other topics include national, state, and local party politics; Booker T. Washington; economic policy; proposed legislation; and the Supreme Court's ruling overturning the grandfather clause.

72. *Washington Bee,* Jan. 22, 1916, p. 4. On Smith's "fulsome praise" of Willis, see *Cleveland Gazette*, May 1, 1915, p. 2, and "'Birth of a Nation,'" ibid., Sept. 4, 1915, p. 2. Smith broke with Willis in February 1916. See ibid., Mar. 4, 1916, p. 2; Apr. 7, 1917, p. 2; and Aug. 7, 1920, p. 1.

73. *Cleveland Gazette*, Feb. 5, 1916, p. 2. Smith also reprinted an article written by a "white friend" in the *Moving Picture World* that called another film Smith sought to ban, *The Nigger,* a "repulsive, harmful" film "that never should have been made." See *Cleveland Gazette*, Apr. 3, 1915, p. 2. For another example of white criticism of the film, see "The Birth of a Nation," ibid., May 12, 1917, p. 2.

74. *Cleveland Gazette*, May 13, 1916, p. 2.

75. Ibid., Mar. 10, 1917, p. 2. John Mitchell also noted that the film "misrepresents the Northerners, much more than it does anybody else." See "'The Birth of a Nation,'" *Richmond Planet,* Oct. 2, 1915, p. 4.

76. "The Infamous Film 'The Birth of a Nation,'" *Cleveland Gazette*, Mar. 3, 1917, p. 1; "The Beatty Bill," ibid., p. 2.

77. "*Birth of a Nation* Won," ibid., Apr. 14, 1917, p. 1.

78. Ibid., Mar. 4, 1916, pp. 1, 2.

79. E. Franklin Frazier, *Black Bourgeoisie* (New York: Free Press, 1957), 24–26, 179–94.

80. *New York Age,* Feb. 11, 1915, p. 4. Not every black newspaper used the same tactics Smith used against *Birth of a Nation.* The *Baltimore Afro-American,* for example, focused more on how the film injured blacks than on how it insulted whites. The paper also optimistically exaggerated the degree of white opposition to the film, arguing that "no thinking man" accepted its historical premise and that praise of the film focused mainly on its production techniques instead of its message, which received "universal condemnation." But like the *Cleveland Gazette*, the *Baltimore Afro-American* tried to use the black vote to convince local officials to censor the film and sought to discredit Dixon, calling him a "criminally vicious" "yellow dramatist." The *Afro-American* also reprinted critiques of the film from white publica-

tions, including the *Congregationalist and Christian World,* which confronted
Dixon in an interview with the fact that white southern men more often
crossed the color line for sex than black men; the *National Tribune,* which
wrote a scathing indictment of the "cowardly and infamous" Ku Klux Klan;
and the *Boston Herald,* which quoted Moorefield Storey's criticisms of the
film. When the "Hate of a Nation" left town, an editorial advised theater
owners to "fumigate" their theaters. See *Baltimore Afro-American,* Aug. 7,
1915, p. 4; Mar. 4, 1916, p. 4; Apr. 1, 1916, p. 4; June 5, 1915, p. 4; and
May 6, 1916, p. 4.

81. On this reading of the film, see Rogin, *Ronald Reagan, the Movie,* 211–12.

82. See, for example, Smith's comparison of Dixon and the northern abo-
litionist novelist, Harriet Beecher Stowe, whom Dixon had consciously
sought to rebut, in *Cleveland Gazette,* Mar. 10, 1917, p. 2.

83. In addition to the officials in localities already mentioned, some officials
in other places banned the film during the war to prevent race riots and
assure the loyalty of blacks.

84. Cripps, *Slow Fade to Black,* 66–69.

85. Quoted in Henri, *Black Migration,* 230.

86. " 'Birth of a Nation,' " *Washington Bee,* Apr. 1, 1916, p. 4. On the *Bee's* criticism of the film, see "Violence vs. Common Sense," ibid., Oct. 2, 1915,
p. 4; " 'The Birth of the Nation,' " ibid., Feb. 19, 1916, p. 4; and " 'The Birth
of a Nation,' " ibid., Apr. 22, 1916, p. 4.

87. See Cripps, *Slow Fade to Black,* 61, 67. Cripps says a negative impact of
the film was that Hollywood also shied away from positive portrayals of
blacks. This seems doubtful. Hollywood may well have dropped unflattering black roles because of the protest against *Birth of a Nation,* but flattering
roles did not exist in any case.

88. Rogin, *Ronald Reagan, the Movie,* 195; Cripps, *Slow Fade to Black,* 62; Henri,
Black Migration, 231. See also Woodrow Wilson to Joseph P. Tumulty, Apr.
28, 1915, in Wilson, *Papers,* 33:86.

89. Daniel M. Smith, *The Great Departure: The United States and World War I,
1914–1920* (New York: Alfred A. Knopf, 1965), 2.

90. For an account of "Americanization," see John Higham, *Strangers in the
Land: Patterns of American Nativism, 1860–1925* (1963; reprint, New York:
Atheneum, 1977), 234–63.

91. Ibid., 243. On Kellor, see Lucille O'Connell, "Kellor, Frances," in Barbara
Sicherman et al., eds., *Notable American Women: The Modern Period* (Cambridge: Harvard University Press, 1980), 393–95.

92. Frederick C. Luebke, *Bonds of Loyalty: German-Americans and World War I*
(De Kalb: Northern Illinois University Press, 1974), 68–69.

93. See Theodore Roosevelt, "Americanism," in Theodore Roosevelt, *Fear God
and Take Your Own Part* (1916), vol. 20 of *The Works of Theodore Roosevelt,* ed.
Hermann Hagedorn (New York: Charles Scribner's Sons, 1925), 457.

94. David M. Kennedy, *Over Here: The First World War and American Society* (New
York: Oxford University Press, 1980), 24.

95. Arthur S. Link, *Wilson: Confusions and Crises, 1915–1916* (Princeton: Princeton University Press, 1964), 37.

96. Roosevelt, *Fear God and Take Your Own Part,* 330–31, 328.

97. Woodrow Wilson, "An Address on the American Spirit," July 13, 1916, in Wilson, *Papers,* 37:414–18.

98. In spite of Wilson's intentions, the theme that "he kept us out of war" supplanted Americanism as the dominant note of his reelection campaign. See Woodrow Wilson, *Facing War, 1915–1917,* vol. 6 of *Woodrow Wilson, Life and Letters,* ed. Ray Stannard Baker (Garden City, N.Y.: Doubleday, Doran, 1937), 249–58.

99. Ralph W. Tyler, "Proper Name for Race Discussed," *Appeal,* Mar. 6, 1915, p. 1; untitled editorial, ibid., p. 2. The discussion of the issue continued. See also ibid., May 1, 1915, pp. 1, 2; June 5, 1915, p. 2; Aug. 7, 1915, p. 2; and Oct. 2, 1915, p. 2.

100. *Baltimore Afro-American,* Dec. 11, 1915, p. 4. See also ibid., Mar. 31, 1917, p. 4.

101. *California Eagle,* Mar. 3, 1917, p. 1.

102. "Governor Praises Negro Loyalty," *Norfolk Journal and Guide,* Dec. 16, 1916, p. 1.

103. *New York Age,* Mar. 15, 1917, p. 4.

104. "Our Defense Plan," *Chicago Defender,* Sept. 18, 1915, p. 10.

105. *Louisville Courier-Journal,* quoted in *Chicago Broad Ax,* Mar. 17, 1917, p. 1. See also *Baltimore Afro-American,* Mar. 31, 1917, p. 4. The *Cleveland Gazette* labeled Wilson's adoption of the hyphenate issue a transparent political ploy but joined most other black newspapers in accepting the language of Americanism. The *Gazette*'s criticism of hyphenism was itself driven by partisan politics since it singled out the Democrat Wilson while ignoring the far more impassioned rhetoric of the Republican Roosevelt. See *Cleveland Gazette,* Nov. 6, 1915, p. 2, and William A. Byrd, "Americanism," ibid., July 29, 1916, p. 2.

106. Untitled editorial, *Richmond Planet,* Apr. 14, 1917, p. 4.

107. *California Eagle,* Mar. 17, 1917, p. 1. The desire to keep the black war record intact was another reason many editors supported the war effort. On similar themes, see also, for example, *Baltimore Afro-American Ledger,* Aug. 8, 1914, p. 4; *Appeal,* June 24, 1916, p. 2; *Savannah Tribune,* July 1, 1916, p. 2; *New York Age,* Apr. 5, 1917, p. 4; and *Chicago Broad Ax,* Apr. 21, 1917, p. 1.

108. Kennedy, *Over Here,* 31; Nathan Miller, *Theodore Roosevelt: A Life* (New York: William Morrow, 1992), 540–52.

109. Theodore Roosevelt, *The Writings of Theodore Roosevelt,* ed. William H. Harbaugh (Indianapolis: Bobbs-Merrill, 1967), 362. Roosevelt made the statement on abolitionists in a paper presented to the American Sociological Congress in Washington, D.C., December 28–30, 1914. See also Theodore Roosevelt, "Peace Insurance by Preparedness against War," in Roosevelt, *Fear God and Take Your Own Part,* 349.

110. Link, *Wilson: Confusions and Crises,* 15–18, 23–30.
111. *Chicago Broad Ax,* Jan. 8, 1916, p. 1.
112. Untitled editorial, *Savannah Tribune,* June 17, 1916, p. 4.
113. "Our Defense Plan," *Chicago Defender,* Sept. 18, 1915, p. 10; "A Step Backward," ibid., Nov. 4, 1916, p. 12.
114. "Wilson and Congress," *Cleveland Gazette,* Mar. 4, 1916, p. 2. See also ibid., Nov. 6, 1915, p. 2. On Smith's support of preparedness, see ibid., May 13, 1916, p. 2.
115. The major alteration Congress made was to eliminate the proposed national reserve force in favor of strengthening the existing National Guard. Southern Democrats had opposed the national force because they "feared formation of Negro volunteer units." See Link, *Wilson: Confusions and Crises,* 327–38.
116. "Are We to Get into the War?," *Appeal,* Mar. 3, 1917, p. 2.
117. *California Eagle,* Feb. 3, Mar. 17, 1917.
118. William A. Byrd, "The War," *Cleveland Gazette,* Apr. 7, 1917, p. 2.
119. *Chicago Broad Ax,* Mar. 31, 1917, p. 1; Mar. 17, 1917, p. 1. For a similarly ambivalent response by William Monroe Trotter, see Fox, *Guardian of Boston,* 215–17.
120. *Louisville Courier-Journal,* quoted in *Chicago Broad Ax,* Mar. 17, 1917, p. 1.
121. See, for example, "First in Everything America," *Chicago Defender,* May 6, 1916, p. 8.
122. Roosevelt, "Americanism," 459; James W. Johnson, "Wake Up Colored Men! Wake Up!," *New York Age,* Nov. 2, 1916, p. 4.
123. "Saluting the Flag," *Richmond Planet,* Apr. 1, 1916, p. 4.
124. "Teaching Treason," *Appeal,* Apr. 1, 1916, p. 2; "Negro Boy Sentenced for Insult to Flag," *Chicago Broad Ax,* Apr. 8, 1916, p. 1.
125. "Saluting the Flag," *New York Age,* Apr. 6, 1916, p. 4.
126. "Saluting the Flag," *Richmond Planet,* Apr. 1, 1916, p. 4.

CHAPTER THREE

1. "German Plots among Negroes," *Literary Digest,* Apr. 21, 1917, p. 1153; *New York Tribune,* quoted in Franklin F. Johnson, "German Agents Try to Start Rebellion," *Baltimore Afro-American,* Apr. 7, 1917, p. 1; "Detain Three in South as German Plotters," *New York Times,* Apr. 7, 1917, p. 3; "Inciter of Negroes Held," ibid., Apr. 9, 1917, p. 2.
2. On Frissell, see "Says Negroes Are Loyal," *New York Times,* Apr. 6, 1917, p. 11. On the *Macon Telegraph* and *Montgomery Advertiser,* see "German Plots among Negroes," *Literary Digest,* Apr. 21, 1917, p. 1153, and "A Futile Attempt at Sedition," *Outlook,* Apr. 18, 1917, p. 648.
3. The account of Harris's remarks to the *New York Tribune* is from Franklin F. Johnson, "German Agents Try to Start Rebellion," *Baltimore Afro-American,* Apr. 7, 1917, p. 1.
4. Woodrow Wilson, "An Address to a Joint Session of Congress," Apr. 2,

1917, in Woodrow Wilson, *The Papers of Woodrow Wilson*, ed. Arthur S. Link (Princeton: Princeton University Press, 1983), 41:524; "Sixty German Suspects in New York and Other Cities Locked Up," *New York Times*, Apr. 7, 1917, p. 1.

5. "Patriotic Meetings Held during Week," *Norfolk Journal and Guide*, Apr. 14, 1917, p. 1; *Boston Guardian*, quoted in "German Plots among Negroes," *Literary Digest*, Apr. 21, 1917, p. 1153; Franklin F. Johnson, "German Agents Try to Start Rebellion," *Baltimore Afro-American*, Apr. 7, 1917, p. 1; "German Plot Fails to Work," ibid., Apr. 14, 1917, p. 1; "Pledge Loyalty on Part of Negro," ibid., Apr. 21, 1917, p. 1; "Emphasize Loyalty and Preparedness," ibid., May 5, 1917, p. 1; "The Afro-American Loyal," *Cleveland Gazette*, Apr. 14, 1917, p. 2. On the *Nashville Globe*'s affirmations of loyalty immediately after the outbreak of war, see Yollette Trigg Jones, "The Black Community, Politics, and Race Relations in the 'Iris City': Nashville, Tennessee, 1870–1954" (Ph.D. diss., Duke University, 1985), 181–85.

6. "Loyalty to the Flag," *Richmond Planet*, Apr. 14, 1917, p. 4. See also "10,000 Suspects Arrested," *Norfolk Journal and Guide*, Apr. 28, 1917, p. 4.

7. "Loyalty," *Crisis* 14 (May 1917): 8.

8. "The Afro-American Loyal," *Cleveland Gazette*, Apr. 14, 1917, p. 2; "No Time Now for Rebellion," *Baltimore Afro-American*, Apr. 7, 1917, p. 4.

9. "The Afro-American Loyal," *Cleveland Gazette*, Apr. 14, 1917, p. 2. William Monroe Trotter of the *Boston Guardian* also both discounted reports of black disloyalty and warned that discrimination would affect the level of black participation. See Stephen R. Fox, *The Guardian of Boston: William Monroe Trotter* (New York: Atheneum, 1970), 215–16.

10. Woodrow Wilson, "An Address to the Senate," Jan. 22, 1917, in Wilson, *Papers*, 40:533–39, and "An Address to a Joint Session of Congress," Apr. 2, 1917, in ibid., 41:525.

11. Arthur S. Link, *Wilson: Campaigns for Progressivism and Peace* (Princeton: Princeton University Press, 1965), 269–70. See also Woodrow Wilson, *Facing War, 1915–1917*, vol. 6 of *Woodrow Wilson, Life and Letters*, ed. Ray Stannard Baker (Garden City, N.Y.: Doubleday, Doran, 1937), 430, and Robert C. Hilderbrand, *Power and the People: Executive Management of Public Opinion in Foreign Affairs, 1897–1921* (Chapel Hill: University of North Carolina Press, 1981), 136.

12. David M. Kennedy, *Over Here: The First World War and American Society* (New York: Oxford University Press, 1980), 50, 53.

13. Nathan Miller, *Theodore Roosevelt: A Life* (New York: William Morrow, 1992), 554–55.

14. Link, *Wilson: Campaigns for Progressivism and Peace*, 269, 426, 430, 429 (n. 103).

15. "The Great Decision," *New Republic*, Apr. 7, 1917, pp. 279–80.

16. "The Decision for War," *Nation*, Apr. 5, 1917, p. 388.

17. Quoted in Link, *Wilson: Campaigns for Progressivism and Peace*, 428.

18. "America in the Battle Line of Democracy," *World's Work* 33 (Apr. 1917): 581–86. See also "Why This Is America's War," ibid. 34 (May 1917): 9.

19. "Consistency Thou Art a Jewel," *Baltimore Afro-American Ledger,* Jan. 27, 1917, p. 4.

20. "Talk Is Cheap," *Chicago Defender,* Feb. 3, 1917, p. 10. For a similar analogy, see "Who Are the Autocrats?," *Baltimore Afro-American,* May 5, 1917, p. 4.

21. "Well Worth Thinking About," *New York Age,* Feb. 15, 1917, p. 4; "The President's Opportunity," ibid., Mar. 8, 1917, p. 4.

22. "No Time Now for Rebellion," *Baltimore Afro-American,* Apr. 7, 1917, p. 4.

23. Untitled editorials, *Richmond Planet,* Apr. 7, 1917, p. 4; May 20, 1917, p. 4.

24. William A. Byrd, "Things Must Change," *Cleveland Gazette,* June 2, 1917, p. 2. On the Persons lynching, see Robert L. Zangrando, *The NAACP Crusade against Lynching, 1909–1950* (Philadelphia: Temple University Press, 1980), 35.

25. "Democrat," *Baltimore Afro-American,* Apr. 28, 1917, p. 4; "Who Are the Autocrats?," ibid., May 5, 1917, p. 4.

26. James W. Johnson, "The Duty of the Hour," *New York Age,* Apr. 5, 1917, p. 4.

27. Roscoe Conkling Simmons, untitled editorial, *Chicago Defender,* Nov. 3, 1917, p. 12.

28. "Shall We Have a Real Democracy," *Cleveland Gazette,* Dec. 1, 1917, pp. 1, 2.

29. "A National Crisis," *Richmond Planet,* Apr. 7, 1917, p. 4.

30. "Progress of the Horrible War in Europe," *Norfolk Journal and Guide,* Feb. 17, 1917, p. 4; "War," ibid., Mar. 30, 1917, p. 4; "War Has Been Declared," ibid., Apr. 7, 1917, p. 4.

31. "Resolutions of the Washington Conference," *Crisis* 14 (June 1917): 59–60. Editor Harry Smith printed Roosevelt's praise of Wilson's war address in the *Cleveland Gazette.* Smith himself offered no direct comment on the war message, but a scathing editorial by Reverend William A. Byrd that pronounced America unfit to promote democracy in Europe pledged black loyalty in the fight. The *Chicago Defender* hoped America's stated war aims would stimulate foreigners to ask America embarrassing questions about the status of African Americans. See "Roosevelt Praises Wilson's Document," *Cleveland Gazette,* Apr. 7, 1917, p. 1; William A. Byrd, "The War," ibid., p. 2; and "A Pertinent Question," *Chicago Defender,* May 12, 1917, [p. 10].

32. "The Why of the Thing," *Chicago Defender,* Oct. 6, 1917, p. 12; Roscoe Conkling Simmons, untitled editorial, ibid., Nov. 3, 1917, p. 12.

33. *Savannah Tribune,* Apr. 7, 1917, p. 4; "What Savings May Mean," ibid., May 4, 1918, p. 4.

34. James W. Johnson, " 'Why Should a Negro Fight?,' " *New York Age,* June 29, 1918, p. 4.

35. "Dr. J. E. Spingarn Explains," *Cleveland Gazette,* Mar. 10, 1917, p. 1. On the officer-training camp for blacks, see Charles Flint Kellogg, *The National Association for the Advancement of Colored People* (Baltimore: Johns Hopkins University Press, 1967), 250–56; Joyce B. Ross, *J. E. Spingarn and the Rise of the NAACP, 1911–1939* (New York: Atheneum, 1972), 92–95; David Levering Lewis, *W. E. B. Du Bois: Biography of a Race, 1868–1919* (New York:

Henry Holt, 1993), 528–32; and Arthur E. Barbeau and Florette Henri, *The Unknown Soldiers: Black American Troops in World War I* (Philadelphia: Temple University Press, 1974), 56–57.

36. *Crisis* 13 (Apr. 1917): 270–71; "We Need Trained Officers," *Norfolk Journal and Guide*, Apr. 14, 1917, p. 4. See also W. E. B. Du Bois, *The Autobiography of W. E. B. Du Bois* (New York: International Publishers, 1968), 265–66.

37. *Savannah Tribune*, Mar. 31, 1917, p. 4. See also *Norfolk Journal and Guide*, May 12, 1917, p. 4; untitled editorial, *Richmond Planet*, May 20, 1917, p. 4; and "A Word about the Training Camp," ibid., June 2, 1917, p. 4.

38. "The Perpetual Dilemma," *Crisis* 13 (Apr. 1917): 270–71.

39. Trotter opposed and helped to keep out of Boston a black hospital, a black hotel, and a black YMCA. "The minute we accept a separate branch or place, the segregationists get the argument on us that we practice and accept it when we can get money or position out of it. We ruin our cause by advising separation," he said. See William Monroe Trotter to A. P. Russell, June 9, 1920, box 3, A. P. Russell Papers, Mugar Library, Boston University, Boston, Massachusetts. On Smith's opposition to separate YMCAs and hospitals, see "The 'Jim Crow' Y.M.C.A.," *Cleveland Gazette*, Mar. 3, 1918, p. 2, and "New Segregation Efforts," ibid., July 3, 1915, p. 2.

40. According to one editor, a black YMCA was "a blessing to the community and should receive the unbiased support of every race-loving Negro in the city and country" (*Pittsburgh Courier*, Nov. 11, 1911, p. 4). See also "Opposes Colored Y.M.C.A.'s," *Indianapolis Freeman*, Feb. 11, 1911, p. 4. On Johnson's support of a separate YMCA, see Eugene Levy, *James Weldon Johnson: Black Leader, Black Voice* (Chicago: University of Chicago Press, 1973), 156. The *Washington Bee* was ambivalent about the training camp: "Colored people should never accept any separation or distinction based on race alone, except where they must do so, in spite of objection and protest, and then only with the understanding that they do so until they can change conditions" ("The Summer Military Camp," *Washington Bee*, Mar. 24, 1917, p. 4). But the paper consistently defended segregated public schools. See Hal S. Chase, "Chase, W[illiam] Calvin," *Dictionary of American Negro Biography*, ed. Rayford Logan (New York: W. W. Norton, 1982), 100.

41. " 'Jim Crow' Training Camps—No!," *Chicago Defender*, Apr. 7, 1917, p. 10; "A Little Previous," ibid., Aug. 19, 1916, p. 12. For examples of the *Defender*'s call for black participation, see editorials in ibid., Apr. 28, 1917, [p. 10]; May 19, 1917, p. 10; and Nov. 3, 1917, p. 12.

42. "Dr. Spingarn's Army Call," *Cleveland Gazette*, Mar. 10, 1917, p. 2; " 'Jim Crow' Training Camps—No!," *Chicago Defender*, Apr. 7, 1917, p. 10.

43. "Dr. Spingarn's Explanation," *Cleveland Gazette*, Mar. 10, 1917, p. 2.

44. Untitled editorial, ibid., June 9, 1917, p. 2.

45. On Smith's support of Ohio recruitment and war stamps, see ibid., May 11, 1918, p. 2. On comparison of loyal blacks with disloyal socialists and members of the Industrial Workers of the World, see "Patriots Disfranchised," ibid., Apr. 13, 1918, p. 2. Smith also endorsed the governor of North Carolina's statement that " 'in this crucial hour' " the African American could

be " 'counted upon to do his full part' " ("Patting 'Ham' on the Back," ibid., Apr. 14, 1917, p. 2).

46. "Army Enlistment Barrier," ibid., Apr. 1, 1916, p. 2.

47. Ibid., June 2, 1917, p. 1.

48. "We Have No Duties Where We Have No Rights," *Baltimore Afro-American*, Mar. 17, 1917, p. 4.

49. "On Compromisers," ibid., Mar. 31, 1917.

50. "O.R.T.C. Now a Fact," ibid., May 19, 1917, p. 4. On the newspaper's support of the camp, see "O.R.T.C.," ibid., May 26, 1917, p. 4.

51. "The Summer Military Camp," *Washington Bee*, Mar. 24, 1917, p. 4; "Speak for Yourself," ibid., Apr. 17, 1917, p. 4; *New York Age*, Mar. 22, 1917, p. 4; Mar. 1, 1917, p. 4; Mar. 15, 1917, p. 4; *Appeal*, Mar. 3, 1917, p. 2.

52. *Savannah Tribune*, Mar. 31, 1917, p. 4; *Washington Bee*, May 19, 1917, p. 4; *Norfolk Journal and Guide*, May 12, 1917, p. 4; Ross, J. E. *Spingarn and the Rise of the NAACP*, 84–97; Barbeau and Henri, *Unknown Soldiers*, 56–59.

53. *Boston Guardian* clipping, Oct. 31, 1918, folder 91, box 5, William Monroe Trotter Papers, Mugar Library, Boston University, Boston, Massachusetts.

54. Joel E. Spingarn to W. E. B. Du Bois, Feb. 26, 1917, W. E. B. Du Bois Papers, W. E. B. Du Bois Library, University of Massachusetts, Amherst, Massachusetts.

55. "Bourbonism and Progress," *New York Age*, Sept. 6, 1917, p. 4.

56. "This Is No Soldier!," *Chicago Defender*, May 4, 1918, p. 16. See also "Mr. Phillips of Memphis Would Like to Know," ibid., Jan. 5, 1918, p. 12; "Heflin with the Bunch," *Baltimore Afro-American*, Nov. 1, 1918, p. 4; and "The East St. Louis Massacre," *Cleveland Gazette*, July 28, 1917, p. 2.

57. *Savannah Tribune*, Sept. 1, 1917, p. 4.

58. "Heflin with the Bunch," *Baltimore Afro-American*, Nov. 1, 1918, p. 4; Wilson, quoted in Kennedy, *Over Here*, 284. See also *New York Age*, Jan. 19, 1918, p. 4, and May 18, 1918, p. 4.

59. *Cleveland Gazette*, May 4, 1918, p. 2; May 11, 1918, p. 2; "Although Outnumbered," *Chicago Defender*, May 12, 1917, p. 10.

60. On black contributions to the Liberty Loan drive and other voluntary war work, see Henry Lewis Suggs, *P. B. Young, Newspaperman: Race, Politics, and Journalism in the New South, 1910–1962* (Charlottesville: University Press of Virginia, 1988), 37, and Andrew Buni, *Robert L. Vann of the "Pittsburgh Courier": Politics and Black Journalism* (Pittsburgh: University of Pittsburgh Press, 1974), 103. On enlistment of blacks in the military, see Jane Lang Scheiber and Harry N. Scheiber, "The Wilson Administration and the Wartime Mobilization of Black Americans, 1917–18," *Labor History* 10 (Summer 1967): 433–58.

61. "German Propaganda," *Cleveland Gazette*, July 27, 1918, p. 2; ibid., Feb. 16, 1918, p. 2.

62. On Johnson, see Barbeau and Henri, *Unknown Soldiers*, 116.

63. "Southern Democracy," *Cleveland Gazette*, May 4, 1918, p. 2. After a black physician attending a Liberty Loan meeting in Houston was punched by a white man, the *Cleveland Gazette* observed that "police refused to arrest

the brutal and cowardly Texan . . . and yet this country is helping to fight for world democracy and calling on the Afro-American to help" (ibid.).

64. "Mr. Phillips of Memphis Would Like to Know," *Chicago Defender*, Jan. 5, 1918, p. 12.

65. "South Opposes Negro Soldiers," *Baltimore Afro-American*, Apr. 14, 1917, p. 1.

66. James W. Johnson, "The Danger of Treason," *New York Age*, May 3, 1917, p. 4.

67. James W. Johnson, "Taking Their Measure," ibid., Jan. 19, 1918, p. 4; "Fix the Responsibility," ibid., Aug. 30, 1917, p. 4; "Bourbonism and Progress," ibid., Sept. 6, 1917, p. 4; and "Ridicule for Our Soldiers in France," ibid., Sept. 7, 1918, p. 4.

68. James W. Johnson, "The First Six Months," ibid., July 13, 1918, p. 4.

69. *Baltimore Afro-American*, Sept. 27, 1918, p. 4. On the "work or fight" laws, see James W. Johnson, " 'Work or Fight' Laws for Women," *New York Age*, Nov. 2, 1918, p. 4, and Barbeau and Henri, *Unknown Soldiers*, 9–10. An Arkansas law aimed at forcing black women to work in the cotton fields was unpatriotic, *Chicago Defender* columnist W. Allison Sweeney suggested; if cotton was necessary for the war effort, then both white and black Arkansas women should pick the crop to "prove that patriotism is not onesided" ("The Last Straw," *Chicago Defender*, Oct. 5, 1918, p. 16).

70. "Some More American 'Huns,' " *Cleveland Gazette*, June 8, 1918, p. 2; ibid., Sept. 7, 1918, p. 2. For another use of "Hun," see "The Hun Still Unleashed in America," *Savannah Tribune*, Nov. 16, 1918, p. 4.

71. "The Jim Crow Car or the Kaiser on Wheels," *Chicago Defender*, Nov. 3, 1917, p. 12; Ben Baker, "Our Political and Economic Status," ibid., Apr. 6, 1918, p. 16.

72. See, for example, "Bourbonism and Progress," *New York Age*, Sept. 6, 1917, p. 4.

73. In an untitled editorial, Harry Smith commented: "The South favors a maximum of representation with a minimum of taxation and it comes pretty near getting it" (*Cleveland Gazette*, July 27, 1918, p. 2).

74. The recent study is Stewart E. Tolnay and E. M. Beck, *A Festival of Violence: An Analysis of Southern Lynchings, 1882–1930* (Urbana: University of Illinois Press, 1995), 271–72. Tuskegee statistics are cited in Zangrando, *NAACP Crusade against Lynching*, 6. The figures printed in the black press sometimes vary slightly from Zangrando's figures. For example, the *Cleveland Gazette* reported that 36 African Americans were lynched in 1917 and 58 in 1918, whereas Zangrando lists 36 in 1917 and 60 in 1918. See "The Lynching Record for 1917," *Cleveland Gazette*, Jan. 5, 1918, p. 1, and ibid., Jan. 4, 1919, p. 1.

75. William A. Byrd, "Things Must Change," *Cleveland Gazette*, June 2, 1917, p. 2. On the lynchings, see Zangrando, *NAACP Crusade against Lynching*, 41–42.

76. William A. Byrd, "A Southern Man Flays the South," *Cleveland Gazette*, July 7, 1917, p. 2; "Shall We Have a Real Democracy," ibid., Dec. 1, 1917,

p. 1; and "Why Democratic Party Should Be Defeated Now and in 1920!," ibid., Oct. 5, 1918, p. 1.

77. Johnson erroneously reported the number as 34. See James W. Johnson, "No Cause for Congratulations," *New York Age*, Jan. 19, 1918, p. 4. See also "Our Foreign Reputation," ibid., May 18, 1918, p. 4.

78. Kelly Miller, "The Disgrace of Democracy," *Baltimore Afro-American*, Aug. 25, 1917, p. 4.

79. Elliott M. Rudwick, *Race Riot at East St. Louis, July 2, 1917* (Carbondale: Southern Illinois University Press, 1964). On labor problems, see ibid., 16–26. On the killing of police officers, see ibid., 38–40.

80. Ibid., 50–53.

81. Ibid., 59.

82. "The Negro and the Nation," *Nation*, July 26, 1917, p. 86.

83. "East St. Louis Riots," *Norfolk Journal and Guide*, July 7, 1917, p. 4.

84. "The White Man's Burden," *Chicago Defender*, July 14, 1917; "East St. Louis Aftermath," ibid., July 28, 1917, p. 12.

85. "Frightfulness in America Puts Europe to Shame," *Baltimore Afro-American*, July 7, 1917, p. 1; "Will Congress Act?," *New York Age*, July 26, 1917, p. 4.

86. "Roosevelt Scores Gompers," *Cleveland Gazette*, July 14, 1917, p. 1; "Will Congress Act?," *New York Age*, July 26, 1917, p. 4. See also Philip G. Peabody, "Hypocrisy and 'Democracy,'" ibid., July 26, 1917, p. 4, and "Must Settle Race Issue," *Baltimore Afro-American*, July 14, 1917, p. 4. Du Bois was willing to forget Roosevelt's previous sins against blacks because of his "strong word" on East St. Louis ("Roosevelt," *Crisis* 14 [Aug. 1917]: 164). The *Chicago Defender* focused on less enlightened responses of whites to the riot in a July 28, 1917, editorial but earlier had expressed faith that the American legal system ultimately "cannot fail" to redress black grievances and that "surely the good people must predominate." See "East St. Louis Aftermath," *Chicago Defender*, July 28, 1917, p. 12, and "The White Man's Burden," ibid., July 14, 1917. During a congressional inquiry into the riot, a *Defender* reporter wrote: "The St. Louis papers keep a watch on these things and give them much needed publicity and it all adds to the justice which the Negro may get out of the thing" (ibid., Nov. 3, 1917, p. 1).

87. "Responsibility for Murder," *Richmond Planet*, July 21, 1917, p. 4.

88. "Echoes of East St. Louis," *Norfolk Journal and Guide*, July 14, 1917, p. 4.

89. For a sampling of white newspapers' views, see ibid.

90. Untitled editorial, *Cleveland Gazette*, June 2, 1917, p. 2; "The East St. Louis Massacre," ibid., July 28, 1917, p. 2.

91. "Memphis Lynching Real Cause of Illinois Riot," *Chicago Defender*, June 2, 1917, p. 1.

92. James W. Johnson, "Senator Tillman Not Yet Dead," *New York Age*, July 26, 1917, p. 4; "The Negro and the Nation," *Nation*, July 26, 1917, p. 86.

93. "Afro-American Cullings," *Cleveland Gazette*, Oct. 7, 1916, p. 1.

94. William A. Byrd, "A Southern Man Flays the South," ibid., July 7, 1917, p. 2, and "Why Democratic Party Should Be Defeated Now and in 1920!," ibid., Oct. 5, 1918, p. 1.

95. "Humanity and the Negro," ibid., Apr. 6, 1918, p. 2. Smith also wrote: "A little 'democracy' is sadly needed these days, in Georgia, Alabama, Tennessee and indeed the entire south."

96. "Roosevelt's Opportunity," *Baltimore Afro-American*, July 14, 1917, p. 4. The *Afro-American* also accused the mayor of Baltimore of being "unpatriotic and un-American" when he signaled his support for a new residential segregation ordinance. The mayor, the paper suggested, should "lose sight of caste and autocracy for a while and get into his system a mite of the kind of democracy we are trying to beat into the Huns." See "Segregation Fever Again in the Air," ibid., July 5, 1918, p. 4.

97. "White Labor in the South," *New York Age*, Oct. 11, 1917, p. 4.

98. Yet in the context of the war, the paper often blamed the nation as a whole for race problems, thereby highlighting the hypocrisy of the war effort. See, for example, "A Pertinent Question," *Chicago Defender*, May 12, 1917, p. 10; "Not Belgium—America," ibid., Sept. 8, 1917, p. 1; and "And a Lady Applauds," ibid., Mar. 2, 1918, p. 12.

99. "The Jim Crow Car or the Kaiser on Wheels," ibid., Nov. 3, 1917, p. 12.

100. "Echoes of East St. Louis," *Norfolk Journal and Guide*, July 14, 1917, p. 4; *Savannah Tribune*, Mar. 2, 1918, p. 4.

101. *Savannah Tribune*, Mar. 2, 1918, p. 4.

102. On the Houston riot, see Robert V. Haynes, *A Night of Violence: The Houston Riot of 1917* (Baton Rouge: Louisiana State University Press, 1976).

103. Ibid., 96.

104. Ibid., 140–41.

105. Ibid., 167–68.

106. Quoted in ibid., 193.

107. On the *Outlook* as Theodore Roosevelt's "spokesman," see Link, *Wilson: Campaigns for Progressivism and Peace*, 391.

108. "The Houston Mutiny," *Outlook*, Sept. 5, 1917, pp. 10–11.

109. *Nation*, Aug. 30, 1917, pp. 212–13.

110. "The Houston Outbreak," *New York Times*, Aug. 25, 1917, p. 6. See also House Resolution 131, by Texas representative Jeff McLemore, which asked the secretary of war to return the mutineers to Houston for trial and protested against sending black soldiers to the South (*Congressional Record*, 65th Cong., 1st sess., 1917, vol. 55, pt. 7:6467).

111. "Houston," *Crisis* 14 (Oct. 1917): 284–85.

112. *Cleveland Gazette*, Dec. 15, 1917, p. 4.

113. Quoted in Mark Ellis, "America's Black Press, 1914–18," *History Today* 41 (Sept. 1991): 25.

114. Willard Utley, report on *San Antonio Inquirer*, Nov. 27, 1917, in Theodore Kornweibel Jr., ed., *Federal Surveillance of Afro-Americans, 1917–1925: The First World War, the Red Scare, and the Garvey Movement* (Frederick, Md.: University Publications of America, 1986, microfilm), reel 9, frames 903–4.

115. Ellis, "America's Black Press," 26.

116. "Houston," *Crisis* 14 (Oct. 1917): 284–85.

117. "In the Enemy's Camp," *Chicago Defender*, Sept. 1, 1917, [p. 12]. To confuse

matters further, the same editorial concluded with a warning to whites who provoke mob violence: "What the white man starts, the Colored man unquestionably will finish." The *Cleveland Advocate* said every colored man in America regretted the mutiny but at the same time was "tired" of the "wholesale" executions of black soldiers who allegedly participated. "Yet," another editorial added, "we are standing and will continue to stand by the flag, ready to protect its graceful folds with the last drop of our blood. . . . Was there ever a more sublime patriotism?" See "That Texas Affair," *Cleveland Advocate*, Sept. 1, 1917, p. 6, and "Tired of Wholesale Killing," ibid., Jan. 12, 1918, p. 8.

118. Quoted in Buni, *Robert L. Vann of the "Pittsburgh Courier,"* 105. In the same editorial, the *Pittsburgh Courier* also criticized "crackers" for abusing black soldiers in every southern town.

119. "The Rioting of Negro Soldiers," *Messenger,* Nov. 1917, p. 6. The *Baltimore Afro-American* opposed the swiftness of the executions of some of the soldiers but conceded that they were guilty and deserved punishment. See "Houston Incident Closed—Not Forgotten," *Richmond Planet,* Jan. 5, 1918, p. 7.

120. "The Houston Uprising," *Baltimore Afro-American,* Sept. 1, 1917, p. 4.

121. *Cleveland Gazette,* Dec. 15, 1917, p. 1.

122. "In the Enemy's Camp," *Chicago Defender,* Sept. 1, 1917, [p. 12]; James W. Johnson, "Houston," *New York Age,* Aug. 30, 1917, p. 4. See also "The Rioting of Negro Soldiers," *Messenger,* Nov. 1917, p. 6. On the *Pittsburgh Courier's* use of "human" in this context, see Buni, *Robert L. Vann of the "Pittsburgh Courier,"* 105. The *Chicago Defender* used "human" in a similar context. See "Our Responsibilities," *Chicago Defender,* Apr. 4, 1918, p. 16. For other references to the provocations directed at the soldiers, see *Chicago Broad Ax,* Sept. 1, 1917, p. 1; *Cleveland Gazette,* Sept. 8, 1917, pp. 1, 2; and "That Texas Affair," *Cleveland Advocate,* Sept. 1, 1917, p. 6.

123. "The Trouble at Houston," *Norfolk Journal and Guide,* Sept. 1, 1917, p. 4; "The Trouble at Houston, Tex.," *Richmond Planet,* Sept. 1, 1917, p. 4; "Six More Die," ibid., Sept. 14, 1918, p. 4.

124. On tensions between black soldiers and civilians, see Barbeau and Henri, *Unknown Soldiers,* 38–42.

125. "In the Enemy's Camp," *Chicago Defender,* Sept. 1, 1917, [p. 12].

126. Buni, *Robert L. Vann of the "Pittsburgh Courier,"* 105.

127. "Five More Sentenced to Die," *Cleveland Gazette,* Jan. 1, 1918, p. 2.

128. "Fix the Responsibility," *New York Age,* Aug. 30, 1917, p. 4.

129. *Savannah Tribune,* Oct. 6, 1917, p. 4; Dec. 1, 1917, p. 4.

130. "The Firing Line," *Chicago Defender,* Apr. 6, 1918, p. 16; cartoon, ibid., Mar. 31, 1917, p. 10.

131. Wilson, quoted in James Weldon Johnson, *Along This Way: The Autobiography of James Weldon Johnson* (New York: Viking Press, 1933), 324.

132. Zangrando, *NAACP Crusade against Lynching,* 38.

133. Ibid., 42–45.

134. "Tennessee's Bi-Monthly Lynching," *Baltimore Afro-American,* May 3, 1918,

p. 4; "Lynching," ibid., May 31, 1917, p. 4. See also James W. Johnson, "For Executive Clemency," *New York Age,* Apr. 6, 1918, p. 4.

135. House Committee on the Judiciary, *To Protect Citizens of the United States against Lynching in Default of Protection by the States,* 65th Cong., 2d sess., 1918, H.R. 11279, pp. 3–14.

136. *Nashville Globe,* May 17, 1918, quoted in Jones, "Black Community, Politics, and Race Relations in the 'Iris City,' " 186.

137. "What the Parade Showed," *New York Age,* Aug. 2, 1917, p. 4.

138. "To Introduce a Bill to Prevent Lynching," ibid., Sept. 6, 1917, p. 1.

139. "Mr. Scott's Appointment," ibid., Oct. 11, 1917, p. 4.

140. Jones, "Black Community, Politics, and Race Relations in the 'Iris City,' " 194.

141. Untitled editorial and "America's Changing Heart," *Savannah Tribune,* Mar. 2, 1918, p. 4.

142. "A Change for the Better," *Richmond Planet,* Nov. 3, 1917, p. 4.

143. "A Common Ground," *Chicago Defender,* July 6, 1918, p. 16.

144. "Humanity for the Negro," *Cleveland Gazette,* Apr. 6, 1918, p. 2.

145. "Law and Order League against Lynching," *Baltimore Afro-American,* May 3, 1918, p. 1; "Seeing the Light Slowly," ibid., June 28, 1918, p. 4; "Lynching," ibid., July 5, 1918, p. 4.

146. "Anti-Lynching Movement," *New York Age,* June 15, 1918, p. 4; James W. Johnson, "Reactionary Journalism," ibid., June 15, 1918, p. 4.

147. Zangrando, *NAACP Crusade against Lynching,* 34; " 'The Infamous Film' Worse Than Poison Gas!," *Cleveland Gazette,* Oct. 5, 1918, p. 1; untitled editorial, *Richmond Planet,* Aug. 3, 1917, p. 4.

148. "No Peace Talks for Colored Folks," *Richmond Planet,* Oct. 13, 1917, p. 4.

CHAPTER FOUR

1. Hay T. Thornton to Solicitor, U.S. Post Office, Aug. 3, 1917, in Theodore Kornweibel Jr., ed., *Federal Surveillance of Afro-Americans, 1917–1925: The First World War, the Red Scare, and the Garvey Movement* (Frederick, Md.: University Publications of America, 1986, microfilm), reel 13, frame 744; Uzziah Miner, "American Negro and World Democracy," *Richmond Planet,* Aug. 4, 1917, p. 1.

2. John Mitchell Jr. to Albert S. Burleson, Aug. 6, 1917, in Kornweibel, *Federal Surveillance of Afro-Americans,* reel 13, frames 745–46; John Mitchell Jr. to Thomas S. Martin, Aug. 6, 1917, in ibid., frames 747–48; Thomas S. Martin to Albert S. Burleson, Aug. 6, 1917, in ibid., frame 749; "The *Planet* Is Held Up by the Post Office Authorities Here," *Richmond Planet,* Aug. 11, 1917, p. 1.

3. "Throttling the *Planet,*" *Richmond Planet,* Aug. 11, 1918, p. 4; "Suppression of Sedition and Suppression of Criticism," ibid., Oct. 20, 1917, p. 4; "The Right of Free Speech," *Norfolk Journal and Guide,* Aug. 18, 1917, p. 4.

4. David M. Kennedy, *Over Here: The First World War and American Society* (New

York: Oxford University Press, 1980), 80; H. C. Peterson and Gilbert C. Fite, *Opponents of War, 1917–1918* (Madison: University of Wisconsin Press, 1957), 16, 95–99; O. A. Hilton, "Public Opinion and Civil Liberties in Wartime, 1917–1919," *Southwestern Social Science Quarterly* 28 (Dec. 1947): 201–24, and "Freedom of the Press in Wartime, 1917–1919," ibid. 28 (Mar. 1948): 346–61; Frederick C. Luebke, *Bonds of Loyalty: German-Americans and World War I* (Dekalb: Northern Illinois University Press, 1974), 241, 271, 319.

5. *Baltimore Afro-American,* Apr. 14, 1917, p. 4; *Cleveland Gazette,* Dec. 15, 1917, p. 4; untitled editorial, *Richmond Planet,* Aug. 4, 1917, p. 4.

6. See Willard Utley, report on *San Antonio Inquirer,* Nov. 27, 1917, in Kornweibel, *Federal Surveillance of Afro-Americans,* reel 9, frames 903–4, and B. C. Baldwin, report on *San Antonio Inquirer,* Nov. 25, 1917, in ibid., frame 902.

7. See *Messenger,* Nov. 1911, pp. 7, 9, 10, 11, 20, 31.

8. Theodore Kornweibel Jr., *"Seeing Red": Federal Campaigns against Black Militancy, 1919–1925* (Bloomington: Indiana University Press, 1998), 75–78, 81; Jervis Anderson, *A. Philip Randolph: A Biographical Portrait* (New York: Harcourt Brace Jovanovich, 1972), 104–9; Mark Ellis, "America's Black Press, 1914–18," *History Today* 41 (Sept. 1991): 20–27.

9. W. E. B. Du Bois to F. E. Young, Aug. 8, 1918, in W. E. B. Du Bois Papers, W. E. B. Du Bois Library, University of Massachusetts, Amherst, Massachusetts.

10. "Quotations from Several Issues of the *Crisis,*" in Kornweibel, *Federal Surveillance of Afro-Americans,* reel 19, frames 667–78; Harry A. Taylor, "Memorandum for Colonel Coxe," July 19, 1918, in ibid., frame 679.

11. Howell B. Jackson, " 'Crisis,' Possible Pro-German Publication," May 10, 1918, in ibid., frame 640; Albert Neunhoffer to A. Bruce Bielaski, May 10, 1918, in ibid., reel 9, frame 111. See also James L. Bruff, "Memorandum re. Officers and Directors of the National Association for the Advancement of Colored People," July 13, 1918, p. 3, in ibid., reel 19, frames 802–4.

12. A. Bruce Bielaski to Charles DeWoody, June 4, 1918, in ibid., reel 19, frame 646.

13. Charles H. Studin to W. E. B. Du Bois, May 1, 1918, Du Bois Papers.

14. Marlborough Churchill to Charles H. Studin, June 3, 1918, in Kornweibel, *Federal Surveillance of Afro-Americans,* reel 9, frame 636; minutes, NAACP Board of Directors meeting, June 10, 1918, Du Bois Papers.

15. Charles H. Studin to Marlborough Churchill, June 12, 1918, in Kornweibel, *Federal Surveillance of Afro-Americans,* reel 9, frame 637.

16. W. E. B. Du Bois, "Close Ranks," *Crisis* 16 (July 1918): 111.

17. Joel E. Spingarn to Marlborough Churchill, July 6, 1918, in Kornweibel, *Federal Surveillance of Afro-Americans,* reel 9, frame 767.

18. For the interpretation that Du Bois wrote "Close Ranks" as a condition for receiving a commission as captain in the army, see Mark Ellis, " 'Closing Ranks' and 'Seeking Honors': W. E. B. Du Bois in World War I," *Journal of American History* 79 (June 1992): 96–124. For the opposing view that "Close Ranks" was in keeping with Du Bois's accommodationist approach

to the war and that he would not have required a quid pro quo to write it, see William Jordan, "'The Damnable Dilemma': African-American Accommodation and Protest during World War I," ibid. 81 (Mar. 1995): 1562–83. Ellis's rebuttal is in Mark Ellis, "W. E. B. Du Bois and the Formation of Black Opinion in World War I: A Commentary on 'The Damnable Dilemma,'" ibid., 1584–90.

19. The act of participating in this dialogue likely modified the view of the censors. According to Hans-Georg Gadamer, "One is required to take account of the positions of others in discussing an issue or subject-matter with them. Here, even if one holds to one's initial point of view one has nevertheless to deal with the objections, considerations and counter-examples that others introduce. In the end, whether one changes one's position or maintains it, the view that results is more developed than the one with which one began" (Georgia Warnke, *Gadamer: Hermeneutics, Tradition, and Reason* [Stanford, Calif.: Stanford University Press, 1987], 169–70).

20. L. How to U.S. Assistant District Attorney, June 27, 1918, in Kornweibel, *Federal Surveillance of Afro-Americans*, reel 13, frame 1158.

21. L. How to U.S. Assistant District Attorney, May 16, 1918, in ibid., frames 1132–33.

22. Kornweibel, *"Seeing Red,"* 50.

23. Robert A. Bowen to U.S. Assistant District Attorney, June 13, 1918, in Kornweibel, *Federal Surveillance of Afro-Americans*, reel 13, frame 1136; [L. How] to U.S. Assistant District Attorney, Aug. 22, 1918, in ibid., frames 1142–43.

24. Robert A. Bowen to William H. Lamar, July 18, 1918, in ibid., frame 1141; Robert A. Bowen to U.S. Assistant District Attorney, June 6, 1918, in ibid., frame 1135.

25. L. How to U.S. District Attorney, May 2, 1918, in ibid., frames 1150–51.

26. L. How to U.S. Assistant District Attorney, June 13, 1918, in ibid., frame 1155.

27. L. How to U.S. Assistant District Attorney, Oct. 17, 1918, in ibid., frame 1145; L. How to U.S. District Attorney, May 2, 1918, in ibid., frame 1130.

28. Letter to U.S. Assistant District Attorney, Aug. 22, 1918, in ibid., frame 1142.

29. Robert A. Bowen to U.S. Assistant District Attorney, June 13, 1918, in ibid., frame 1136. See also L. How to U.S. Assistant District Attorney, June 13, Aug. 15, 1918, in ibid., frames 1155, 1163.

30. L. How to U.S. Assistant District Attorney, July 4, 1918, in ibid., frame 1159. The same censor made a similar criticism of the *New York Age* on the same date. See ibid., frames 1138–39. See also L. How to U.S. Assistant District Attorney, May 23, 1918, in ibid., frame 1154. How believed the *Age's* mention of the navy's discriminatory treatment of blacks "would tend directly to discourage Negroes from enlisting in the Navy" and was therefore objectionable (L. How to U.S. Assistant District Attorney, Mar. 22, 1918, in ibid., frame 1125).

31. *New York News,* Aug. 14, 1918, p. 8, quoted in W. S. to J. E. E., Aug. 28, 1918, in ibid., frame 1166; Robert A. Bowen to J. Bond Smith, Jan. 2, 1919, in ibid., frame 1175. On the threat of militant returning black soldiers, see L. How to U.S. Assistant District Attorney, Mar. 28, 1918, in ibid., frame 1148.

32. See L. How to U.S. Assistant District Attorney, June 13, Oct. 17, Mar. 28, Apr. 25, 1918, in ibid., frames 1155, 1145, 1148–49, 1129; Robert A. Bowen to U.S. Assistant District Attorney, June 13, 1918, in ibid., frame 1136; L. How to U.S. Assistant District Attorney, July 26, May 16, 23, Aug. 29, 1918, in ibid., frames 1160–61, 1132–33, 1154, 1167.

33. How was referring to the practice of "race angling," in which black papers emphasized the racial aspects of the news by paying close attention to the activities of African Americans.

34. L. How to U.S. Assistant District Attorney, June 20, 1918, in ibid., frames 1156–57.

35. L. How to U.S. Assistant District Attorney, June 13, 1918, in ibid., frame 1155.

36. L. How to U.S. Assistant District Attorney, Apr. 25, 1918, in ibid., frame 1129. See also L. How to U.S. Assistant District Attorney, May 30, 1918, in ibid., frame 1134.

37. L. How to U.S. Assistant District Attorney, July 4, 1918, in ibid., frame 1138.

38. Robert A. Bowen to William H. Lamar, July 18, 1918, in ibid., frame 1141.

39. James W. Johnson, "Faith and Works," *New York Age,* Mar. 23, 1918, p. 4; L. How to U.S. Assistant District Attorney, Mar. 22, 1918, in Kornweibel, *Federal Surveillance of Afro-Americans,* reel 13, frame 1125.

40. Roy F. Britton to Chief, Military Intelligence Branch, May 6, 1918, in Kornweibel, *Federal Surveillance of Afro-Americans,* reel 19, frame 684. See also Roy F. Britton to E. J. Brennan, May 27, 1918, in ibid., frame 697.

41. Roy F. Britton to Chief, Military Intelligence Branch, June 25, 1918, in ibid., frame 700.

42. W. H. Loving to Chief, Military Intelligence Branch, May 10, 1918, in ibid., frame 611.

43. R. H. Van Deman to W. H. Loving, May 3, 1918, in ibid., frame 617.

44. M. E. Nash to Solicitor, U.S. Post Office, June 22, 1918, in ibid., reel 13, frame 769. On the threat to southern agriculture, see E. J. Kerwin to A. Bruce Bielaski, May 2, 1918, in ibid., reel 9, frames 70–71.

45. See Denison, Texas, Postmaster to Solicitor, U.S. Post Office, June 8, 1918, in ibid., reel 13, frame 755; F. B. Zock, Justice Department report, Dec. 28, 1917, in ibid., reel 9, frames 57–58; D. Whipple to A. M. Briggs, July 5, 1917, in ibid., frame 49; E. J. Kerwin to A. Bruce Bielaski, May 2, 1918, in ibid., frames 70–71; F. Pendleton, Justice Department report, [Apr. 1917], in ibid., frame 50; Edward S. Chestalb, Justice Department report, Apr. 24, 1917, in ibid., frame 39; Bolton Smith to W. D. Kyser, Jan. 14, 1918, in ibid., reel 13, frame 764; T. M. Diskin to Chief Inspector, U.S. Post Office, Jan. 29, 1918, in ibid., frame 766; Justice Department report, Mo-

bile, Alabama, Sept. 14, 1918, in ibid., reel 9, frame 66; and Charles F. Lorenzen to A. Bruce Bielaski, Oct. 3, 1918, in ibid., frame 67.

46. Denison, Texas, Postmaster to Solicitor, U.S. Post Office, June 8, 1918, in ibid., reel 13, frame 755. On other southerners who accused the *Chicago Defender* of being part of a German conspiracy, see memorandum on *Chicago Defender*, Apr. 24, 1917, in ibid., reel 9, frame 39; D. Whipple to A. M. Briggs, July 5, 1917, in ibid., frame 49; and memorandum on German activities, Tucson, Arizona, Dec. 28, 1917, in ibid., frames 57–58.

47. Post Office Department report on *Chicago Defender*, July 6, 1918, in ibid., reel 13, frame 771.

48. R. H. Van Deman to W. H. Loving, May 3, 1918, in ibid., reel 19, frame 617. On Van Deman's position in the military, see Kornweibel, *"Seeing Red,"* 10.

49. C. E. B. to editor, *Chicago Defender*, June 13, 1918, in Kornweibel, *Federal Surveillance of Afro-Americans*, reel 13, frames 756–57.

50. Justice Department report, Dec. 22, 1917, in ibid., reel 9, frames 55–56.

51. Bolton Smith to W. D. Kyser, Jan. 14, 1918, in ibid., reel 13, frame 764.

52. John Sharp Williams to Albert S. Burleson, June 22, 1918, in ibid., frame 768.

53. J. E. Hawkins, memorandum on *Chicago Defender*, Apr. 15, 1917, in ibid., reel 9, frame 41.

54. C. E. B. [to Robert S. Abbott], June 13, 1918, in ibid., reel 13, frames 756–57.

55. W. H. Loving to Chief, Military Intelligence Branch, May 10, 1918, in ibid., reel 19, frame 611.

56. Robert S. Abbott to W. H. Loving, May 11, 1918, in ibid., frame 612.

57. W. H. Loving to J. E. Mitchell, May 28, 1918, in ibid., frames 687–88.

58. Joel E. Spingarn, memorandum to Marlborough Churchill, June 22, 1918, in ibid., frames 733–35.

59. It is not clear how many newspapermen attended the meeting. A list compiled by the government includes forty African Americans who did not represent the government. Of these, twenty-seven were associated with black publications. The *Cleveland Gazette* puts the number of newspapermen at "thirty or forty." Du Bois states that "thirty-one representatives of the Negro press" endorsed a statement issued by the conference. A photograph of the conference shows fifty-one people, including two French and two American military officers and an unidentified white man. See "Conference of Colored Editors: List of Conferees," June 19–21, 1918, in ibid., frames 739–41; "Members of the Great Race Conference," *Cleveland Gazette*, July 6, 1918, p. 1; and "Conference of Colored Editors: Address to the Committee on Public Information," June 21, 1918, in Kornweibel, *Federal Surveillance of Afro-Americans*, reel 19, frames 736–38.

60. Newton D. Baker to Woodrow Wilson, July 1, 1918, in Woodrow Wilson, *The Papers of Woodrow Wilson*, ed. Arthur S. Link (Princeton: Princeton University Press, 1985), 48:475–76; Joel E. Spingarn, memorandum to Marlborough Churchill, in Kornweibel, *Federal Surveillance of Afro-Americans*, reel 19, frames 733–35.

61. "Excerpts from Addresses at Colored Liberty Congress," [July 1, 1918], in Kornweibel, *Federal Surveillance of Afro-Americans,* reel 19, frames 720–21.

62. "The Two Washington Conferences," *Cleveland Gazette,* Aug. 3, 1918, p. 2.

63. Newton D. Baker to Woodrow Wilson, July 1, 1918, in Wilson, *Papers,* 48: 475–76; J. E. Spingarn, "Report on Conference of Colored Editors," June 22, 1918, in Kornweibel, *Federal Surveillance of Afro-Americans,* reel 19, frame 734·

64. "Conference of Colored Editors: Address to the Committee on Public Information," June 21, 1918, in ibid., frames 736–38.

65. Marlborough Churchill, memorandum for Chief of Staff, n.d., in ibid., frame 732.

66. Bill of Particulars, Conference of Editors, June 19–21, 1918, in ibid., frame 742·

67. George Creel to Woodrow Wilson, June 17, 1918, in Wilson, *Papers,* 48: 341–42.

68. Woodrow Wilson to George Creel, June 18, 1918, in ibid., 346.

69. George Creel to Woodrow Wilson, July 5, 1918, and Emmett J. Scott to Woodrow Wilson, June 26, 1918, in ibid., 528–30.

70. Newton D. Baker to Woodrow Wilson, July 1, 14, 1918, in ibid., 475–76, 607.

71. See, for example, "Well, It Has Happened," *Cleveland Gazette,* July 6, 1918, p. 2.

72. Ben Baker, "Must All Work Together to Get Somewhere," *Chicago Defender,* July 6, 1918, p. 16. On the same page, an editorial entitled "A Common Ground" predicted that the experience of fighting in a common struggle for democracy would mend the rifts between classes and races: "Strange indeed it will be if a new society does not emerge from the democratic spirit that is being evidenced more and more as the war goes on. Worth and not birth will determine one's standing."

73. "Red Cross Nurses," *Baltimore Afro-American,* July 26, 1918, p. 4; "New Draft Age Limit," ibid., July 26, 1918, p. 4; "Good Results Already Evident from Conference of Editors," ibid., Aug. 2, 1918, p. 1. See also untitled editorial, *Cleveland Gazette,* July 27, 1918, p. 2. Young was ordered back into active military service just as the war ended. See *Savannah Tribune,* Nov. 16, 1918, p. 1.

74. In an editorial on Wilson's lynching speech, the *New York Times* called the lynching of Prager "the most conspicuous example of the mob mind." A news report on the speech asserted that although Wilson did not mention the lynchings of southern blacks, "it is known that he included them in his characterization of mob spirit." See "Mr. Wilson on the Mob Spirit," *New York Times,* July 27, 1918, p. 8, and "President Demands That Lynchings End," ibid., July 27, 1918, p. 7. William B. Hale had urged Wilson shortly after the Prager lynching to form a special commission to safeguard the lives of Americans of Eastern European heritage. Wilson promised to give the matter serious attention. See William B. Hale to Woodrow Wilson, Apr. 6, 1918, in Wilson, *Papers,* 47:275–76, 276 (n. 4). For the view that

Wilson's statement was a response—albeit a late one—to the Prager lynching, see Luebke, *Bonds of Loyalty*, 13–14. For an account that emphasizes the fact that Wilson's statement contained no reference to race, see Jane Lang Scheiber and Harry N. Scheiber, "The Wilson Administration and the Wartime Mobilization of Black Americans, 1917–18," *Labor History* 10 (Summer 1967): 433–58. Robert C. Hilderbrand, in *Power and the People: Executive Management of Public Opinion in Foreign Affairs, 1897–1921* (Chapel Hill: University of North Carolina Press, 1981), 163, claims the statement was aimed at winning the support of blacks and emphasizes the role of Committee on Public Information chairman George Creel in influencing Wilson.

75. Woodrow Wilson, "A Statement to the American People," [July 26, 1918], in Wilson, *Papers*, 49:97–98.

76. Woodrow Wilson to Emmett J. Scott, July 31, 1918, in ibid., 139.

77. Woodrow Wilson to George Foster Peabody, Aug. 7, 1918, in ibid., 204.

78. Woodrow Wilson, statement, Aug. 31, 1918, in ibid., 401.

79. "Six More Die," *Richmond Planet*, Sept. 14, 1918, p. 4.

80. National Race Congress Memorial, Oct. 1, 1918, in Wilson, *Papers*, 51:191–93; "Remarks to a Group of American Blacks," Oct. 1, 1918, in ibid., 168; "Colored Men Hold a Conference with President," *Richmond Planet*, Oct. 12, 1918, p. 1.

81. "Good Results Already Evident from Conference of Editors," *Baltimore Afro-American*, Aug. 2, 1918, p. 1; Reverend William H. Weaver, "Weekly Views and Comments," ibid., Aug. 9, 1918, p. 4.

82. "Mob Rule Helps Kaiser," *Cleveland Gazette*, Aug. 3, 1918, p. 1; "Great Anti-Lynch-Murder Plea," ibid., Aug. 3, 1918, p. 2.

83. Andy Dawson, "We Second the Motion," *Chicago Defender*, July 6, 1918, p. 1.

84. A. N. Fields, "President Wilson against Mob Rule," ibid., Aug. 3, 1918, p. 1. See also "Editors' Conference Yields Big Results," ibid., Aug. 3, 1918, p. 1, and "Our President Has Spoken," ibid., Aug. 3, 1918, p. 16.

85. "The President Speaks," *New York Age*, Aug. 3, 1918, p. 4.

86. James W. Johnson, "The President on Mob Violence," ibid., Aug. 10, 1918, p. 4. Johnson noted that when he led a delegation to the White House in February to plead for clemency for some of the convicted Houston soldiers, he asked Wilson to speak out against lynching. Although Wilson at first "demurred," he finally agreed that "he would 'seek an opportunity' to say something." Johnson believed the July 26 statement was the fulfillment of that pledge. See James Weldon Johnson, *Along This Way: The Autobiography of James Weldon Johnson* (New York: Viking Press, 1933), 324–25.

87. John Mitchell credited Scott and Moton for the president's statement rather than the black press. See "President Wilson's Deliverances," *Richmond Planet*, Aug. 3, 1917, p. 4. On Moton's request after the murder of Mary Turner and after the editors' conference that Wilson make a statement condemning lynching, see Robert Russa Moton to Woodrow Wilson, June 15, 24, 1918, in Wilson, *Papers*, 48:323–24, 416. See also Robert Russa Moton to Woodrow Wilson, July 27, 1918, in ibid., 49:113–14, and

Woodrow Wilson to Robert Russa Moton, June 18, Aug. 2, 1918, in ibid., 48:346, 49:166.

88. "The President's Appeal," *St. Louis Argus*, Aug. 2, 1918, in Kornweibel, *Federal Surveillance of Afro-Americans*, reel 19, frame 704.

89. James W. Johnson, "The First Six Months," *New York Age*, July 13, 1918, p. 4. On Bolton Smith, see Lester C. Lamon, *Black Tennesseans, 1900–1930* (Knoxville: University of Tennessee Press, 1977), 242.

90. "Seeing the Light Slowly," *Baltimore Afro-American*, June 28, 1918, p. 4. See also Reverend William H. Weaver, "Weekly Views and Comments," ibid.; "Lynching," ibid., July 5, 1918, p. 4; and "Anti-Lynching Movement," *New York Age*, June 22, 1918, p. 4. On the University Commission on Southern Race Relations, see James Dillard to Woodrow Wilson, June 28, 1918, in Wilson, *Papers*, 48:462–63.

91. A. N. Fields, "President Wilson against Mob Rule," *Chicago Defender*, Aug. 3, 1918, p. 1.

92. James W. Johnson, "The President on Mob Violence," *New York Age*, Aug. 210, 1918, p. 4.

93. Nan Elizabeth Woodruff, "African-American Struggles for Citizenship in the Arkansas and Mississippi Deltas in the Age of Jim Crow," *Radical History Review* 55 (Winter 1993): 33–51.

94. "Our President Has Spoken," *Chicago Defender*, Aug. 3, 1918, p. 16.

95. "Now Is the Accepted Time," *Richmond Planet*, July 27, 1918, p. 4.

96. "Contend While You Wait!," *Cleveland Gazette*, Aug. 3, 1918, p. 2.

97. Moton corresponded with Wilson on lynching a month before the president's statement. See Robert Russa Moton to Woodrow Wilson, June 15, 1918, in Wilson, *Papers*, 48:323–24.

98. Arthur E. Barbeau and Florette Henri, *The Unknown Soldiers: Black American Troops in World War I* (Philadelphia: Temple University Press, 1974), 71–88.

99. On black resistance to the war, see Theodore Kornweibel Jr., "Apathy and Dissent: Black America's Negative Responses to World War I," *South Atlantic Quarterly* 80 (Summer 1981): 322–38. On black militancy during the war, see Stephen A. Reich, "Soldiers of Democracy: Black Texans and the Fight for Citizenship, 1917–1921," *Journal of American History* 82 (Mar. 1996): 1478–1504.

100. Particulars 10 and 11 had to do with wartime press coverage, and the federal government relinquished control of the railroads before abolishing Jim Crow on them.

101. William L. Ziglar, "The Decline of Lynching in America," *International Social Science Review* 63 (Winter 1988): 14–25. On the interracial commission, see Jacquelyn Dowd Hall, *Revolt against Chivalry: Jessie Daniel Ames and the Women's Campaign against Lynching* (New York: Columbia University Press, 1979), 60–65; George Brown Tindall, *The Emergence of the New South, 1913–1945* (Baton Rouge: Louisiana State University Press, 1967), 177–83; and Morton Sosna, *In Search of the Silent South: Southern Liberals and the Race Issue* (New York: Columbia University Press, 1977), 20–41.

1. Bolton Smith, "The Negro in War-Time," *Public,* Aug. 31, 1918, pp. 1110–13. On Smith, see Bolton Smith, "A Philosophy of Race Relations," *Congressional Record,* 66th Cong., 2d sess., 1919, vol. 59, pt. 1:963–69, and *The National Cyclopaedia of American Biography* (New York: James T. White, 1930), s.v. "Smith, Bolton," A:381–82.

2. James Weldon Johnson, "The Negro in Wartime," *Public,* Sept. 21, 1918, pp. 1218–19.

3. "From the Diary of Dr. Grayson," Mar. 10, 1919, in Woodrow Wilson, *The Papers of Woodrow Wilson,* ed. Arthur Link (Princeton: Princeton University Press, 1986), 55:471.

4. "Unrest among the Negroes," Oct. 7, 1919, in Theodore Kornweibel Jr., ed., *Federal Surveillance of Afro-Americans, 1917–1925: The First World War, the Red Scare, and the Garvey Movement* (Frederick, Md.: University Publications of America, 1986, microfilm), reel 13, frames 982–1003. On authorship of the document, see Theodore Kornweibel Jr., *"Seeing Red": Federal Campaigns against Black Militancy, 1919–1925* (Bloomington: Indiana University Press, 1998), 72.

5. "Returning Soldiers," *Crisis* 18 (May 1919): 13–14; Kornweibel, *"Seeing Red,"* 36–75; Bowen and Lamar, quoted in ibid., 57.

6. Robert A. Bowen, "Radicalism and Sedition among the Negroes as Reflected in Their Publications," July 2, 1919, in Kornweibel, *Federal Surveillance of Afro-Americans,* reel 13, frames 806–11.

7. Quoted in Chicago Commission on Race Relations, *The Negro in Chicago: A Study of Race Relations and a Race Riot* (Chicago: University of Chicago Press, 1922), 476–77; Patrick S. Washburn, *A Question of Sedition: The Federal Government's Investigation of the Black Press during World War II* (New York: Oxford University Press, 1986), 27.

8. *Congressional Record,* 66th Cong., 1st sess., 1919, vol. 58, pt. 5:4302–5. See also "Blames Race Riots on Negro Leaders," *New York Times,* Aug. 26, 1919, p. 14.

9. William M. Tuttle Jr., "Violence in a 'Heathen' Land: The Longview Race Riot of 1919," *Phylon* 33 (Winter 1972): 324–33; "The Riot at Longview, Texas," *Crisis* 18 (Oct. 1919): 297–98; Arthur I. Waskow, *From Race Riot to Sit-in, 1919 and the 1960s: A Study in the Connections between Conflict and Violence* (Garden City, N.Y.: Doubleday, 1966), 16–20. Their statement also condemned the white mob for burning blacks' homes.

10. Resolution, Atlanta, Georgia, Apr. 1, 1920, in Kornweibel, *Federal Surveillance of Afro-Americans,* reel 13, frame 905. The individual listed as secretary of this meeting also wrote to the U.S. Post Office asking that it ban the *Chicago Defender,* the *New York Age,* the *Indianapolis Freeman,* the *Boston Guardian,* and the *Crisis* from the mails. See W. H. Rossman to William H. Lamar, June 28, 1919, in ibid., frame 783.

11. On Pine Bluff, see A. Smith to Postmaster General, Feb. 23, 1920, in ibid., frames 975–76. On Monticello, see anonymous to Solicitor, U.S. Post

Office, Aug. 7, 1919, in ibid., frame 868. On Helena, see Committee of Seven in Charge [of the Race Trouble in This County] to W. L. Jarman, Oct. 9, 1919, in ibid., frame 889. On Greenville, see John H. Small to William H. Lamar, Aug. 12, 1919, in ibid., frame 1034. On Macon, see Aucil Milarn to First Assistant Postmaster, Aug. 2, 1919, in ibid., frame 866. On Marks, see Thirza I. Clarke to Pat Harrison, Aug. 7, 1919, in ibid., frame 869. On Baldwin, see John B. Sewell to [U.S. Postmaster], Apr. 27, 1920, in ibid., frame 909.

12. Special Agent in Charge to Chief, Bureau of Investigation, July 14, 1919, in ibid., reel 9, frame 76.

13. William D. Upshaw to J. C. Koons, July 2, 1919, in ibid., reel 13, frame 852.

14. Roi Ottley, *The Lonely Warrior: The Life and Times of Robert S. Abbott* (Chicago: Henry Regnery, 1955), 144–46; Tuttle, "Violence in a 'Heathen' Land," 326; Chicago Commission on Race Relations, *Negro in Chicago*, 564; *New York Age*, Apr. 5, 1919, p. 4. The Athens lynching was reported in *Philadelphia American*, Feb. 19, 1921. See also Frederick G. Detweiler, *The Negro Press in the United States* (Chicago: University of Chicago Press, 1922), 20.

15. Charles H. Brough to Albert S. Burleson, Oct. 17, 1919, in Kornweibel, *Federal Surveillance of Afro-Americans*, reel 13, frames 894–95; Charles H. Brough to H. L. Donnelly, Nov. 4, 1919, in ibid., frames 901–2; Walter F. White, "Expose Arkansas Peonage System," *Chicago Defender*, Nov. 1, 1919, p. 1. On the Phillips County riot, see Richard C. Cortner, *A Mob Intent on Death: The NAACP and the Arkansas Riot Cases* (Middletown, Conn.: Wesleyan University Press, 1988), 5–47; William M. Tuttle Jr., *Race Riot: Chicago in the Red Summer of 1919* (New York: Atheneum, 1970), 246–48; Waskow, *From Race Riot to Sit-in*, 121–42; Nan Elizabeth Woodruff, "African-American Struggles for Citizenship in the Arkansas and Mississippi Deltas in the Age of Jim Crow," *Radical History Review* 55 (Winter 1993): 33–51; and Steven A. Reich, "Soldiers of Democracy: Black Texans and the Fight for Citizenship, 1917–1921," *Journal of American History* 82 (Mar. 1996): 1478–1504.

16. On estimates of the number of deaths, see Cortner, *Mob Intent on Death*, 30.

17. Detweiler, *Negro Press in the United States*, 21.

18. Robert Kerlin, *The Voice of the Negro, 1919* (New York: E. P. Dutton, 1920), x–xi; "White Professor Writes Book — *Voice of the Negro*," *Chicago Broad Ax*, Feb. 14, 1920. Academic interest in African Americans went beyond the black press. Black historian Carter Woodson published an essay in the July 1919 *Journal of Negro History* in which he said that an " 'enlightened class' of southern whites was taking an interest in black history: 'seeing that a better understanding of the races is now necessary to maintain that conservatism to prevent this country from being torn asunder by Socialism and Bolshevism, they are now making an effort to effect a closer relation between . . . blacks and whites by making an intensive study of the Negro' " (quoted in Clarence E. Walker, "The American Negro as Historical Outsider, 1836–1935," *Canadian Review of American Studies* 17 [Summer 1986]: 148.

19. Chicago Commission on Race Relations, *Negro in Chicago*, 556–57, 650–51.

20. Clayton R. Lusk, Chair, Joint Committee Investigating Seditious Activities, New York State Legislature, "Propaganda among the Negroes," in *Revolutionary Radicalism*, Apr. 24, 1920, pp. 1476–1520; Robert K. Murray, *Red Scare: A Study in National Hysteria, 1919–1920* (Minneapolis: University of Minnesota Press, 1955), 101–2.

21. Quoted in *New York Age*, Aug. 9, 1919, p. 4.

22. "Soldiers Try to Terrorize Colored Folk; *Afro* Agent Held Up in Washington," *Baltimore Afro-American*, July 25, 1919, pp. 1, 4.

23. Quoted in Chicago Commission on Race Relations, *Negro in Chicago*, 556. For a black response to Taft, see "Plea for Education of the White Man," *New York Age*, Aug. 23, 1919, p. 4.

24. "The Mob!: A Warning," *Cleveland Gazette*, Aug. 2, 1919, p. 2; "Chief of Police Smith Refuses to Be 'Used' by a 'Cracker' Reporter," ibid., Aug. 16, 1919, p. 4.

25. *New York Age*, Oct. 18, 1919, p. 4.

26. "Ohio Afro-American Heroes of the Old Ninth Battalion," *Cleveland Gazette*, Mar. 1, 1919, p. 1.

27. "Mistakes That Will Continually Happen," *Chicago Defender*, July 5, 1919, p. 20.

28. Chicago Commission on Race Relations, *Negro in Chicago*, 565.

29. Nahum Daniel Brascher, "Getting America Told," *Chicago Defender*, June 7, 1919, p. 20.

30. On the social forces leading to the creation of the New Negro, see Albert Lee Kreiling, "The Making of Racial Identities in the Black Press: A Cultural Analysis of Race Journalism in Chicago, 1878–1929" (Ph.D. diss., University of Illinois at Urbana, 1973), 387ff.; Leroi Jones, *Blues People: Negro Music in White America* (New York: William Morrow, 1963), chap. 8; Nathan I. Huggins, *Harlem Renaissance* (London: Oxford University Press, 1971), chap. 2; Tuttle, *Race Riot*, 208–22; Gerald Early, "Introduction," in *My Soul's High Song: The Collected Writings of Countee Cullen, Voice of the Harlem Renaissance*, ed. Gerald Early (New York: Anchor Books, 1991), 1–73; and Reich, "Soldiers of Democracy," 1503.

31. Most historical accounts of the connection between the black press and the New Negro see the black press as a manifestation, a cause, or an accurate reflection of the New Negro. For accounts that treat the black press as a manifestation of the New Negro or an institution that both reflected and encouraged the phenomenon, see Kreiling, "Making of Racial Identities in the Black Press," chap. 9; Theodore G. Vincent, "Preface," in *Voices of a Black Nation: Political Journalism in the Harlem Renaissance* (San Francisco: Ramparts Press, 1973), 19–38; and Tuttle, *Race Riot*, 208–26. For accounts that are primarily interested in how promoters of the New Negro movement sought to create a new image of blacks in the popular imagination, see Henry Louis Gates Jr., "The Trope of a New Negro and the Reconstruction of the Image of the Black," *Representations* 24 (Fall 1988): 129–55;

Houston A. Baker Jr., "Modernism and the Harlem Renaissance," in *Modernist Culture in America*, ed. Daniel Joseph Singal (Belmont, Calif.: Wadsworth, 1991), 107–25; and Early, "Introduction."

32. "New York 15th Has Fine Record," *Baltimore Afro-American*, Feb. 14, 1919, p. 1. See also W. S. Braddan, "Col. Thomas A. Roberts," *Chicago Broad Ax*, June 28, 1919, p. 1; "Ohio Afro-American Heroes of the Old Ninth Battalion," *Cleveland Gazette*, Mar. 1, 1919, p. 1; Daniel T. Brantley, "Possibilities Abroad Coming after the War," *New York Age*, Nov. 2, 1918, p. 4; Lester A. Walton, "War Correspondent Lauds Negro Soldier Fighting in France," ibid., Nov. 9, 1918, p. 1; "Brave Deeds of 'Black Devils' Told," *Chicago Defender*, Feb. 22, 1919, p. 1; and *New York Age*, Jan. 11, 1919, p. 1; Feb. 8, 1919, p. 1; May 3, 1919, p. 1.

33. "Welcome, Eighth!," *Chicago Defender*, Feb. 22, 1919, p. 24.

34. Charles A. Smith, "A Word from a Soldier," *Baltimore Afro-American*, May 16, 1919, p. 4.

35. "Sergt. Webb Tells of 808th Pioneer Infantry in France," ibid., Mar. 21, 1919, p. 4.

36. Edward Lyon Jones, "A Letter from an Eye-Witness," *Cleveland Gazette*, Feb. 1, 1919, p. 2. In a similar vein, the *Baltimore Afro-American* reported that a black sergeant *did* kill two men in Georgia after they tried to "Jim Crow" him. See "Shabuta," *Baltimore Afro-American*, Dec. 27, 1918, p. 4.

37. "Negroes Determined to Get Justice in This Country," *Savannah Tribune*, Apr. 5, 1919, p. 1; "The Rights of Africans and Peoples of African Origin," ibid., June 7, 1919, p. 7; ibid., July 3, 1920, p. 4.

38. "Present Day Conditions," *Richmond Planet*, Aug. 9, 1919, p. 4.

39. William A. Byrd, "Southern American Villain Abroad," *Cleveland Gazette*, Aug. 2, 1919, p. 1.

40. James W. Johnson, "Psychology of the Present Situation," *New York Age*, Aug. 2, 1919, p. 4.

41. "Editor's Mail," *Chicago Defender*, May 3, 1919, p. 20. See also "Justice or Death Is Watchword," *Baltimore Afro-American*, Apr. 4, 1919, p. 4.

42. "The Chicago Riots," *Richmond Planet*, Aug. 9, 1919, p. 4.

43. On the death tolls, see Tuttle, *Race Riot*, 10, and "Violence in a 'Heathen' Land," 324. On riots other than those in Washington and Phillips County, see Waskow, *From Race Riot to Sit-in*, chaps. 2, 3, and 6. See also "Thirty-two Killed in Fierce Race Riot," *Savannah Tribune*, Aug. 2, 1919, p. 1; "Negroes of Washington Were Forced to Protect Themselves," *New York Age*, Aug. 2, 1919, p. 1; and "More Than a Score Killed and Hundreds Wounded since Sunday Afternoon," ibid.

44. William A. Byrd, "Hiding the Truth," *Cleveland Gazette*, Aug. 2, 1919, p. 1; "Soldiers Try to Terrorize Colored Folk," *Baltimore Afro-American*, July 25, 1919, p. 1. Ten whites and five blacks were killed in Washington, according to Waskow, *From Race Riot to Sit-in*, 27.

45. William A. Byrd, "Hiding the Truth," *Cleveland Gazette*, Aug. 2, 1919, p. 1; "Southern American Villain Abroad," ibid.; "The Mob!: A Warning," ibid., Aug. 2, 1919, p. 2.

46. "The Mob," *Savannah Tribune*, Sept. 6, 1919, p. 4.
47. "Reaping the Whirlwind," *Chicago Defender*, Aug. 2, 1919, p. 16.
48. James W. Johnson, "More of the Fruits of Lawlessness," *New York Age*, Sept. 6, 1919, p. 4.
49. "The Chicago Riots," *Richmond Planet*, Aug. 9, 1919, p. 4. On the right of blacks and whites to defend themselves, see "Congressman Byrnes' Declaration," ibid., Aug. 30, 1919, p. 4.
50. "Washington Riots," *Baltimore Afro-American*, July 25, 1919, p. 4.
51. "Trouble at Washington," *Richmond Planet*, July 26, 1919, p. 4.
52. "A Misleading Report," ibid., Dec. 27, 1918, p. 4. On Mitchell's soft-pedaling of black radicalism, see "Congressman Byrnes' Declaration," ibid., Aug. 30, 1919, p. 4.
53. "Let 'U.S.' Mean Us," *Chicago Defender*, May 3, 1919, p. 20; "Federal Agents," ibid., Dec. 13, 1919, p. 20.
54. "Mistakes That Will Continually Happen," ibid., July 5, 1919, p. 20; "That Omaha Affair," ibid., Oct. 4, 1919, p. 4.
55. "The Bolshevist Movement," *New York Age*, Feb. 8, 1919, p. 4.
56. William A. Byrd, "Our Bishops' Riot Views," *Cleveland Gazette*, Aug. 16, 1919, p. 1.
57. James W. Johnson, "Radicalism and the Negro," *New York Age*, Aug. 9, 1919, p. 4, and "Some More about Radicalism and the Negro," ibid., Sept. 6, 1919, p. 4.
58. Vincent, "Preface," 25.
59. " 'Social Equality,' " *Baltimore Afro-American*, Mar. 21, 1919, p. 4; "The Case of the Rand School," ibid., July 18, 1919, p. 4; "Listening to Socialism," ibid., Aug. 8, 1919, p. 4; "As to Radicals," ibid., Dec. 5, 1919, p. 4.
60. "Listening to Socialism," ibid., Aug. 8, 1919, p. 4; "As to Radicals," ibid., Dec. 5, 1919, p. 4.
61. "Stifling Liberty!," *Chicago Defender*, May 15, 1920, p. 16.
62. "The Mob!: A Warning," *Cleveland Gazette*, Aug. 2, 1919, p. 2.
63. "Southern 'Crackers' in the North," ibid., Aug. 16, 1919, p. 2. For similar interpretations, see William A. Byrd, "The Washington Riot," ibid., Aug. 16, 1919, p. 1; James W. Johnson, "Chicago's Present Need," *New York Age*, Aug. 9, 1919, p. 4; and "Troops Wrest Omaha from Mob," *Chicago Defender*, Oct. 4, 1919, p. 1.
64. "Seeking the Cause," *Chicago Defender*, Aug. 9, 1919, p. 20; "Another Angle of the Trouble," ibid., Sept. 6, 1919, p. 20. For a similar interpretation, see "The Mob!: A Warning," *Cleveland Gazette*, Aug. 2, 1919, p. 2.
65. "North and South," *Baltimore Afro-American*, Aug. 8, 1919, p. 4.
66. James W. Johnson, "Justice toward the Negro, North and South," *New York Age*, Aug. 16, 1919, p. 4. For an editorial that argues that the northern riots were preferable to the constant brutal oppression of blacks in the South, see William A. Byrd, "Dr. Wm. A. Byrd on Race Riots," *Cleveland Gazette*, Aug. 30, 1919, p. 1.
67. "The Temper of Rural Life," *Savannah Tribune*, Nov. 1, 1919, p. 4.

68. James W. Johnson, "Justice toward the Negro, North and South," *New York Age*, Aug. 16, 1919, p. 4.

69. "Sham of American Democracy Exposed," *New York Age*, Oct. 4, 1919, p. 2.

70. *Chicago Defender*, Mar. 1, 1919, p. 20; *Baltimore Afro-American*, Mar. 21, 1919, p. 4.

71. *Chicago Defender*, Feb. 22, 1919, p. 24.

72. William A. Byrd, "Dr. Wm. A. Byrd on Race Riots," *Cleveland Gazette*, Aug. 30, 1919, p. 1.

73. For the use of the term "southern Hun," see William A. Byrd, "The Washington Riot," ibid., Aug. 16, 1919, p. 1, and William A. Byrd, "Dr. Wm. A. Byrd on Race Riots," ibid., Aug. 30, 1919, p. 1.

74. "Another Angle of the Trouble," *Chicago Defender*, Sept. 6, 1919, p. 20.

75. For an example of an article that categorizes racist southerners as "the leading exponents of Bolshevism . . . in the United States to-day," see "Sham of American Democracy Exposed," *New York Age*, Oct. 4, 1919, p. 2.

76. William A. Byrd, "Dr. Wm. A. Byrd on Race Riots," *Cleveland Gazette*, Aug. 30, 1919, p. 1, and "The Washington Riot," ibid., Aug. 16, 1919, p. 1. Another editorial that claims that black self-defense saved the nation's capital from disgrace is "Reaping the Whirlwind," *New York Age*, Aug. 2, 1919, p. 4.

77. "The Hun Still Unleashed in America," *Savannah Tribune*, Nov. 16, 1918, p. 4.

78. Georgia's status as the second most violent state is based on lynching totals from 1882 to 1930. See Stewart E. Tolnay and E. M. Beck, *A Festival of Violence: An Analysis of Southern Lynchings, 1882–1930* (Urbana: University of Illinois Press, 1995), 270, and "Georgia Famed in Blood and Burning," *Savannah Tribune*, June 7, 1919, p. 4.

79. "An Outrageous Assault," *Richmond Planet*, Aug. 30, 1919, p. 4.

80. "Editor H. C. Smith and His Traducers," ibid., Sept. 6, 1919, p. 4; "The Riot at Knoxville," ibid.

81. Launey J. Benjamin, "Hopes of the Soldiers," *New York Age*, Dec. 7, 1918, p. 4.

82. "Danger," *Crisis* 19 (Feb. 1920): 169.

83. "The Graham Sedition Bill," *Cleveland Gazette*, Feb. 7, 1920, p. 2; "Helpless!," *Chicago Defender*, Feb. 7, 1920, p. 20.

84. On the peacetime sedition bills, see Murray, *Red Scare*, 230–31, and Charles Flint Kellogg, *NAACP: A History of the National Association for the Advancement of Colored People* (Baltimore: Johns Hopkins University Press, 1967), 289–90.

85. "A Misleading Report," *Richmond Planet*, Dec. 27, 1918, p. 4.

86. A. E. Thompson, "Editor's Mail: South Heard From," *Chicago Defender*, June 7, 1919, p. 20.

87. Launey J. Benjamin, "Hopes of the Soldiers," *New York Age*, Dec. 7, 1918, p. 4.

88. "Local Ministers Discuss Race Riots," *Baltimore Afro-American*, Aug. 8, 1919, p. 1.

CONCLUSION

1. Walter Lippmann, *Public Opinion* (New York: Free Press, 1922); David M. Kennedy, *Over Here: The First World War and American Society* (New York: Oxford University Press, 1980), 90–92.

2. See Michael Schudson, *Discovering the News: A Social History of American Newspapers* (New York: Basic Books, 1978), chap. 4. On the exclusion of dissident voices from the mainstream press, see Lauren Kessler, *The Dissident Press: Alternative Journalism in American History* (Beverly Hills: Sage Publications, 1984), chap. 1. For a modern critique of the news media, see Lance Bennett, *News: The Politics of Illusion*, 2d ed. (New York: Longman, 1988).

3. See, for example, H. C. Peterson and Gilbert C. Fite, *Opponents of War, 1917–1918* (Madison: University of Wisconsin Press, 1957), and Robert K. Murray, *Red Scare: A Study in National Hysteria, 1919–1920* (Minneapolis: University of Minnesota Press, 1955).

4. See Patrick S. Washburn, *A Question of Sedition: The Federal Government's Investigation of the Black Press during World War II* (New York: Oxford University Press, 1986), 4, and Theodore Kornweibel Jr., *"Seeing Red": Federal Campaigns against Black Militancy, 1919–1925* (Bloomington: Indiana University Press, 1998), 39, 181. On the rise of violence against blacks, see Steven A. Reich, "Soldiers of Democracy: Black Texans and the Fight for Citizenship, 1917–1921," *Journal of American History* 82 (Mar. 1996): 1478–1504.

5. Quoted in David Morgan, *Suffragists and Democrats: The Politics of Woman Suffrage in America* (East Lansing: Michigan State University Press, 1972), 124.

6. Kornweibel, *"Seeing Red,"* 39.

7. Stewart E. Tolnay and E. M. Beck, *A Festival of Violence: An Analysis of Southern Lynchings, 1882–1930* (Urbana: University of Illinois Press, 1995), 202–38.

8. Washburn, *Question of Sedition*, 52–56, 201.

9. Ibid., 90–93, 98, 131, 152.

10. A recent account that emphasizes the similarities between the black responses to the two wars is Harvard Sitkoff, "African-American Militancy in the World War II South: Another Perspective," in *Remaking Dixie: The Impact of World War II on the American South*, ed. Neil R. McMillen (Jackson: University Press of Mississippi, 1997). On evidence of progress gained by the black press, see Washburn, *Question of Sedition*, 198–202.

11. On Biddle's pivotal role, see Washburn, *Question of Sedition*.

SELECT BIBLIOGRAPHY

NEWSPAPERS AND MAGAZINES

Appeal
Baltimore Afro-American
Boston Guardian
California Eagle
Chicago Broad Ax
Chicago Defender
Cleveland Gazette
Crisis
Indianapolis Freeman

Messenger
New York Age
New York Times
Norfolk Journal and Guide
Pittsburgh Courier
Richmond Planet
Savannah Tribune
Washington Bee

PUBLISHED PRIMARY SOURCES

Bass, Charlotta A. *Forty Years: Memoirs from the Pages of a Newspaper.* Los Angeles: Charlotta A. Bass, 1960.

Chicago Commission on Race Relations. *The Negro in Chicago: A Study of Race Relations and a Race Riot.* Chicago: University of Chicago Press, 1922.

Du Bois, W. E. B. *The Autobiography of W. E. B. Du Bois.* New York: International Publishers, 1968.

———. *The Correspondence of W. E. B. Du Bois.* 3 vols. Edited by Herbert Aptheker. Amherst: University of Massachusetts Press, 1973.

———. *Dusk of Dawn: An Essay toward an Autobiography of a Race Concept.* New York: Harcourt, Brace, 1940.

Johnson, James Weldon. *Along This Way: The Autobiography of James Weldon Johnson.* New York: Viking Press, 1933.

Kerlin, Robert. *The Voice of the Negro, 1919.* New York: E. P. Dutton, 1920.

Knox, George L. *Slave and Freeman: The Autobiography of George L. Knox.* Edited by Willard B. Gatewood Jr. Lexington: University Press of Kentucky, 1979.

Kornweibel, Theodore, Jr., ed. *Federal Surveillance of Afro-Americans, 1917–1925: The First World War, the Red Scare, and the Garvey Movement.* Frederick, Md.: University Publications of America, 1986. Microfilm.

Lunardini, Christine, ed. "Standing Firm: William Monroe Trotter's Meetings with Woodrow Wilson, 1913–1914." *Journal of Negro History* 64 (Summer 1979): 244–64.

Roosevelt, Theodore. *The Works of Theodore Roosevelt.* 24 vols. Edited by Hermann Hagedorn. New York: Charles Scribner's Sons, 1923–26.

————. *The Writings of Theodore Roosevelt.* Edited by William H. Harbaugh. Indianapolis: Bobbs-Merrill, 1967.

Vincent, Theodore G., ed. *Voices of a Black Nation: Political Journalism in the Harlem Renaissance.* San Francisco: Ramparts Press, 1973.

Washington, Booker T. *The Booker T. Washington Papers.* 14 vols. Edited by Louis R. Harlan and Raymond W. Smock. Chicago: University of Chicago Press, 1972–89.

Wells, Ida B. *Crusader for Justice: The Autobiography of Ida B. Wells.* Chicago: University of Chicago Press, 1970.

Wilson, Woodrow. *The Papers of Woodrow Wilson.* 69 vols. Edited by Arthur S. Link. Princeton: Princeton University Press, 1966–94.

————. *Facing War, 1915–1917.* Volume 6 of *Woodrow Wilson, Life and Letters.* Edited by Ray Stannard Baker. Garden City, N.Y.: Doubleday, Doran, 1937.

SECONDARY SOURCES

Baker, Houston A., Jr. "Modernism and the Harlem Renaissance." In *Modernist Culture in America,* edited by Daniel Joseph Singal. Belmont, Calif.: Wadsworth, 1991.

Bakhtin, M. M. *The Dialogic Imagination: Four Essays.* Translated by Caryl Emerson and Michael Holquist; edited by Michael Holquist. Austin: University of Texas Press, 1981.

Baldwin, James. *The Fire Next Time.* New York: Laurel, 1977.

————. *Notes of a Native Son.* 1955. Reprint, Boston: Beacon Press, 1990.

Barbeau, Arthur E., and Florette Henri. *The Unknown Soldiers: Black American Troops in World War I.* Philadelphia: Temple University Press, 1974.

Beard, Richard L., and Cyril E. Zoerner II. "Associated Negro Press: Its Founding, Ascendancy, and Demise." *Journalism Quarterly* 46 (Spring 1969): 47–52.

Beasley, Maurine. "The Muckrakers and Lynching: A Case Study in Racism." *Journalism History* 9 (Autumn–Winter 1982): 86–91.

Beatty, Jack. *The Rascal King: The Life and Times of James Michael Curley, 1874–1958.* Reading, Mass.: Addison-Wesley, 1992.

Bederman, Gail. "'Civilization,' the Decline of Middle-Class Manliness, and Ida B. Wells's Antilynching Campaign, 1892–94." *Radical History Review* 52 (Winter 1992): 5–30.

Bennett, Lance. *News: The Politics of Illusion.* 2d ed. New York: Longman, 1988.

Berardi, Gayle K., and Thomas W. Segady. "The Development of African-American Newspapers in the American West: A Sociohistorical Perspective." *Journal of Negro History* 75 (Summer/Fall 1990): 96–109.

Bitner, Katherine A. "The Role of the *Chicago Defender* in the Great Migration of 1916–1918." *Negro History Bulletin* 48 (April–June 1985): 20–26.

Blassingame, John W. "The Press and American Intervention in Haiti and the Dominican Republic, 1904–1920." *Caribbean Studies* 9 (July 1969): 27–43.

Brooks, Maxwell R. *The Negro Press Re-Examined: Political Content of Leading Negro Newspapers.* Boston: Christopher Publishing House, 1959.

Brown, Elsa Barkley. "Uncle Ned's Children: Negotiating Community and Freedom in Postemancipation Richmond, Virginia." Ph.D. diss., Kent State University, 1994.

Brundage, W. Fitzhugh. *Lynching in the New South: Georgia and Virginia, 1880–1930.* Urbana: University of Illinois Press, 1993.

————. "Mob Violence North and South, 1865–1940." *Georgia Historical Quarterly* 75 (Winter 1991): 748–70.

————. "'To Howl Loudly': John Mitchell Jr. and His Campaign against Lynching in Virginia." *Canadian Review of American Studies* 22 (Winter 1991): 325–41.

Buni, Andrew. *Robert L. Vann of the "Pittsburgh Courier": Politics and Black Journalism.* Pittsburgh: University of Pittsburgh Press, 1974.

Burkett, Randall K., Nancy Hall Burkett, and Henry Louis Gates Jr., eds. *Black Biographical Dictionaries, 1790–1950.* Alexandria, Va.: Chadwyck-Healey, 1988.

Campbell, Georgetta Merritt, ed. *Extant Collections of Early Black Newspapers: A Research Guide to the Black Press, 1880–1915.* Troy, N.Y.: Whitson, 1981.

Carey, James W. *Communication as Culture: Essays on Media and Society.* Boston: Unwin Hyman, 1988.

Chalmers, David M. *Hooded Americanism: The History of the Ku Klux Klan.* Durham: Duke University Press, 1987.

Chartier, Roger. "Texts, Printing, Readings." In *The New Cultural History,* edited by Lynn Hunt, 154–75. Berkeley: University of California Press, 1989.

Coben, Stanley. *Rebellion against Victorianism: The Impetus for Cultural Change in 1920s America.* New York: Oxford University Press, 1991.

Cortner, Richard C. *A Mob Intent on Death: The NAACP and the Arkansas Riot Cases.* Middletown, Conn.: Wesleyan University Press, 1988.

Cripps, Thomas. *Slow Fade to Black: The Negro in American Film, 1900–1942.* New York: Oxford University Press, 1977.

Dann, Martin E., ed. *The Black Press, 1827–1890: The Quest for National Identity.* New York: G. P. Putnam's Sons, 1971.

Detweiler, Frederick G. *The Negro Press in the United States.* Chicago: University of Chicago Press, 1922.

Devlin, Patrick. *Too Proud to Fight: Woodrow Wilson's Neutrality.* New York: Oxford University Press, 1975.

Dinnerstein, Leonard. *The Leo Frank Case.* Birmingham: Notable Trials Library, 1991.

Downey, Dennis B., and Raymond M. Hyser. *No Crooked Death: Coatsville, Pennsylvania, and the Lynching of Zachariah Walker.* Urbana: University of Illinois Press, 1991.

Early, Gerald. "Introduction." In *My Soul's High Song: The Collected Writings of Countee Cullen, Voice of the Harlem Renaissance,* edited by Gerald Early, 1–73. New York: Anchor Books, 1991.

Ellis, Mark. "America's Black Press, 1914–18." *History Today* 41 (September 1991): 20–27.

————. "Joel Spingarn's 'Constructive Programme' and the Wartime Antilynching Bill of 1918." *Journal of Policy History* 4 (1992): 134–61.

————. "W. E. B. Du Bois and the Formation of Black Opinion in World War I: A Commentary on 'The Damnable Dilemma.'" *Journal of American History* 81 (March 1995): 1584–90.

Farrar, Hayward. *The "Baltimore Afro-American," 1892–1950.* Westport, Conn.: Greenwood Press, 1998.

Finkle, Lee. *Forum for Protest: The Black Press during World War II.* Rutherford, N.J.: Fairleigh Dickinson University Press, 1975.

Foucault, Michel. *The History of Sexuality.* Volume 1, *An Introduction.* Translated by Robert Hurley. New York: Vantage Books, 1990.

Fox, Stephen R. *The Guardian of Boston: William Monroe Trotter.* New York: Atheneum, 1970.

Franklin, V. P. "'Voice of the Black Community': The *Philadelphia Tribune,* 1912–1941." *Pennsylvania History* 51 (1984): 261–84.

Frazier, E. Franklin. *Black Bourgeoisie.* New York: Free Press, 1957.

Fredrickson, George M. *The Arrogance of Race: Historical Perspectives on Slavery, Racism, and Social Inequality.* Hanover, N.H.: Wesleyan University Press, 1988.

————. *The Black Image in the White Mind: The Debate on Afro-American Character and Destiny, 1817–1914.* 1971. Reprint, Middletown, Conn.: Wesleyan University Press, 1987.

Gaines, Kevin K. *Uplifting the Race: Black Leadership, Politics, and Culture in the Twentieth Century.* Chapel Hill: University of North Carolina Press, 1996.

Gates, Henry Louis, Jr. "Editor's Introduction: Writing 'Race' and the Difference It Makes." In *"Race," Writing, and Difference,* edited by Henry Louis Gates Jr., 1–20. Chicago: University of Chicago Press, 1985.

————. *Figures in Black: Words, Signs, and the "Racial Self."* New York: Oxford University Press, 1987.

————. *Loose Cannons: Notes on the Culture Wars.* New York: Oxford University Press, 1992.

————. "The Trope of a New Negro and the Reconstruction of the Image of the Black." *Representations* 24 (Fall 1988): 129–55.

Gerber, David A. *Black Ohio and the Color Line, 1860–1915.* Urbana: University of Illinois Press, 1976.

Gossett, Thomas F. *Race: The History of an Idea in America.* 1963. Reprint, New York: Schocken Books, 1965.

Gramsci, Antonio. *Selections from the Prison Notebooks.* Edited and translated by Quintin Hoare and Geoffrey Nowell Smith. New York: International Publishers, 1971.

Grant, Donald L. *The Anti-Lynching Movement, 1883–1932.* San Francisco: R and E Research Associates, 1975.

Gross, Bella. *"Freedom's Journal* and the *Rights of All." Journal of Negro History* 17 (July 1932): 241–86.

Grossman, James R. *Land of Hope: Chicago, Black Southerners, and the Great Migration.* Chicago: University of Chicago Press, 1989.

Gutman, Herbert. "The Black Family in Slavery and Freedom: A Revised Perspective." In *Power and Culture: Essays on the American Working Class,* edited by Ira Berlin, 357–79. New York: Pantheon Books, 1987.

Habermas, Jurgen. *The Structural Transformation of the Public Sphere: An Inquiry into a Category of Bourgeois Society.* Translated by Frederick Lawrence. Cambridge: MIT Press, 1995.

Hall, Jacquelyn Dowd. *Revolt against Chivalry: Jesse Daniel Ames and the Women's Campaign against Lynching.* New York: Columbia University Press, 1979.

Harris, J. William. "Etiquette, Lynching, and Racial Boundaries in Southern History: A Mississippi Example." *Journal of American History* 100 (April 1995): 387–410.

Hellwig, David J. "The Afro-American Press and United States Involvement in Cuba, 1902–1912." *Mid-America* 71 (April–July 1990): 135–45.

Henri, Florette. *Black Migration: Movement North, 1900–1920.* Garden City, N.Y.: Anchor Press/Doubleday, 1975.

Herbst, Susan. *Politics at the Margin: Historical Studies of Public Expression outside the Mainstream.* New York: Cambridge University Press, 1994.

Higginbotham, Evelyn Brooks. *Righteous Discontent: The Women's Movement in the Black Baptist Church, 1880–1920.* Cambridge: Harvard University Press, 1993.

Higham, John. *Strangers in the Land: Patterns of American Nativism, 1860–1925.* 1963. Reprint, New York: Atheneum, 1977.

Hilderbrand, Robert C. *Power and the People: Executive Management of Public Opinion in Foreign Affairs, 1897–1921.* Chapel Hill: University of North Carolina Press, 1981.

Hill, Robert A. " 'The Foremost Radical among His Race': Marcus Garvey and the Black Scare, 1918–1921." *Prologue* 16 (Winter 1984): 215–31.

Hilton, O. A. "Freedom of the Press in Wartime, 1917–1919." *Southwestern Social Science Quarterly* 28 (March 1948): 346–61.

———. "Public Opinion and Civil Liberties in Wartime, 1917–1919." *Southwestern Social Science Quarterly* 28 (December 1947): 201–24.

Holt, Thomas C. "Marking: Race, Race-making, and the Writing of History." *American Historical Review* 100 (February 1995): 1–20.

Howard-Pitney, David. "Calvin Chase's *Washington Bee* and Black Middle-Class Ideology, 1882–1900." *Journalism Quarterly* 63 (Spring 1986): 89–97.

Huggins, Nathan I. "The Deforming Mirror of Truth: Slavery and the Master Narrative of American History." *Radical History Review* 49 (Winter 1991): 25–46.

———. *Harlem Renaissance.* London: Oxford University Press, 1971.

Hunter, Tera. *To 'Joy My Freedom: Southern Black Women's Lives and Labors after the Civil War*. Cambridge: Harvard University Press, 1997.
Hutton, Frankie. *The Early Black Press in America, 1827–1860*. Westport, Conn.: Greenwood Press, 1993.
Jackson, Luther P., Jr. "Foreword: Toward an Appreciation of the Black Press." In *Extant Collections of Early Black Newspapers: A Research Guide to the Black Press, 1880–1915*, edited by Georgetta Merritt Campbell, ix–xviii. Troy, N.Y.: Whitson, 1981.
Jacobs, Alan. "The Man Who Heard Voices." *Books & Culture*, January/February 1996, 24–26.
Jacoby, Russell. "A New Intellectual History?" *American Historical Review* 97 (June 1992): 405–24.
Jay, Martin. "Should Intellectual History Take a Linguistic Turn?: Reflections on the Habermas-Gadamer Debate." In *Modern European History: Reappraisals and New Perspectives*, edited by Dominick LaCapra and Steven L. Kaplan, 86–110. Ithaca: Cornell University Press, 1982.
Johnson, Abby Arthur, and Ronald M. Johnson. "Away from Accommodation: Radical Editors and Protest Journalism, 1900–1910." *Journal of Negro History* 62 (October 1977): 325–38.
Jones, Leroi. *Blues People: Negro Music in White America*. New York: William Morrow, 1963.
Jones, Yollette Trigg. "The Black Community, Politics, and Race Relations in the 'Iris City': Nashville, Tennessee, 1870–1954." Ph.D. diss., Duke University, 1985.
Jordan, William. " 'The Damnable Dilemma': African-American Accommodation and Protest during World War I." *Journal of American History* 81 (March 1995): 1562–83.
Kelley, Robin D. G. "Notes on Deconstructing 'The Folk.' " *American Historical Review* 97 (December 1992): 1400–1408.
———. " 'We Are Not What We Seem': Rethinking Black Working-Class Opposition in the Jim Crow South." *Journal of American History* 80 (June 1993): 75–112.
Kellogg, Charles Flint. *NAACP: A History of the National Association for the Advancement of Colored People*. Baltimore: Johns Hopkins University Press, 1967.
Kennedy, David M. *Over Here: The First World War and American Society*. New York: Oxford University Press, 1980.
Kessler, Lauren. *The Dissident Press: Alternative Journalism in American History*. Beverly Hills: Sage Publications, 1984.
Klassen, Teresa C., and Owen V. Johnson. "Sharpening the Blade: Black Consciousness in Kansas, 1892–97." *Journalism Quarterly* 63 (Summer 1986): 298–304.
Kornweibel, Theodore, Jr. "Apathy and Dissent: Black America's Negative Responses to World War I." *South Atlantic Quarterly* 80 (Summer 1981): 322–38.

————. *"Seeing Red": Federal Campaigns against Black Militancy, 1919–1925*. Bloomington: Indiana University Press, 1998.

Kramer, Lloyd S. "Literature, Criticism, and Historical Imagination: The Literary Challenge of Hayden White and Dominick LaCapra." In *The New Cultural History*, edited by Lynn Hunt, 97–128. Berkeley: University of California Press, 1989.

Kreiling, Albert Lee. "The Making of Racial Identities in the Black Press: A Cultural Analysis of Race Journalism in Chicago, 1878–1929." Ph.D. diss., University of Illinois at Urbana, 1973.

Kusmer, Kenneth L. "The Black Urban Experience in American History." In *The State of Afro-American History: Past, Present, and Future*, edited by Darlene Clark Hine, 91–129. Baton Rouge: Louisiana State University Press, 1986.

————. *A Ghetto Takes Shape: Black Cleveland, 1870–1930*. Urbana: University of Illinois Press, 1976.

LaCapra, Dominick. "Intellectual History and Its Ways." *American Historical Review* 97 (April 1992): 425–39.

————. *Rethinking Intellectual History: Texts, Contexts, Language*. Ithaca: Cornell University Press, 1983.

Lamon, Lester C. *Black Tennesseans, 1900–1930*. Knoxville: University of Tennessee Press, 1977.

Lears, T. J. Jackson. "The Concept of Cultural Hegemony: Problems and Possibilities." *American Historical Review* 90 (June 1985): 567–93.

————. "Making Fun of Popular Culture." *American Historical Review* 97 (December 1992): 1427–30.

Levine, Lawrence W. "The Folklore of Industrial Society: Popular Culture and Its Audiences." *American Historical Review* 97 (December 1992): 1369–99.

Levy, Eugene. " 'Is the Jew a White Man?': Press Reaction to the Leo Frank Case, 1913–1915." *Phylon* 35 (June 1974): 212–22.

————. *James Weldon Johnson: Black Leader, Black Voice*. Chicago: University of Chicago Press, 1973.

Lewis, David Levering. *W. E. B. Du Bois: Biography of a Race, 1868–1919*. New York: Henry Holt, 1993.

————. "W. E. B. Du Bois and the Dilemma of Race." *Prologue* 27 (Spring 1995): 37–44.

Lewis, Earl. *In Their Own Interests: Race, Class, and Power in Twentieth-Century Norfolk, Virginia*. Berkeley: University of California Press, 1991.

Link, Arthur S. *Wilson: Confusions and Crises, 1915–1916*. Princeton: Princeton University Press, 1964.

————. *Wilson: The New Freedom*. Princeton: Princeton University Press, 1956.

Lippmann, Walter. *Public Opinion*. New York: Free Press, 1922.

Logan, Rayford, ed. *Dictionary of American Negro Biography*. New York: W. W. Norton, 1982.

Luebke, Frederick C. *Bonds of Loyalty: German-Americans and World War I.* De Kalb: Northern Illinois University Press, 1974.

McFeely, William S. *Frederick Douglass.* New York: Touchstone, 1991.

McGovern, James R. *Anatomy of a Lynching: The Killing of Claude Neal.* Baton Rouge: Louisiana State University Press, 1992.

MacLean, Nancy. *Behind the Mask of Chivalry: The Making of the Second Ku Klux Klan.* New York: Oxford University Press, 1994.

———. "The Leo Frank Case Reconsidered: Gender and Sexual Politics in the Making of Reactionary Populism." *Journal of American History* 78 (December 1991): 917–48.

McMillen, Neil R. "Black Journalism in Mississippi: The Jim Crow Years." *Journal of Mississippi History* 49 (1987): 129–38.

———. *Dark Journey: Black Mississippians in the Age of Jim Crow.* Urbana: University of Illinois Press, 1989.

McMurry, Linda O. *Recorder of the Black Experience: A Biography of Monroe Nathan Work.* Baton Rouge: Louisiana State University Press, 1985.

Martindale, Carolyn. "Coverage of Black Americans in Five Newspapers since 1950." *Journalism Quarterly* 62 (Summer 1985): 321–28.

———. *The White Press and Black America.* Westport, Conn.: Greenwood Press, 1986.

Matthews, John M. "Black Newspapermen and the Black Community in Georgia, 1890–1930." *Georgia Historical Quarterly* 68 (Fall 1984): 356–81.

May, Henry F. *The End of American Innocence: A Study of the First Years of Our Own Time, 1912–1917.* New York: Alfred A. Knopf, 1959.

Meier, August. *Negro Thought in America, 1880–1915: Racial Ideologies in the Age of Booker T. Washington.* 1963. Reprint, Ann Arbor: University of Michigan Press, 1988.

Miller, Nathan. *Theodore Roosevelt: A Life.* New York: William Morrow, 1992.

Moore, Leonard J. *Citizen Klansmen: The Ku Klux Klan in Indiana, 1921–1928.* Chapel Hill: University of North Carolina Press, 1991.

Morgan, David. *Suffragists and Democrats: The Politics of Woman Suffrage in America.* East Lansing: Michigan State University Press, 1972.

Morris, Aldon. "Centuries of Black Protest: Its Significance for America and the World." In *Race in America: The Struggle for Equality,* edited by Herbert Hill and James E. Jones Jr., 19–69. Madison: University of Wisconsin Press, 1993.

Mott, Frank Luther. *American Journalism: A History of Newspapers in the United States through 250 Years, 1690–1940.* New York: Macmillan, 1941.

Murray, Robert K. *Red Scare: A Study in National Hysteria, 1919–1920.* Minneapolis: University of Minnesota Press, 1955.

Myrdal, Gunnar. *An American Dilemma: The Negro Problem and Modern Democracy.* 1944. Reprint, New York: Harper and Row, 1962.

Nalty, Bernard C. *Strength for the Fight: A History of Black Americans in the Military.* New York: Free Press, 1986.

Neal, Diane. "Seduction, Accommodation, or Realism?: Tabbs Gross and the *Arkansas Freedman.*" *Arkansas Historical Quarterly* 48 (1989): 57–64.

Nerone, John. *Violence against the Press: Policing the Public Sphere in U.S. History.* New York: Oxford University Press, 1994.

Oak, Vishnu V. *The Negro Newspaper.* Yellow Springs, Ohio: Antioch Press, 1948.

O'Kelly, Charlotte G. "Black Newspapers and the Black Protest Movement: Their Historical Relationship, 1827–1945." *Phylon* 43 (March 1982): 1–14.

Ottley, Roi. *The Lonely Warrior: The Life and Times of Robert S. Abbott.* Chicago: Henry Regnery, 1955.

————. *New World A-Coming: Inside Black America.* 1943. Reprint, New York: Arno Press and New York Times, 1968.

Park, Robert Ezra. *Race and Culture.* New York: Free Press, 1950.

Paxson, Frederic L. *Pre-War Years, 1913–1917.* Volume 1 of *American Democracy and the World War.* Boston: Houghton Mifflin, 1936.

Paz, D. G. "John Albert Williams and Black Journalism in Omaha, 1895–1929." *Midwest Review* 10 (1988): 14–32.

Penn, I. Garland. *The Afro-American Press and Its Editors.* 1891. Reprint, New York: Arno Press and New York Times, 1969.

Peterson, Dale E. "Response and Call: The African-American Dialogue with Bakhtin." *American Literature* 65 (December 1993): 761–75.

Peterson, H. C., and Gilbert C. Fite. *Opponents of War, 1917–1918.* Madison: University of Wisconsin Press, 1957.

Plummer, Brenda Gayle. "The Afro-American Response to the Occupation of Haiti, 1915–1934." *Phylon* 43 (June 1982): 125–43.

Pocock, J. G. A. "Introduction: State of the Art." In *Virtue, Commerce, and History: Essays on Political Thought and History, Chiefly in the Eighteenth Century,* 1–34. New York: Cambridge University Press, 1985.

Poster, Mark. "Foucault and History." *Social Research* 49 (Spring 1982): 116–42.

Pride, Armistead Scott. "Negro Newspapers: Yesterday, Today, and Tomorrow." *Journalism Quarterly* 28 (Spring 1951): 179–88.

Quarles, Benjamin. *Black Abolitionists.* New York: Oxford University Press, 1969.

Rable, George C. "The South and the Politics of Antilynching Legislation, 1920–1940." *Journal of Southern History* 51 (May 1985): 201–20.

Reich, Steven A. "Soldiers of Democracy: Black Texans and the Fight for Citizenship, 1917–1921." *Journal of American History* 82 (March 1996): 1478–1504.

Roberts, Randy. *Papa Jack: Jack Johnson and the Era of White Hopes.* New York: Free Press, 1983.

Rodgers, Daniel T. "Republicanism: The Career of a Concept." *Journal of American History* 79 (June 1992): 11–38.

Rogin, Michael. *Ronald Reagan, the Movie, and Other Episodes in Political Demonology.* Berkeley: University of California Press, 1987.

Rorty, Richard. *Achieving Our Country: Leftist Thought in Twentieth-Century America.* Cambridge: Harvard University Press, 1998.

Ross, Joyce B. *J. E. Spingarn and the Rise of the NAACP, 1911–1939*. New York: Atheneum, 1972.

Rudwick, Elliott M. *Race Riot at East St. Louis, July 2, 1917*. Carbondale: Southern Illinois University Press, 1964.

———. *W. E. B. Du Bois: Propagandist of the Negro Protest*. 2d ed. Philadelphia: University of Pennsylvania Press, 1968.

Sanders, M. L., and Philip M. Taylor. *British Propaganda during the First World War, 1914–1918*. London: MacMillan, 1982.

Scheiber, Jane Lang, and Harry N. Scheiber. "The Wilson Administration and the Wartime Mobilization of Black Americans, 1917–18." *Labor History* 10 (Summer 1967): 433–58.

Schudson, Michael. *Advertising, the Uneasy Persuasion: Its Dubious Impact on American Society*. New York: Basic Books, 1984.

———. *Discovering the News: A Social History of American Newspapers*. New York: Basic Books, 1978.

———. "Preparing the Minds of the People: Three-Hundred Years of the American Newspaper." In *Three-Hundred Years of the American Newspaper*, edited by John B. Hench, 421–43. Worcester, Mass.: American Antiquarian Society, 1991.

Scott, Emmett J. "Letters of Negro Migrants of 1916–1918." *Journal of Negro History* 4 (July 1919): 290–340.

Sealander, Judith. "Antebellum Black Press Images of Women." *Western Journal of Black Studies* 6 (Fall 1982): 159–65.

Seaman, William R. "Active Audience Theory: Pointless Populism." *Media, Culture, and Society* 14 (April 1992): 301–11.

Semmes, Clovis E. *Cultural Hegemony and African American Development*. Westport, Conn.: Praeger, 1992.

Sim, John Cameron. *The Grass Roots Press: America's Community Newspapers*. Ames: Iowa State University Press, 1969.

Simmons, Charles A. *The African American Press: A History of News Coverage during National Crises, with Special Reference to Four Black Newspapers, 1827–1965*. Jefferson, N.C.: McFarland, 1998.

Singal, Daniel Joseph, ed. *Modernist Culture in America*. Belmont, Calif.: Wadsworth, 1991.

Singleton, Gregory Holmes. "Birth, Rebirth, and the 'New Negro' of the 1920s." *Phylon* 43 (Spring 1982): 29–45.

Sitkoff, Harvard. "African-American Militancy in the World War II South: Another Perspective." In *Remaking Dixie: The Impact of World War II on the American South*, edited by Neil R. McMillen, 70–92. Jackson: University Press of Mississippi, 1997.

———. "Racial Militancy and Interracial Violence in the Second World War." *Journal of American History* 58 (December 1971): 661–81.

Smead, Howard. *Blood Justice: The Lynching of Mack Charles Parker*. New York: Oxford University Press, 1986.

Snorgrass, William J. "The Black Press in the San Francisco Bay Area, 1856–1900." *California History* 60 (1981–82): 306–17.

SoRelle, James M. "The 'Waco Horror': The Lynching of Jesse Washington." *Southwestern Historical Quarterly* 86 (1983): 517–36.

Spear, Allan H. *Black Chicago: The Making of a Negro Ghetto, 1890–1920.* Chicago: University of Chicago Press, 1967.

Spivey, Donald. *Schooling for the New Slavery: Black Industrial Education, 1868–1915.* Westport, Conn.: Greenwood Press, 1988.

Stanton, Bill. *Klanwatch: Bringing the Ku Klux Klan to Justice.* New York: Grove Weidenfeld, 1991.

Stepan, Nancy Leys, and Sander L. Gilman. "Appropriating the Idioms of Science: The Rejection of Scientific Racism." In *The Bounds of Race: Perspectives on Hegemony and Resistance,* edited by Dominick LaCapra, 72–103. Ithaca: Cornell University Press, 1991.

Stepto, Robert B. *From behind the Veil: A Study of Afro-American Narrative.* Urbana: University of Illinois Press, 1979.

Stevens, John D. "Black Journalism: Neglected No Longer." In *Mass Media and the National Experience,* edited by John D. Stevens and Ronald T. Farrar, 97–111. New York: Harper and Row, 1971.

———. "The Black Press Looks at 1920's Journalism." *Journalism History* 7 (Autumn–Winter 1980): 109–13.

Stevens, Summer E., and Owen V. Johnson. "From Black Politics to Black Community: Harry C. Smith and the *Cleveland Gazette.*" *Journalism Quarterly* 67 (Winter 1990): 1090–1102.

Stovall, Mary E. "The *Chicago Defender* in the Progressive Era." *Illinois Historical Journal* 83 (Autumn 1990): 159–72.

Stuckey, Sterling. *Slave Culture: Nationalist Theory and the Foundations of Black America.* New York: Oxford University Press, 1987.

Suggs, Henry Lewis. *P. B. Young, Newspaperman: Race, Politics, and Journalism in the New South, 1910–1962.* Charlottesville: University Press of Virginia, 1988.

———. "The Response of the African American Press to the United States Occupation of Haiti, 1915–1934." *Journal of Negro History* 73 (Spring–Fall 1988): 33–45.

———, ed. *The Black Press in the South, 1865–1979.* Westport, Conn.: Greenwood Press, 1983.

Sullins, William S., and Paul Parsons. "Roscoe Dunjee: Crusading Editor of Oklahoma's *Black Dispatch,* 1915–1955." *Journalism Quarterly* 69 (Spring 1992): 204–13.

Thompson, E. P. *The Poverty of Theory and Other Essays.* New York: Monthly Review Press, 1978.

Thompson, Julius E. *The Black Press in Mississippi, 1865–1985.* Gainesville: University Press of Florida, 1993.

Thompson, Mildred I. *Ida B. Wells-Barnett: An Exploratory Study of an American Black Woman, 1893–1930.* Black Women in United States History. Edited by Darlene Clark Hine et al. Volume 4. Brooklyn: Carlson, 1990.

Thornbrough, Emma Lou. "American Negro Newspapers, 1880–1914." *Business History Review* 40 (Winter 1966): 467–90.

————. *T. Thomas Fortune: Militant Journalist.* Chicago: University of Chicago Press, 1972.

Toews, John E. "Intellectual History after the Linguistic Turn: The Autonomy of Meaning and the Irreducibility of Experience." *American Historical Review* 92 (October 1987): 879–907.

Tolnay, Stewart E., and E. M. Beck. *A Festival of Violence: An Analysis of Southern Lynchings, 1882–1930.* Urbana: University of Illinois Press, 1995.

Trotter, Joe William, ed. *The Great Migration in Historical Perspective: New Dimensions of Race, Class, and Gender.* Bloomington: Indiana University Press, 1991.

Tuttle, William M., Jr. *Race Riot: Chicago in the Red Summer of 1919.* New York: Atheneum, 1970.

————. "Violence in a 'Heathen' Land: The Longview Race Riot of 1919." *Phylon* 33 (Winter 1972): 324–33.

Vaughn, Stephen. *Holding Fast the Inner Lines: Democracy, Nationalism, and the Committee on Public Information.* Chapel Hill: University of North Carolina Press, 1980.

Vincent, Theodore G. "Preface." In *Voices of a Black Nation: Political Journalism in the Harlem Renaissance,* edited by Theodore G. Vincent, 19–38. San Francisco: Ramparts Press, 1973.

Walker, Clarence E. "The American Negro as Historical Outsider, 1836–1935." *Canadian Review of American Studies* 17 (Summer 1986): 137–54.

————. *Deromanticizing Black History: Critical Essays and Reappraisals.* Knoxville: University of Tennessee Press, 1991.

Walters, Ronald G. "Signs of the Times: Clifford Geertz and Historians." *Social Research* 47 (Autumn 1980): 537–56.

Warnke, Georgia. *Gadamer: Hermeneutics, Tradition, and Reason.* Stanford, Calif.: Stanford University Press, 1987.

Washburn, Patrick S. *A Question of Sedition: The Federal Government's Investigation of the Black Press during World War II.* New York: Oxford University Press, 1986.

Waskow, Arthur I. *From Race Riot to Sit-in, 1919 and the 1960s: A Study in the Connections between Conflict and Violence.* Garden City, N.Y.: Doubleday, 1966.

Westbrook, Robert. "Good-bye to All That: Aileen Kraditor and Radical History." *Radical History Review* 28–30 (1984): 69–89.

Williams, Nudie. "The Black Press in Oklahoma: The Formative Years, 1899–1907." *Chronicles of Oklahoma* 61 (1983): 308–19.

Wilson, Clint C., II. *Black Journalists in Paradox: Historical Perspectives and Current Dilemmas.* New York: Greenwood Press, 1991.

Wolseley, Roland E. *The Black Press, U.S.A.* Ames: Iowa State University Press, 1971.

Woodruff, Nan Elizabeth. "African-American Struggles for Citizenship in the Arkansas and Mississippi Deltas in the Age of Jim Crow." *Radical History Review* 55 (Winter 1993): 33–51.

Yohn, Susan M. "Will the Real Conservative Please Stand Up? or, The

Pitfalls Involved in Examining Ideological Sympathies: A Comment on Alan Brinkley's 'Problem of American Conservatism.' " *American Historical Review* 99 (April 1994): 430–37.

Zangrando, Robert L. *The NAACP Crusade against Lynching, 1909–1950.* Philadelphia: Temple University Press, 1980.

Ziglar, William L. "The Decline of Lynching in America." *International Social Science Review* 63 (Winter 1988): 14–25.

INDEX

Abbott, Robert S., 119, 123, 140; leadership of, 14; and profitability of *Chicago Defender*, 32; conservative views of, 33; and war effort, 33; integration versus separate black institutions stance of, 79–80; statement of patriotism, 121; on Chicago riot, 150. See also *Chicago Defender*

Accommodation/protest dichotomy: Washington and, 6, 10, 13, 18–19, 22, 25, 34, 35; and reactions to World War I, 6, 35, 105; and rise of activism, 10–14; leading activist editors and, 10–14, 23–24, 31–35; in black press, 16–25, 35, 71–72, 105, 109, 165–66; and personal success ideology, 17–18; and erosion of southern black rights, 28; New Negro's place in, 28; and Johnson's editorial objectives, 31; and Young as accommodationist, 34; and Smith's integrationist beliefs, 53–56; and responses to *Birth of a Nation*, 57–58; and loyalty issues, 105; and wartime issues, 165–66. See also Militancy; Tuskegee philosophy

Adams, John Quincy (*St. Paul Appeal* editor), 22, 62

Addams, Jane, 52

"Afro-American Agitators," 21–25, 27, 53, 79

"Afro-American Cullings" (syndicated column), 90

Afro-American League, 25

Agitators. See "Afro-American Agitators"

Alabama, 16, 19

Alexander's Magazine, 24

Alger, Horatio, 17–18

Aluminum Ore Company strike, 87

American Federation of Labor, 103

Americanism, 5, 59–62

American Revolution, 59, 62, 63, 85

"American Spirit, The" (Wilson speech), 61

Amsterdam News, 34, 137

Anarchism, 152

Antebellum black journalism, 14–16

Antilynching campaign, 7; Wells and, 19–20, 24; Johnson and, 31, 42–43, 48, 76, 86, 100, 103, 129–30; reports of European atrocities linked with, 39–41, 76; NAACP and, 43, 76, 98, 100, 167; and critics of *Birth of a Nation*, 50–58; Smith and, 56; white southerners and, 103, 133, 165; success of, 165

Antilynching legislation, 23, 52, 54, 73, 119, 165; Spingarn's testimony on, 100–101, 106; conference of black editors calls for, 125; Wilson's failure to call for, 132

Antislavery movement, 14–16

Arkansas, 16, 141–42, 148, 149

Arkansas Gazette, 141

Armed forces: and officer-training segregation issue, 78–82, 105, 106, 166; and Bulletin 35, 101, 117; and attitudes of returning black soldiers, 138, 146–47. See also Houston mutiny

Armenian massacre, 40, 42, 45–46, 76, 88

Assimilation. See Integrationists

Associated Negro Press, 145, 146, 147–48

Atlanta, Georgia, 45, 140

Atlanta Constitution, 21, 130

Coolidge, Calvin, 34
Copperheads, 63, 82
Cornish, Samuel E., 1, 14, 15
Creel, George, 122, 123, 127, 132
Cripps, Thomas, 56
Crisis, 8; Du Bois's editorship of,
8, 14, 28–29, 40–41; support of
World War I, 65, 77; on African
American loyalty, 70; Du Bois's
"Close Ranks" editorial in, 113–
15, 131, 138, 167, 172 (n. 21); and
conference of black editors, 123;
and federal surveillance, 137–38,
141; and radicalism charges, 138,
143
Crusader, 137, 152
Curley, James Michael, 52, 101

Dallas Express, 21
Daniels, Rufus, 93
Daughters of the American Revolu-
tion, 59
Davis, Richard Harding, 50
Declaration of Independence, 155
Delany, Martin R., 14
Democracy, 37, 39, 88, 146, 164
Democratic Party, 10, 11, 12, 22, 61,
90
Detweiler, Frederick G., 2
Disenfranchisement. *See* Voting
rights
Dix, Dorothea, 50
Dixon, Thomas, 48, 49, 50, 52, 53,
55
Dominican Republic, 43, 44
Donnelly, H. L., 141
Double V campaign, 167
Douglass, Frederick, 15
Du Bois, W. E. B.: "Close Ranks"
editorial, 5–6, 113–15, 131, 138,
167, 172 (n. 21); opposition to ac-
commodationism, 6, 26; as *Crisis*
editor, 8, 14, 28–29, 113–15; jour-
nalistic practices of, 14; leadership
of, 14, 26, 28–29; and Washington's black uplift philosophy, 18;

on "vast veil" hiding blacks, 25;
and Niagara Movement, 26; and
support of war effort, 33, 64, 69,
112, 113, 131; on Belgian atrocities in Congo, 40–41; on *Birth
of a Nation,* 49; affirmation of
black loyalty, 69, 70; on southern
plot to halt black migration to
North, 70; and segregated officer-
training camp, 79, 82; on separate
black institutions, 80; on Houston
mutiny, 94, 95, 96; and conference of black editors, 123, 125;
statement on black loyalty, 125;
"Returning Soldiers" editorial,
138; on sedition laws, 160
Duke, Jesse C., 19, 20, 21
Dyer, Leonidas, 100, 101

Easton, William, 52
East St. Louis race riot (1917), 86–
92, 93, 98, 101, 105, 155
Eaves, Hubert, 65–67
Ellis, James G., 146
Emancipation, 15, 16, 131
Emancipation Proclamation, 16, 59
Espionage and Sedition Acts (1917,
1918): censorship under, 5, 110–
12, 164; jailing of black publisher
under, 94–95, 111, 112; and Houston mutiny, 94–95, 112; Miner's
letter and, 107; suspect black
publications and, 111–12, 115–16;
New York Age and, 118; postwar
enforcement of, 136–37; 1920
peacetime sedition law and, 160

Federal government: investigatory
agencies, 4, 135, 163, 164, 167;
segregation in departments of,
10–11, 12, 13, 36, 79, 111, 125;
black accommodationist/protest
dichotomy and, 10–14; segregation sanctions by, 17; and race
relations, 73, 121, 122; and race
riots, 88; black press as Afri-

can American link with, 106;
sponsorship of conference of
black editors by, 110, 122–29,
132; manipulation of public opinion by, 163. *See also* Antilynching
legislation; Censorship; Loyalty;
World War I

Fields, A. N., 129, 130

Fisk University, 82

Fleming, J. L., 20

Florida, 16

Florida Sentinel, 18

Florida Times-Union, 89, 103, 130

Fortune, T. Thomas, 22, 26; activism
as Agitator, 24–25, 53. See also
New York Age

Fox, Stephen R., 26

Frazier, E. Franklin, 3, 56

Freedom's Journal, 1, 14, 15, 66

Free speech. *See* Censorship

Frissell, Hollis, 68

Frissell, S. S., 50

Gard, Warren, 100

Garvey, Marcus, 34, 137, 145, 152

German Americans, 59, 127; and
German-language newspaper
censorship, 111

Germany: alleged atrocities by,
39–41, 44, 45, 76, 100; alleged
incitement of southern blacks by,
68–71, 79, 81, 120; and submarine
warfare, 72. *See also* World War I

"Gospel of Wealth" (Carnegie doctrine), 17

Grady, Henry, 21

Grant, Ulysses S., 54

Great Britain, 40, 41

Gregory, Thomas, 69

Griffith, D. W., 48–58

Hackett, Francis, 52

Haiti, 44, 182 (n. 30)

Hampton Institute, 82

Harlem Renaissance, 29

Harris, George W., 68–69, 70, 71,
123

Harrison, Hubert, 123

Harvard College, 25, 26

Hearst, William Randolph, 32, 33

Heflin, J. Thomas, 83

Henry, Vida, 93

Hobby, William, 159

Hodges, William A., 14–15

House Judiciary Committee, 100

Housing segregation, 17, 35

Houston Informer, 140

Houston mutiny (1917), 92–98, 101,
105, 113, 132; and Johnson's clemency appeal, 31, 100; and Wilson's
commutation of death sentences,
31, 128; white press's reaction to,
93–94; black press's reaction to,
96–98, 106, 166; and *Crisis*, 113

Houston Post, 130

Howard University, 86, 107

Hughes, Charles Evans, 60

Hull House, 59

Hyphenated Americans: loyalty
concerns about, 59–62, 64, 65,
166

Immigration: and Americanization
campaigns, 59–61, 62; movement
to restrict, 60; African American dissociation from, 62; and
newspaper censorship, 111

Independent, 46

Indianapolis Freeman, 8, 17, 24, 123;
advocacy of Tuskegee philosophy,
23; on segregated officer-training
camp, 81; and federal surveillance, 140

Indianapolis World, 22

Industrial capitalism, 17–18

Industrial Workers of the World
(IWW), 137, 152

Influenza epidemic, 135

Integrationists: Agitators as, 23;
Smith's beliefs and, 23, 53, 79;

on wartime fostering of black-
white unity, 103, 129; and Miner's
letter, 107–9; mailing privileges
of, 111; on censorship, 112; and
conference of black editors, 123;
and race riots, 143, 150; and New
Negro, 148; and radicalism, 152;
on northern democratic principles, 159. *See also* Mitchell, John
L., Jr.
Riots. *See* Race riots
Rogin, Michael, 50
Roosevelt, Franklin Delano, 34, 123,
167
Roosevelt, Theodore: Washington as
black spokesman to, 10, 13; loyalty
standards of, 59, 61; opposition
to hyphenism, 60–61; advocacy
of preparedness, 62–63; and Wilson's war declaration, 73; on race
riots, 88–89; on Houston mutiny,
93–94
Russia, 40, 137
Russwurm, John B., 1, 14, 15

St. Louis Argus, 21, 119, 122, 123, 130
St. Paul Appeal, 8, 17; editorial militancy of, 22; on black Americanism, 62; opposition to war, 64;
and Eaves case, 66; on segregated
officer-training camp, 81
St. Philip's Church, 98
San Antonio Inquirer, 95, 112
Savannah Tribune, 8, 19; on World
War I issues, 41, 45, 63, 78, 83; on
lynchings, 48, 91, 92, 98, 159; and
segregated officer-training camp,
79; on improvement in race relations, 103; and conference of
black editors, 123; on returning black soldiers, 146; on race
riots, 149, 150, 156; and black
migration, 156
School segregation, 17
Scott, Emmett, 34, 57, 101, 132; and

conference of black editors, 122,
123, 127, 130
Scott, Ligon, 86
Sedition Act. *See* Espionage and
Sedition Acts
Segregation, 2; in federal government, 10–11, 12, 13, 36, 111, 125;
southern legalization of, 17, 85;
Agitators' denunciation of, 23,
24; integration versus, 23, 78–
80; appeals against, 36, 84, 90;
and Wilson's war declaration, 75;
and officer-training camp, 78–
82, 105, 106, 165; and Houston
mutiny, 92–98; and Bulletin 35,
101, 117; conference of black
editors' statement on, 125
Self-improvement, 18, 28, 33
Selma Independent, 19
Selznick, Lewis, 52
Sherman, William Tecumseh, 54
Shillady, John R., 159
Silent Protest Parade (1917), 98, 101
Simmons, Charles A., 2
Simmons, Roscoe Conkling, 77
Smiley, J. Hockley, 32–33
Smith, Bolton, 120, 130, 134, 135
Smith, Frank W., 143–44, 159
Smith, Harry C., 8; opposition to
Tuskegee philosophy, 22; and
integration, 23, 53, 79; criticism
of Trotter's militancy, 27; as critic
of South, 53, 56, 83, 90; campaign against *Birth of a Nation,* 53–
56, 83, 103–4; and World War I,
58, 105–6; on preparedness, 63–
64; on black loyalty, 70–71; on
black army officers, 78, 80–81;
opposition to segregated officer-
training camp, 80; on Houston
mutiny, 94; on improved race
relations, 103, 131; and conference of black editors, 123; on
Liberty Congress, 124; on Wilson's
antilynching statement, 129; and

White, Walter, 141, 142
White supremacy doctrine, 15, 18, 139, 143; and *Birth of a Nation,* 48–50
Williams, John Sharp, 83, 121
Willis, Frank, 54, 56
Wilmington (N.C.) riot (1898), 22
Wilmington Daily Record, 20
Wilson, Woodrow: and *Birth of a Nation,* 7, 12–13, 49–50, 58, 183–84 (n. 57); and black press, 7, 13; and lynchings, 7, 31, 86, 100, 125, 127–30, 131–32, 139, 164; and treatment of African Americans, 10–11, 13, 31, 69, 73, 85, 104–5, 128; Trotter's meeting with, 10–14, 27, 31, 126; and black activism, 10–14, 36, 58, 138; Johnson's meeting with, 31–32, 100; advocacy of neutrality, 39; intervention in Latin America, 43–44; and reports of Turkish atrocities, 45–46; and loyalty issues, 59, 61, 65, 69; on hyphenated Americans, 60, 61; and preparedness policies, 63–64, 65, 98; declaration of war by, 72–76, 164, 166; Miller's open letter to, 86; commutes death sentences of Houston mutineers, 100, 128; and Miner's letter, 107; and conference of black editors, 110, 126–30; antilynching state-·ment, 127–30, 131–32; and fears

of African American bolshevism, 137
Wise, Stephen A., 52
Woman suffrage, 131, 164
World's Work, 75
World War I: African Americans' responses to, 2, 3, 5–6, 33–39, 64–67, 73–78, 113–15, 131, 138, 145, 165, 167, 168, 172 (n. 21); role of black press in, 5, 33, 35; black conditions in context of, 6–7, 36–37, 100–101; and *Chicago Defender,* 33; and preparedness campaigns, 36, 62–65, 80, 83, 98, 166; nationalism as force behind, 37, 39; and neutrality issues, 39, 41; reports of atrocities in, 39–41; and interventionists, 42–45; and Wilson's declaration of war, 72–76, 164, 166; New Negro's emergence and, 135, 138, 146–47; conclusion of, 136, 160, 164; official end of, 136–37; black contribution in, 144–46; government manipulation of public opinion in, 163; U.S. propaganda in, 163. *See also* Loyalty
World War II, 34, 166–67
Worth County Local, 48
Wright, Richard, 1, 150

Young, Charles, 126, 127
Young, P. B., 34, 123